D1564417

ORDER, FAMILY, AND COMMUNITY IN
BUENOS AIRES
1810-1860

ORDER, FAMILY, AND COMMUNITY IN
BUENOS AIRES
1810-1860

Mark D. Szuchman

STANFORD UNIVERSITY PRESS   Stanford, California

Stanford University Press
Stanford, California
© 1988 by the Board of Trustees of the
Leland Stanford Junior University
Printed in the United States of America

CIP data appear at the end of the book

Published with the assistance of
the Andrew W. Mellon Foundation and
Florida International University

To Jeffrey,
the most patient

Preface

The thinking behind this work began over a decade ago, as I completed a previous study in the historical sociology of fin-de-siècle Argentina. I began to sense at that time an attraction toward the investigation of an earlier era, the first half of the nineteenth century, curious about the possibilities of discovering the threads that bound together a society mired in political turmoil—a society that appeared to have come apart, that did not possess even the minimal benefits of a constitution, and that indeed was devoid of a national ethos.

Students of Latin American societies have a rich historiographical cache from which to draw, but which also serves to demonstrate a basic literary imbalance: despite our awareness of the patriarchal nature of Latin America's social systems, our literature is oriented preponderantly toward the epic figures—the political patriarchs—while the corpus of studies addressing the subject of their clients, dependents, and kin remains relatively scanty. As I sat in the Researchers' Room of the Archivo General de la Nación in Buenos Aires fourteen years ago, poring over manuscript census schedules of the late nineteenth century and sampling individuals, I knew that my intellectual challenge in the future was nestled within the deeper recesses of the Argentine past, and would begin by sampling households.

Family history was then being practiced by very few historians of the United States and even fewer specialists in Latin America. By the late 1970's, when I formally embarked on the present study, the literature on family history in Ibero-America totaled, according to James Milden's contemporaneous compilation *The Family in Past Time*, five works. Since then, the interest of Latin Americanists in family history as a subject for monographic research has expanded, although there is general agreement that we still lag far behind our Europeanist colleagues in quantity and breadth of scholarly production. My own interest was to add to this budding field, but with a research paradigm that would address a traditional problem in Latin American history: the nature of political legitimacy and the means of establishing deference and obligation to authority. Furthermore, I became very conscious of not permitting the heady, and sometimes superficial, sense of achievement that comes from computer runs and statistical significance to become a surrogate for extracting historical signification.

With relatively few monographic materials on Latin America at my disposal, I was (salutarily) required to dig deeply into the literature on family history from other areas, especially the United States and Europe, in order to draw plausible models; furthermore, I depended heavily on exchanges with colleagues here and abroad whose mastery of those cultural regions and their past social realities helped me to see similarities and oppositions to the Argentine experience. Our discussions and their reading of rudimentary versions of the manuscript helped to improve it beyond what I should have expected on my own, and to diminish weaknesses. I thus thank Tulio Halperín Donghi, E. Bradford Burns, Arnold Bauer, Carlos Mayo, David Prochaska, Richard Wall, Robert M. Levine, John Coatsworth, Stuart Voss, Eduardo Saguier, Ralph Clem, Joseph Love, Lowell Gudmundson, Richard Slatta, and for his special intellectual energy, Howard Kaminsky. Adriana Silva del Agua, of the Archivo General de la Nación, once again provided me with documentation that had been freshly discovered and catalogued (and some that was not). My research assistant, Terry Young, worked diligently with me on the tedious labor of data coding. Dan Godfrey provided some essential computer programming to suit the peculiarities of the caseload.

A number of research grants relieved me of teaching responsibilities over the course of time and facilitated several periods of residence in Buenos Aires between 1978 and 1985. They included awards and fellowships from the Social Science Research Council, the National Endowment for the Humanities, the Center for Latin American and Caribbean Studies of the University of Illinois at Urbana-Champaign, Florida International University, and its Latin

American and Caribbean Center. To these institutions I offer my thanks.

My wife, Lenore, more *porteña* than most, has been a good sport about our periodic adventures in relocating, and the best of editors. From her I have also learned several research paradigms and the formulation of causal links among behavioral phenomena that are most applicable to, though not purely of, the field of history. Paula and Jeffrey can tell their own children about all the new places and experiences for which this study is to blame.

M.D.S.

Contents

Ten pages of illustrations follow p. 122

Figures and Tables

Figures

Tables

ORDER, FAMILY, AND COMMUNITY IN
BUENOS AIRES
1810-1860

1

Home, Neighborhood, Power

In the closing years of the Spanish American Empire in the early 1800's, Buenos Aires was an uncomplicated city. Most resident chroniclers of the era felt proud of the city's growth and the dramatic evolution of its cultural and material achievements, but these changes did not much alter the basic nature of this face-to-face society—the onslaught of impersonal exchanges in this urban center would not be felt until the period of mass immigration toward the century's end. A hundred years earlier, Buenos Aires had attracted immigrants on a much smaller, but equally important, scale, as newly arrived Spaniards came looking for wider opportunities in either commerce or public office. Already the city sensed the presence of migrants from different regions: besides the Spanish merchants and officials, there were English traders, Portuguese and Italian fishermen, and peoples from the country's interior, all of them adding their own presence to the city's growing population. Yet regardless of the quantitative changes in the city's human and material composition, they were not accompanied by any alteration of the basic forms of production and exchange. Despite the quickened pace of economic and demographic development on the eve of the nineteenth century, the city of Buenos Aires managed to retain many of its qualities as a terminus of rural and pastoral behaviors, while becoming the hub of the South Atlantic trade with Europe. The hybrid city blended traditional with cosmopolitan elements, providing intriguing contradictions in the social and political practices of this early nineteenth-century Ibero-American society. The city's exterior reflected the presence of modern capitalist relations, especially as they related to the trans-Atlantic trade, but its inner qualities—the belief system of many of its residents, the modus operandi in social and political matters—were all slower to change.

Argentine historical literature is replete with references that equate modernity both with the reification of material progress and with the expressions of updated Western intellectual currents.[1] Because of the central role played by the city of Buenos Aires in shaping and expressing the historical ideology of progress, researchers have long treated it as a crucible in which to observe the achievements of its modernizing leaderships.[2] In matters of form, this is a modern and near-perfect European metropolis; in matters related to quotidian social and political behaviors, however, the record of Europeanization is checkered.[3] Evidently, "modernization" was more easily achieved materially—and then only selectively—than behaviorally.[4]

But are changing urban forms really at odds with the more traditional beliefs and values of Buenos Aires' nineteenth-century residents? Change and tradition are brought together in this book, which investigates how some critically important and historical institutions mediated between Europeanizing ideals and Iberian norms, thereby providing coherence to a society lacking in political consensus. Two of these vintage institutions form the focus of this study of life in Buenos Aires in the first half of the nineteenth century: they are the neighborhood and the family.[5]

Barrio and *casa* are used in this volume as abstract constructions, that is, conceptual variables. Their purpose is to provide a prism through which the intentions and rhetoric of the period's political elites and the observations of the contemporary chroniclers of *porteño* society can be refracted into their practical components. For Argentines of the period before the significant changes of the later nineteenth century, the consequences of the contending elites' designs were, of course, concrete rather than abstract; moreover, these consequences were best understood by the majority of porteños at the level of their daily existence—work, play, school, and home. Their own concept of community, before the transformations that resulted from the alluvion of capital and human resources of the latter part of the century, was in practice reduced to the components that framed their daily environments. They included their friends; the street hawkers of the early mornings and the stall-keepers at the open-air markets in one of the plazas that dotted the city; the parish clergy and the local schoolteacher; the barrio authorities, including the constable on the beat and the justice of the peace (*juez de barrio*); the tavern and dry goods storekeeper, or *pulpero*; the men and women of the block who were notable either because of their superior status or because of their pixilated qualities; and, predictably in this face-to-face society, the neighborhood informants whose gossip, accurate or not, provided the *vecinos* with valued information.

On the whole, these were not worldly people—they were not moved to action by the dictates of fashions or values found in faraway circles of the European haute bourgeoisie. On the contrary, their motivations drew strength from what they sensed to be of immediacy to their spatial and visceral realities: the barrio and the casa. Despite the numbering of houses and the naming of streets, vecinos would continue to give directions in the manner of rural villagers until well past the period covered by this study: "To reach the home of Don Gómez, follow this street until you get to Espinosa's bakery and then turn left and walk two blocks until you see the establishment of Juana Delfino. Gómez lives two doors down . . . anyone can tell you."

By contrast, long-distance merchants, politicos, clerics, and intellectuals, conceptualized their world differently; they had a sense of universality about their existence, and, not surprisingly, their frames of reference stretched well beyond the confines of the less educated majority constituting the popular classes, known as the *gente de pueblo*. For the others, referred to in the contemporary language as the *gente decente*, and especially for those who had political interests, community was defined geopolitically. Their principal goal was the institutionalization of stable systems of community, mechanisms by which links could be established that would be capable of binding a public that shared a common space and heritage. However, the significant differences in scope and sense of purpose between the two groups, the one including the elite and the gentry and the other composed of the lower classes and encompassing the vast majority, served to make it difficult for the elites to implant their own definitions of community. Upon the first moves toward independence, the control of these masses, and the ultimate harnessing of their loyalties, became elusive goals for the majority of the creole elites. Success in such endeavors can be measured temporally—how long did they last in office?—and in most cases, they departed abruptly. And yet, despite the Sisyphean aspects of political and social control during much of the nineteenth century—lamented by many con-

temporaries throughout Spanish America and epitomized by Bo-
livar's memorable analogy of sowing in the seas—there were successful leaders. Of those who in Buenos Aires received significant
loyalties, or who lasted in power the longest, it can be said that they
knew how to deal with vecinos on levels that they could understand.
This meant that the lines of communication between executive officers of the government and neighborhood figures of authority
would remain vital and would thread together the various barrios.
It also suggests, in the context of accumulated circumstantial evidence, the political advantages that would accrue to any political
leader who could demonstrate sufficient degree of sensitivity to the
basic interests of households, including familial security and the
maintenance of valued traditions.

The streets of Buenos Aires have always been conveniently informative. The transition from one barrio to another was (and to
some extent still is) easily achieved by walking; such an exercise
would provide one with a sense of the inner workings of this urban
society and its political currents. At the end of the eighteenth century, the city covered an area of less than ten square kilometers; by
the mid-nineteenth century, the overwhelming majority of the population was spread over an area of barely twelve square kilometers.
Differences among neighborhoods—in architectural styles, fashion
of dress, and racial composition—were palpable. In fact, the choice
of entrance into Buenos Aires afforded the traveler one of two quite
different views of the city. If entry were made by ship, the traveler
was likely to meet a busy commercial center virtually touching the
shore, with a bustling population where traditional dress melded
easily with European fashion. By contrast, anyone who arrived by
horse or carriage from the south or west would traverse emptier
spaces interrupted unpredictably by housing, stores, lean-tos, and
warehouses; such a visitor would also meet up with a much greater
percentage of people of color, including blacks, mulattoes, and mestizos. He would pass fields, only some of which were cultivated with
cash crops, and he might very well find it impossible to escape the
stench of putrefied meat that emanated from slaughterhouses on the
city's outer limits.

The maps of the city of Buenos Aires made during the late eighteenth and early nineteenth centuries replicated the grid pattern
found in all Spanish American cities. Yet the appearance of a neat
and consistent urban design belied the unevenness of urbanization.

At approximately the time of the initial moves for independence in 1810, maps of Buenos Aires traced a city that fanned outward, in stepwise fashion, from the port area in a generally westerly direction, occupying the equivalent of almost 400 square blocks. The area covered by standard Spanish blocks (136 square meters) that were busily filled with buildings and people narrowed considerably as one headed eastward in the direction of the city's center, which ended at the estuary that eventually flows into the Atlantic Ocean further east. This narrowing of urban space was the result of a gradual but considerable drop in elevation. This sloping of the earth extended to a rocky and shallow beach appropriately known as *el Bajo*. It framed the coastal edges of the city and ran from the center almost directly northwest and southwest. Other than a few adventurous people who resided in very humble shacks in the Bajo, porteños lived on the high ground. Where they resided had much to do with the quality and rhythms of their lives.

The barrios of nineteenth-century Buenos Aires revolved around two principal signposts of the Spanish-American city, the parish church and the plaza. The parish, in fact, was the common unit of administrative space—police precincts, judgeships of the peace, state-supported elementary schools, and even barrio names were designated on the basis of the territory covered by each of the different parish churches. Accordingly, the majority of porteños associated their residences and places of work with Catedral, San Telmo, Monserrat, Socorro, and so on. Porteños of the era did not make linguistic use of broad or generic names of sections of the city's geography, such as Barrio Sud or Barrio Norte, until the latter part of the century. Thus, the faithful from any given barrio attended services in a nearby church; litigants, the accused, and the victims of crimes filed into a nearby home to make their appearances before the barrio's justice of the peace; the accused were usually held for questioning at the local police precinct; and children who attended school did not have far to walk. Just how unaccustomed porteños were to straying far from their homes is suggested by complaints lodged by public employees with their superiors that traveling four blocks to work was a regrettable imposition on them.[6] This was indeed a walking city, or rather a city composed of walking neighborhoods, each of which contained solidarities and animosities commonly known to its constituents.

Information was exchanged at a variety of crucial locations: at windowsills and doorways that faced the streets, at the corner *pulpería*, outside the church where people clustered in groups after mass, and especially at the local marketplace, usually situated on a plaza near the church. In fact, each plaza served as the most convenient location for the barrio's circulation of goods, services, and news.[7] Plazas also served as the meeting places for teamsters from different points in the country's interior as they parked their wagons and delivered their freight for urban consumers. Teamsters and wagon masters formed some of the most informative links with events that were taking place far away in other parts of Argentina; even journalists depended on these interprovincial tradesmen for news. As the city's population grew and its area expanded (mostly in a westerly direction), new plazas were built to serve the commercial and marketing needs of the newer sections. The populations circulating around the majority of the plazas, such as Plaza Lorea, Plaza Nueva, and Plaza Monserrat, reflected the socioeconomic position of the barrios' residents. Around these sites a stranger could reasonably be confused: was this a capital city linked to Europe by an international port, or a humble pampean town populated by gauchos, black slaves and servants, and dirt farmers? Roadways were not paved, and sidewalks were rare, as were street signs. Depending on the season, either dust clouds blew around uncontrollably or mud holes made riding a horse or carriage dangerous for both beast and rider. Housing was sporadic: empty spaces between homes were just as likely to be taken up by untended fields as by carefully cultivated vegetable plots, while many homes were constructed in makeshift fashion, often very small, and with furnishings strikingly sparse. Such were the city's rural aspects, further reinforced by the relatively few people who were visible in public, except during shopping periods in and around the nearest plaza, the area of likeliest concentration of people.

As the traveler headed eastward, toward the water, the densities of people, construction, and businesses, the variety of dress, race, and fashion, in addition to other outward signs of social position, increased dramatically, until one reached the principal marketplace located at the Plaza de Mayo. Here there was no doubt about the cosmopolitan aspects of Buenos Aires. This was the first line of communication with European markets and the first point of observation for what was held to be fashionable in both the intellectual and material realms. Some streets were paved, as would be others—but far from all—in the period of time covered by this book; sidewalks were common, although street lighting remained unreliable for many decades. Streets in this hub of the city looked busier than perhaps they actually were, because the narrow sidewalks forced pedestrians to spill onto the streets—and thereby into the paths of speeding horses, wagons, and carriages. Street corners were notoriously difficult to negotiate for both pedestrian and equine traffic, since sidewalks wrapped tightly around buildings, forming blind intersections. Such relics of the colonial urban design would not disappear from the central street scenes of Buenos Aires until virtually the end of the century. In much of the city, but especially in the commercial and residential center, the human bottleneck that formed at the corners attracted small-scale businessmen to open *pulperías*—shops that combined a bar with food and dry goods, their doors invitingly open.[8] Indeed, street corners were made all the more colorful by the rough-hewn porteños, often gauchos and their gaucho-like urban counterparts, who stood at the entrances of these pulperías gazing, drinking, perhaps gambling surreptitiously toward the back, and quite possibly arguing over alleged cheating at cards. Predictably, when street brawls took place, they were likely to develop in and around these corners.

The contrasts between this central neighborhood and others lying further outward were quite visible, but not extreme; the external aspects of physical environments and of the various populations that circulated in the city's barrios differed principally in degree. The percentages of men who wore the traditional ponchos and chiripás and of women dressed in coarse cotton and woolen clothes increased in step with the concentric regions radiating outward from the Plaza de Mayo and its immediate vicinity. More humble dwellings and farms, gardens, and sheds for storing stacks of wool and cured leather were easily observable along the flat terrain as one headed toward the city's outer limits. The ubiquitous pulpería of the center was here more infrequent, although no less characteristic, and it was also less likely to offer European consumer goods. But then, few consumers of such items resided in these neighborhoods.

The detailed listings of the probates and the testamentary proceedings related to those individuals who had enough possessions to divide among survivors limned the simplicity of their material surroundings.[9] The average wardrobe and other personal belongings of the majority of porteños were limited to bare necessities. Women seldom owned more than a couple of shawls and blouses, perhaps as many as three skirts, and one pair of shoes or sandals. Undergarments were similarly few, and most men's clothing was comparably limited. Almost everyone in the barrios slept on beds, although these often stood on dirt floors. Dressers and chiffoniers were almost totally absent, most men and women making do with low chests of regional hardwoods. The interiors of their houses included no more than two rooms, and often only one. The gente de pueblo, hoi polloi in the eyes of the gentry and the elite, appeared not to need much in the way of European goods in the earlier part of the century; much later, consumer habits generally moved closer to the standards observed by the gente decente. Thus, the possessions of humble families toward the 1850's and 1860's might include such frills as bibelots on dressers and tables, framed mirrors on the walls, and white embroidered cloth contrasting with the surrounding dark wooden surfaces. Life in the barrios was relatively simple, people worked but apparently did not accumulate many permanent possessions, and living from day to day could have been a relaxed affair had it not been for the cycles of political turmoil that shook these simple interiors out of their barrio rhythms. In fact, political turbulence, and particularly its militarized aspects, periodically reminded these vecinos that their neighborhoods were not at all isolated from the nation's troubles.

Political problems were visited on virtually everyone, but they were generated by only a few. In Buenos Aires, most of the men who were at the heart of political conflicts and who led armies to resolve them tended to live in interiors considerably different from those of the vecinos who filled the ranks of the porteño infantry. Gente decente invariably lived in housing built of brick and finished with plaster. The coverage of exterior brick with plaster, in fact, was one of the most distinguishing characteristics that separated the upper and the lower segments of the city's gente decente. The facades of most of the homes of the gentry and elite were both unassuming and uninviting. Because of the scarcity of hardwood forests and ironworks in the region of the littoral, the ornamentation that could be given to the exteriors of houses was circumscribed by the very expensive and limited craftsmanship of local stonecutters. Thus, architectural aesthetics in Buenos Aires—until imitations of the French styles during the *belle époque* appeared at the century's end—remained rather sober.[10] Elevations were designed on the basis of flat vertical planes usually without inlets or interruptions of any sort, other than the entrance and the windows. Because taxes on real property were assessed on the basis of frontage, the gentry's housing tended to be narrow in relation to its depth. Home sites very often reached halfway into the interior of the block, lending themselves to the allocation of rooms on the basis of the modified Roman patio home, with one or more interior courtyards bordered by rooms equipped for different functions. Servants' quarters, kitchens, and sanitary facilities were always situated at the rear. The disposition of rooms hardly varied at all during most of the nineteenth century, except for the increase in the number of courtyards to two—the *patio* and the *traspatio*—which became fashionable for the well-to-do. These courtyards were connected by an opening, usually alongside an adjoining wall. Entrances to rooms ringed the front and rear courtyards. In addition, new housing constructed for the wealthier segment of the gente decente, toward the middle of the century, contained two storys. Only a handful of buildings were constructed with three, and these usually served as multiple-family housing.

Rules of conduct for the gente decente required that acts of sociability among themselves take place in the privacy of interior spaces. For them, the public and the private worlds were much more separable than was the case among the gente de pueblo. Outdoor activities were generally associated with either patriotic or religious holidays, and with labor functions, but not with leisure. To be sure, Sunday strolls along the walkway that paralleled the shore, known as the Alameda, became fashionable, but only gradually. In fact, one of the fundamental differences between the gente de pueblo and the gente decente was their respective attitudes toward and definitions of proper behavior. Work and leisure were closely intertwined among the gente de pueblo. Except for domestic labor, much of the work in which the lower classes were engaged brought them outdoors, often away from the watchful eyes of owners and supervisors, ever-mindful of the clock. The pace of labor for most people was relatively casual; moreover, as was typical of many other Latin American economies, most of the manual laborers worked in spasmodic rhythms, job security being unknown. It was therefore quite likely that the men and women who regularly patronized the troublesome pulperías were in the middle of, or in between, jobs. Thus, it is not surprising that the gente decente, who usually worked at home, in offices, and in stores, defined the outdoors in terms of their own sense of division between work and play. The values they as-

signed to each type of activity became more sharply distinct in the
course of time, as capitalism's deepening penetration demanded.

These differences in attitudes and mentalities toward time, discipline, order, and even one's own physical location were sharpened
and became sources of social tensions that deepened into other, more
overtly political and ideological cleavages. Not surprisingly, the level
of frustration with the sociopolitical environment of Buenos Aires
rose among porteños: "Order!, order!," pleaded a frustrated man in
his letter to the editor of a Buenos Aires newspaper in 1821. He was
complaining about the discontinuous regimen of official regulations,
about the lack of obedience to the laws, and about the absence of
deference to established authority. In sum, he was made all the more
upset by a generalized perception of his government's ineffectiveness
in establishing a sense of respect for its wishes.[11] These were the res-
olute pleas for the establishment of order that characterized the collective conscience of the citizenry and that were expressed in many
ways—both in literary and behavioral modalities—throughout
much of the nineteenth century. The public's desire for order is
gleaned from a variety of sources, including personal memoirs, police reports, the concern of school authorities over related issues of
compliance and discipline, and the city's popular press. This collective tension was especially palpable during the first half of the
nineteenth century, the period preceding the era that Argentine historiography appropriately identifies with the "national organization"—the process of institutionalizing constitutional, civil, and
criminal procedures. The prior era, by contrast, is described as one
of "national disorganization," a term employed by adherents to the
Positivist ideology at the century's end.[12] For those latter-day social
critics, the "inescapable" feature of Spanish American history had
been expressed in the series of "endemic convulsions" that followed
immediately upon independence.[13] And indeed, it was a period characterized by military strongmen, ephemeral interprovincial pacts,
and the legitimation of policy on the basis of the authoritativeness
and the force of character of any given leader.

While these, among others, were the rules that governed the political game for the elites who circulated among the players, the majority of the gente decente turned its attention to the self-absorption
of bourgeois private action. Thus, the gente decente who lived in
the city's central areas generally circulated within their own barrios.
Except for men whose professional or business activities required

them to supervise their affairs elsewhere in the city or outside it, residents of the central areas certainly had no need to go far to acquire food, services, and every type of commodity: the Plaza de Mayo and its surrounding blocks contained dry goods stores, specialty shops, cafés, government offices, and ecclesiastical institutions to satisfy virtually all tastes and needs. Yet the city's center, and especially the Plaza de Mayo, were not segregated areas of activity reserved for the elite. On the contrary, the many retail and service-oriented establishments required a wide spectrum of employees, ranging from the unskilled to the administrative, who joined the domestic servants working in the area's home to form a broad socioeconomic sample of the population milling around the *centro*. This was an excellent observation post from which to note the pace and flavor of a walking city. In addition to satisfying the average needs of daily life, political activities and periodic crises also brought thousands of porteños to the Plaza de Mayo. Even before the moves for independence (and down to the present day), the Plaza de Mayo had become the hub of political and military actions of all sorts. From political speeches to public hangings, from divisive political duels between enemies and their supporters contending for power to mass meetings in solidarity with particular personalities, from religious processions to patriotic celebrations, the central plaza was the city's epicenter—a magnet that drew observers of all social and racial origins to come and bear witness to (or stay safely away from) some of the most crucial developments in the country's history.

Such public excitement and externally oriented fanfare, however, are not the stuff of this volume. It delves, instead, into the much less obvious, but equally crucial, domestic affairs of porteños in the troublesome decades before the city's outward signs began to transform it into the "Paris of South America." At first glance, the fundamental questions raised in this book appear deceptively simple. How did the homes of the two broad social groups, the gente decente and the gente de pueblo, fare during these politically turbulent times? What kinds of strategies did these groups follow to fashion some sort of order from the seemingly constant disorder that so many voices lamented? How were familial and political considerations intertwined? As it turns out, however, these are puzzling and difficult issues made still more complex because the subject lacks a cache of solid scholarly literature from which one can draw useful theoretical models, and because meaning must be coaxed out of the actions of the large proportion of the period's men, women, and children who remained inarticulate. And yet if we are ever to have a sense of the history of the mentalities of Buenos Aires' residents—the dwellers of the city that went on to become the richest and most cosmopolitan in Spanish America—a good beginning is to investigate their sense of themselves, of their families, of their neighbors, and of their nation. It is a complex story with myriad connectives, some of which will be disentangled in the chapters that follow.

Thesis The underlying thesis of this book is that the dynamics in the relations between citizen and state were generated by a commonly desired objective: the reestablishment of law and order after the period of social and political turbulence that began with the Revolution of 1810. Furthermore, the links between citizen and state are here considered to have been mediated by familial strategies of survival and the personalist nature of political power. Finally, the construct of the family as an important element in the realm of political leadership is methodologically fundamental to the study of an era when the domination by the state of the citizen was in its formative stages, still far from becoming institutionalized with state apparatuses. In the absence of a reliable and continuous political estate, the domestic estate possessed, in this patrimonial society, some not-so-obvious leverage in determining and defending its own interests. This leverage waned over time, as the political estate became codified in the course of the century's second half.

The period under study covers a historical moment that in several ways typified many of the troublesome events experienced by other Spanish American republics in the process of building their nations. The wars for independence released divisive forces, which balkanized the colonial viceroyalties and regionalized power within many of the new republics. Political leadership came to rest in the hands of strongmen who periodically competed with one another for political supremacy. Argentina's fundamental ideological divisions can be discerned early in this process. Men who considered a centralized authority the superior form of government battled others who saw in a new federalized republic a mechanism for redressing the economic and political imbalances they had been experiencing since the late colonial period. Beyond the welfare of the elites, however, the divisions and ensuing battles over regional privileges took on characteristics that affected thousands of Argentines whose colonial past had not previously admitted much of wars' consequences. An im-

portant feature of the early modern Argentine period was the absence of cogent political philosophies that could be agreed upon
prior to or simultaneously with independence. No consensus was
reached on the role of the public in determining the political leadership; nor was there a general agreement on how to circumscribe
political authority. Much ink was spent proposing the principles of
legitimate representation, redress of grievances, the social contract,
and other theoretical underpinnings of the French and North
American revolutions. These theories, however, tended to be concentrated around the earliest debates on proper government associated with independence, and soon afterward became detached from
the brusquely practical realities that followed in the wake of political
disorder.[14]

The theoretical framework that shapes this book in matters of
political thought is composed of a set of four propositions aimed at
understanding rights and obligations within the formative political
system of nineteenth-century Argentina, and possibly of other regions in Spanish America. These rights and obligations, in turn,
were conditioned by an unarticulated, semicontractual mode of political rule. The four propositions are:

1. That there was a logical and empirical link between the well-
known patriarchal nature of the family and the way porteños perceived their positions in political society.

2. That the absence of consensus in political rule necessitated a
societally valued tradition of authority that could overcome the inability of early republican forms to forge stable communal links, and
that this tradition was patriarchy.

3. That the assumption that the most important element tem-
pering the caudillo's power was the force of his military opponents
results in the overlooking of two important features of his rule: first,
the degree of protection and benefit accorded to the people at
large—not just to his military and elite supporters—and, second,
the mentalities generated within those people. The consideration of
a Spanish American political public composed largely of the lower
classes (and thus largely inarticulate) is essential to an understanding
of the nineteenth-century caudillo as a dynamic ruler whose durability depended in part on his performance record vis-à-vis the maintenance of life among the poor, the likeliest victims of political turbulence and wars.

4. That the nature of political leadership was patriarchal but not

absolute; that is, that unlike the traditional parental absolutism of the paterfamilias, the political patriarchy of Buenos Aires incorporated consent and an unarticulated contract that mediated between ruler and ruled. These three elements of political leadership—patriarchy, consent, and contract—were reconstituted at various levels of civil and political interaction throughout the first half of the nineteenth century in the absence of other formulae that might have established a basis for social peace.

A Western perspective underlies this analysis in order to place the Argentine experience within a cross-cultural framework. Indeed, the research focuses on a region where relatively few Amerindian traditions survived and much Western culture was nurtured, where the principal city forged more links with Western Europe in the nineteenth century than did any other urban area of Latin America, and where the population and its consumption of culture were increasingly European. Buenos Aires, therefore, offers an optimal arena for going beyond the historical tradition of considering only Iberian institutions that had been transplanted to the Americas. To be sure, Argentine institutions operated within a matrix of central beliefs that were derived from Iberian origins, but they certainly went on to evolve—particularly in the urban areas—within the wider panorama of Western European socioeconomic and political ideologies.[15] Still, nineteenth-century Buenos Aires presented an odd and contradictory mix of Ibero-American tradition and Western European development. For example, it represented the archetype of the caudillo-led society peculiar to Spanish America; and its economy acted in the manner of a typical Spanish American periphery within the evolving world system. But at the same time, the porteño elites set their sights, established their goals, and situated their own country's progress according to a Western European standard. Indeed, this was true of virtually all elites to some degree, regardless of ideological bent. Thus, how much Buenos Aires was effectively a part of contemporary Western sociofamilial development is an issue that this book will address among others.

In the chapters that follow, the interplay between the familial and the sociopolitical orders of porteño society will be examined. Each chapter will focus on a different aspect of this fundamental and troublesome relationship between private satisfaction and public purpose. The first will address the institutional means and particularistic styles employed by the criminal justice system in order to analyze the mechanisms through which the variety of participants in that system expanded, while the traditional criteria for the arbiters remained unaltered. Subsequent chapters will reconstruct the city's moral order and educational system in the context of the political strictures that fashioned the world of children and young people. The demographic aspects of the period's social and political conditions will then be discussed by way of a longitudinal analysis of the observed variations in the structure and composition of urban households. Considerable demographic data will be presented to arrive at conclusions concerning the locational and structural patterns of thousands of families who resided in the city of Buenos Aires. Finally, the concluding chapter will analyze the interplay between family and political leadership.

In its totality, this book represents a research endeavor in family history that contains two principal goals. The first is to integrate traditional evidence and quantitative findings from thousands of men, women, and children in Argentina's most important city. These data reach across race and class in an effort to reconstruct the basic features of the quotidian experiences of the common people and the well-to-do. The second goal is to reconcile social history with issues of political legitimacy and social control. One of the criticisms leveled at family historians stems from the apolitical direction they have taken in the course of their research. Despite the acknowledged links between domestic and political societies, the historian's approach has been, in practice, limited to the investigation of the family's internal dynamics, including, for example, its productive capabilities, its patterns of consumption, its procreative strategies, and so forth. To be sure, research in family history has been carried out with great detail, but, as noted by Elizabeth Fox-Genovese and Eugene Genovese, "adequate analysis and interpretation of the role of the family as mediator between the public and private spheres remain difficult, elusive, and necessarily controversial."[16] To the extent that this study succeeds in surveying the obscure labyrinths in which the fundamental concerns and values of the porteño families were stored, we may gain an understanding of the synapses between the private and the public spheres, the domestic and the political domains.

2

Disorder and Social Control

One of the major consequences of the wars for independence in Spanish America was the breakdown of traditional lines of authority. Social and political divisions were blurred in the process of mass mobilization and recruitment of the lower classes for military purposes. Throughout Spanish America, the traditional dynamics of power and deference were challenged well beyond the political questions revolving around loyalty to Spain. One extreme example of these challenges was the bloody insurrection by Mexican Indians and mestizos led by Manuel Hidalgo and José Morelos in 1810, which quickly took on overt racial and social antipathies.[1] Even if matters did not decay into such intensely bloody confrontations elsewhere, a sense of apprehension pervaded the ruling elites of most of the newly independent republics on the issue of maintaining their social control over a citizenry uprooted and dislocated by the misfortunes of war.

The first successful move toward independence in South America took place in the city of Buenos Aires in 1810. The effects this movement had on the criminal justice system and on social control are comparable to contemporary developments in Europe. In fact, Buenos Aires is a particularly useful locus to study social control in Latin America within a Western framework for a number of reasons. Because its urban population contained relatively few Amerindians or their descendants, the issue of social control was not complicated by the image of an "Indian threat," as it was in the Andean and Mesoamerican regions. Indeed, Buenos Aires, more than most urban centers in Spanish America, was in close contact with cultural and social developments in Western Europe. Throughout its republican history, Buenos Aires has been peculiarly sensitive to and affected by cultural currents and economic developments in England, France, and Germany. Visitors and immigrants from Europe were often influential in molding a mentality among literate porteños that spoke of European ideals but that in turn conflicted with Spanish American realities.[2] This chapter addresses the notion of social control as a constant problem sensed by the city's dominant groups during the first half-century of nation building and locates the local porteño responses within contemporary European developments in matters of criminal justice. It argues that the extreme preoccupation with the establishment and maintenance of a regimen of law and order was the common denominator that characterized otherwise widely divergent and inimical political elites. Furthermore, it argues that issues bearing on local autonomy and traditions prevented meaningful changes from developing within the processes of social control. This chapter ultimately aims at analyzing attitudes toward the criminal justice system in Buenos Aires in order to shed some light on the means employed by political authorities to attain their apparently elusive goal: law and order.

Theory and Method

The wars for independence in South America began with the abstractions derived from philosophical and political debates among members of the urban intelligentsia. The city of Buenos Aires witnessed in 1810 the transposition of such argumentation into execution by becoming the first proponent of independence in the River Plate region and by exporting the idea along with its military support elsewhere in South America. Much more complex than a contest for political supremacy between independentists and royalists, the wars quickly broke down into internal struggles that permanently convulsed the social order. During the decade of military strife, from 1810 to 1820, masses of men who had heretofore moved only in the limited human space of their daily activities were mobilized and thrust into different environments and lifestyles. Military needs also caused the arming of a society that, in its urban confines, had previously felt little need for weapons.

The results had serious consequences for the maintenance of social control, particularly because of the threat to the traditional lines of authority and deference, the wide dissemination of weaponry,

and the brutalization that often accompanied fundamental disagreements in civil and political relations. Thus, almost as soon as the
heady expectations of republican theory gave way to the brusque
realities of political instability, the attention of the authorities turned
to reestablishing civil order by police and judicial measures. In the
wake of these macroscopic changes and the dismemberment of the
previously unified Viceroyalty of the Río de la Plata into a number
of regional units of power and government, authorities in Buenos
Aires fell back on the solidarities and linkages within local urban precincts as defenses against violators of established norms.
Throughout the period studied (at least), it is argued, the neighborhood—the barrio—seldom suffered from interference from national or provincial authorities, except to uphold the principle of local option in dispensing judgments. Furthermore, the criminal
justice system failed to provide an integrative mechanism designed
for community or nation building because of its continued adherence to the philosophy of barrio autonomy, and the discontinuous,
bureaucratic structure charged with the conduct of judicial matters.

Because of the tendency to favor the local space, criminal justice
in the city of Buenos Aires is best studied from the available police
records rather than from the records of the courts. The great importance of each precinct's policemen and *juez de paz* (justice of the
peace) in the pretrial process requires that the researcher pay special
attention to police records as heuristic devices. Furthermore, most
criminologists recognize that police data are rich in that, unlike court
records, they do not eliminate as much of the crime that did in fact
occur.[3] The following discussion is thus based on archival materials
culled mostly from the police records of Buenos Aires housed in the
Archivo General de la Nación. Their contents reveal at close range
not only the underworld of Buenos Aires, but also popular and elite
attitudes toward the idea of lawlessness, which figure in the correspondence the public had with police officials and *jueces de paz*.

Constraints on Orderliness

The concept of criminality broadened considerably during the
nineteenth century. But it built on solid foundations, since colonial
society had by no means been totally law-abiding; by the mid-
eighteenth century, urban authorities from Mexico City to Buenos
Aires shared grave concerns for public safety. In 1753, a census was

taken in Mexico City for the specific purpose of designing a better system for controlling crime, beginning with improved mechanisms for patrolling streets.[4] In Buenos Aires, too, new regulations, enacted in 1790, were meant to respond to the rising tide of criminality. The language of the preamble—the *considerandos* that moved officials to action—of these new ordinances indicates that to the authorities crime was linked to the "pernicious" lower classes, a consequence of their own natural predispositions toward lawlessness.

There being many evildoers with which the city is infested, committing robberies, wounding and killing regardless of the zeal applied to the punishment of those convicted of having perpetrated such detestable crimes; and such acts being so offensive to the peace and security that should shelter the good people under the sacred protection of the Laws; wishing to extirpate the causes that produce licentiousness and the continuous habit of delinquency found among the plebeians, principally the Negroes, Mulattoes, Mestizos, and the wandering strangers and vagrants from the countryside, who, under the specious pretexts of their dealings and farming, enter this city and are usually the perpetrators of the robberies and these enormous atrocities.[5]

As the dual process of population growth and geographic mobility swelled the city's ranks, the quantity of crime and punishment expanded. The percentage of in-migrants from the interior to the city of Buenos Aires more than doubled between 1810 and 1827, in great part as a consequence of the generalized geographic mobility created by years of civil war (1810–20) and war with Brazil (1825–28).[6] One of the principal challenges faced by the municipal authorities was, therefore, to arrive at the means through which to foster the internalization by poor urban dwellers and rustic migrants of the civic norms attendant on urban society. Elites found themselves repeatedly reining in what they considered the excessive freedom of action displayed by the lower classes in their misinterpretation of the meaning of republican liberty, in their "foolish belief that freedom means evading the law and mocking the authorities; . . . this mistaken concept carries with it the most harmful licentiousness."[7] Yet the elites' goal of instilling deference to authority became difficult to attain in the wake of the deep and often violent political strife brutalizing the antagonisms of a population that was led by itinerant caudillos, felt increasingly alienated from earlier colonial expecta-

tions of deference, and, in the end, had a smaller stake in the pres-
ervation of the social distance that had previously protected the elites
from the popular classes.

The generalized concern over the potential dismantling of the
traditional social order can be observed in the many edicts throughout the Río de la Plata requiring permission to travel, internal pass-
ports, and work documentation. The insistence on such strict regulations expressed an awareness "of the depth of the crisis provoked
by the protracted war, of the need to impose on those all-too-agitated
lands a strictly enforced order."[8] The same preoccupations that had
motivated the earlier generation of revolutionary leaders were now
felt by the Buenos Aires authorities. For example, in 1827, government officials reiterated the highly restrictive regulations of 1813;
the police edict of 1827 stipulated that "without vigilance the important objectives [of tranquillity and public order] would not be
attained." Once again, neighborhood officials were to provide the
police with a list of residents of each barrio, after which no person
was to move without permission and registration in the police records; similarly, no one was to move into any neighborhood without
first notifying the authorities.[9]

The earlier police edict of 1821 had established specific streets for
entering and leaving the city and had forbidden the use of knives,
blades, and firearms. In a telling construct relating administrative
responsibilities, political stability, and social control, the equation between disorder and treason to the fatherland was made explicit:
"Any barrio *Alcalde* or Lieutenant [*Alcalde*], and any employee or
officer of the Police Department, who, with malicious intent, fails to
comply with the contents of these Regulations, will be declared an
enemy of the Fatherland."[10] The following year, policemen were instructed to round up all vagrants, "regardless of color or status," to
be sent to military duty or, if disabled, to serve in public works for
one to eight years.[11] Special caution was taken with certain groups.
For example, an Italian priest named Giacondo de Costa arrived
from Montevideo in 1822 on his way to visit relatives in Córdoba; in
accordance with the regulations, he presented himself before the
chief of police to have his passport inspected and internal travel documents approved. He did not have, however, the additional permit
required of foreign ecclesiastics, and was therefore required to make
an appearance at the police headquarters twice daily until the higher
authorities decided what to do. Finally, the government ordered

Fray de Costa expelled and shipped to Montevideo "in the briefest time possible."[12] Finally, also in 1822, it became the obligation of every citizen to "cooperate in the prevention of any attempted crime from taking place by way of his own action, and in the apprehension of the crime's perpetrator," under penalty of incarceration.[13] The following passage, written in the 1830's, describes the itinerary that entrants to the city had to follow if they were to avoid arrest and arbitrary imprisonment: "In the first place, one has to go to the Navy Commandant's office to get a visa for the passport; then to the police headquarters to exchange the passport for a *papeleta* [local documentation]; third, foreigners must go to their consuls to *buy* a document for safeconduct; afterward, one must go to the *alcalde* of the barrio to give him the address that one selected to reside in . . . and then to the local police precinct's office just to make oneself known to those authorities."[14] The extreme guardedness with which the national-period authorities viewed mobile people emanated from no tradition: it was the direct legacy of the political and military conflicts arising from the May Revolution. The preceding era, to the contrary, had witnessed municipal ordinances enacted by the authorities in conscious attempts to make it easier for traffic and persons to move into and within the city. In 1808, for example, the *cabildo* ordered that every street carry signs with the street's name and that the entrance door of every house and apartment display its assigned number. The police department was charged with the execution of this municipal ordinance. Considered an enlightened and modernizing move, the ordinance "followed the fashion of European cities, in order for strangers [*forasteros*] to be able to guide themselves easily toward the streets, blocks, or houses they may be looking for, and to be able to be given directions easily for finding the address of anyone."[15] The ordinance failed to instill in porteños a sense of public space that did not contain personally identifiable addresses: well into the century, directions continued to be given in relation to someone's place of business or home, identified by the owner's name. This small-town mentality reflected in part the ready and personal cognition of the immediate environment, the barrio.

The concern for public order in the nineteenth century was not, of course, limited to Argentina or to Latin America; rather, it appears to have been a generalized phenomenon that had begun in earnest in Europe with the Industrial Revolution. The preoccupation with surveillance was a feature of the French authorities in the nine-

teenth century. While each Argentine laborer was required to carry
a *libreta de conchabo*, the French worker had to carry the *livret* properly validated by both employer and police. In France, this identity
card was an innovation of the Revolution and was intended to control the traffic of workers; in Argentina, the *libreta*, generated by the
Revolution of 1810, served a similar function.[16] Fear that the moral
fiber was disintegrating was to many Englishmen a serious fact of
life by 1800. Crime and immorality had become virtually indistin-
guishable among both Argentine and British contemporaries.[17] Positive and reinforcing relationships were asserted to exist among principles of proper morality, legal behavior, and "correct" political
ideology. Illustrations of the role assigned to the criminal justice system in upholding those relationships came from opposite ends of the
political spectrum. This aspect of social control in Buenos Aires,
which may be called moral Jacobinism, can be noted among zealous
liberals, who, during the revolutionary period in Buenos Aires, went
so far as to urge the police to forbid performances of theatrical works
that were "immoral, unimportant, or frivolous. [The Police De-
partment] should permit the showing of dramatic works deemed to
be patriotic, useful in fostering the nation, and instructive. The theater must close in times of adversity, and whenever useful and liberal-
minded productions are unavailable."[18] Approximately a decade
later, one may compare, for example, the philosophical affinity between the British Society for the Reformation of Manners and the
editors of *El Lucero*, a Buenos Aires daily, recognized as the Rosas
government's organ in the late 1820's and 1830's. The Pontefract
branch of the society felt in 1786 that "idle, disorderly and dangerous
persons, of all descriptions, are constantly wandering about, and the
commission of crimes and offences hath increased to an alarming
degree."[19] Forty years later in Buenos Aires, similar apprehensions
were reinforced by the distrust of "a people who lack sufficient
learned qualities to discover the truth . . . and even if one accords
them a degree of enlightenment, their passions are too agitated to
be able to make impartial judgments."[20] Recent war and social agitation had joined the Spanish Americans' long tradition of preferring urban residence to create some of the same results as the Industrial Revolution had in contemporaneous Western Europe;
through different processes, both regions had begun to experience
the centripetal pull of cities on a dispersed mass of rural workers
and the attendant social heterogeneity and friction.[21]

TABLE I
Distribution of Criminal Convictions, Buenos Aires, 1831
(N = 655)

Crime	Percent	Crime	Percent
Robbery	48.1%	Forgery	1.1%
Insult and		Rape	1.1
insubordination	21.1	Debts	0.9
Fighting and		Drunkenness	0.5
aggravated assault	19.5	Bigamy	0.3
Homicide	7.5	TOTAL	100.0%

SOURCE: AGN X-42-8-5, Censos, 1813–61.

The fears of the elites reflected the strain shown by the municipal facilities of police and justice as early as the 1820's. Delays in judicial processes had resulted in public outcries over the trend "for civil and criminal court cases to take an eternity" to be resolved; and generally, on matters related to police and criminal justice, the government was felt to be unaware of popular sentiments.[22] Eventually, the government acknowledged that indeed the judicial system was nearing a breaking point, though no solutions were offered.[23] The late 1820's appear to have been tumultuous for the criminal justice system; to judge by the significant increase in the population serving time in jail, Rosas' coming to power did signal a heavier hand in the treatment of lawbreakers. In February 1827, the incarcerated population of Buenos Aires numbered 317 people.[24] The following April it fell to 236.[25] By 1831, however, a tranquil year by contemporary standards, 900 convicts, or approximately 2 percent of the city's population, were serving their terms in the city's public jail.[26] In the same year, 655 more men and women were sent to this facility for committing a wide range of crimes. On the average, 55 people were convicted monthly of one of the nine crimes listed in Table 1.

The overarching concern about the potential breakdown of the community's moral fiber can be observed in the relatively high proportion (21.1 percent) of men and women who were incarcerated for offending and insulting—presumably but not only—their social superiors. Indeed, after robbery this was the crime most often committed. It was a reality that conflicted most acutely with the objective of all political factions after independence: to inject a tone of respectability into social relations, even within the lower classes. An irreconcilable duality, then, characterized the system of law and order in Buenos Aires: the expectations demanded by the elites and the reality provided by the period's social relations.[27] The few basic transformations in the pastoral and rustic economic system had served to limit the number of citizens imbued with European cosmopolitan norms.[28] Later on, at the close of the nineteenth century, an important segment of the Argentine intelligentsia would lament the country's Europeanization and would recall with fondness the mythical days when native values prevailed—the days of *criollismo*.[29] But now, at the century's start, the ideal of a Europeanized porteño society meant that elites could not accept the participation of the rustic types until after a long period of apprenticeship to the norms of civilized society.

Despite the high frequency of illegal activities evident in the police records of the city of Buenos Aires, criminality was not widely publicized by either the press or government spokesmen. Florencio Varela, who would become a notable legal and political figure, noted this conspicuous silence in his thesis for the law degree at the University of Buenos Aires in 1827. "Who can deny," he lamented, "that only the jurists among us know the laws that rule us, and that the public hardly knows . . . which actions are legal and which are forbidden." He also pointed to the lack of public notice given to the trials, the lack of relationship between the crime and the punishment—the economy of the penal system, according to Foucault— and the terrible conditions inside the jails.[30]

Newspapers echoed instead the political concerns of the day, alternating with financial reports or cultural news from abroad. On only a few occasions did *El Argos de Buenos Ayres*, for example, a widely read newspaper of the early 1820's, devote space in its columns to reporting socially or criminally disruptive behavior; but when it did, it cast such references in a deprecatory tone, with a disdain that would appear to have relieved both the editors and the authorities of the responsibilities of finding causes and applying constructive remedies. Thus, at carnival time in February, *El Argos* devoted a few lines to the excesses of the participants in the festivities, such as the "Best-Known Triumphs of the Carnival of 1822," printed after a particularly chaotic carnival period.

Pedro Luque: wounded by a flying rock. José Villanueva: gravely wounded with a paring-chisel. José Ríos: two fingers cut off with a saber. Francisco Benites: two wounds with a razor. Manuel García: a broken leg. Bernardo

Vidal: lost a slice of flesh from his instep to the lowest parts. Ignacio Capdevila: wounded by a flying stone. Antonio Ariza: wounded by a blow on the head with a club. Joaquín Marco: stabbed to death. José María Condeani: clubbed to death. A young [unidentified] man: legs crushed after being run over by a horse.[31]

The list was meant to be interpreted not as an objective news item, but rather as biting social commentary on the very existence of such loose and uncivilized behavior: in the porteño press, brevity characterized the sarcasm behind criticism. Juan B. Alberdi noted with dismay the offensive, rather than constructive, nature of the city's journalistic traditions: "I do not favor this system employed by writers who would have nothing to do if they had nothing to attack," he wrote in a letter to Domingo Sarmiento in 1853.[32]

Neither public notice nor public participation was a regular feature of social control in Buenos Aires, contrary to developments in France and England. Indeed, ancien régime France had a two-tier system of judicial cases that allowed private parties as well as royal officials to initiate criminal proceedings. Furthermore, the rise in the criminal court caseload in southwestern France beginning in the 1780's resulted from the increase in private initiation.[33] This growth in the French public's involvement in matters related to criminal procedure helped to spread awareness of the issues of crime and danger among popular circles well beyond the circle of officers of the court. By the time of the restoration of the monarchy the notion of social control, particularly over the dangerous classes, had become an issue of general discussion among both the governing circles and the press.[34]

For its part, English political culture and legal tradition had long made crime a consideration of public awareness. The king's courts had been put into action upon presentment by jury, which thereby thrust "the responsibility upon the community and relied on 'common knowledge,' not on detection."[35] Other legal processes, principally assizes, ensured public display of, and public participation in, the criminal justice system. Even justices of the peace, whose medieval form of commission remained essentially the same until 1878, held public session even on occasions when proper courtrooms were not available.[36] The public display given to adjudicating matters of crime and disorder was, by the eighteenth century, a strategy consciously intended by officers of the court. They hoped that the impact of the "majesty" of the procedure, as Douglas Hay termed it, would spread beyond the group of people watching in the court-room: "Within [their] elaborate ritual . . . judge and counsel displayed their learning with an eloquence that often rivalled that of leading statesmen. There was an acute consciousness that the courts were platforms for addressing the multitude."[37]

By contrast, the reading public of Buenos Aires was very much aware of the differences between the porteño majority's attitudes and mentalities on the subject of criminal justice and those of their European contemporaries. Some worldly porteños recognized their countrymen's collective ignorance of matters of crime and disorder that in other countries, according to a commentator, "would be a cause of general interest and of great alarm among all types of citizens for such things as aggravated assaults, robberies, arson, [and] attempted murder of women by their own husbands. [An occasional] bulletin informs us of the deeds, but who ever speaks about the consequences of those deeds? How are we to know if the accused have been convicted or found innocent? Who has been charged with the duty of assuring us that the ends of justice have been satisfied?"[38]

The Buenos Aires authorities could point to failed experiments in popular participation in the criminal justice system of neighboring Brazil, a frequent point of comparison for Argentine leaders. During the first three decades of independence, reformist Brazilians had succeeded in opening the judicial processes to the public at the local and regional levels. But by the mid-1830's, conservative reaction and the candid disappointment of some liberals resulted in an ideological turn to elitism that closed the system to all but the university-trained *letrados*. Reformers had intended popular involvement, by way of the jury system, to limit the otherwise unilateral power of magistrates. But the reforms resulted in a criminal justice system that contained two conflicting elements, the popular and the professional personnel, whose animosities threatened to immobilize the wheels of justice.[39] In the end, conservatives in Brazil and Argentina shared the elitist philosophy that emphasized the inherent limitations of the lower classes in making positive contributions to the judicial process. The tendency in Buenos Aires to restrict the conduct of legal procedure to *letrados*, however, took place very early in the region's independence. The Appeals Court established in January 1812 had been composed of five men, two of whom were not *letrados*, but rather respectable and patriotic citizens of merit—*vecinos de capa y espada.*[40] Only five years later, the Provisional Regulations governing the administration of justice redefined the criteria for positions on the Court of Appeals to effectively remove laymen from all proceedings: "No one may be named from this moment on, not even temporarily, to any post on the Court of Appeals, unless he is above the age of twenty-five, and a *letrado* with a minimum of six years of professional experience."[41]

Thus, in contrast to the English custom of using judicial proceedings to lecture the public in the courtroom about the virtues and majesty of the law, no audience was available to Argentine judges: they sat behind closed doors and reviewed all evidence and arguments that had been presented in writing, and in writing they passed sentence. Reformers called for the systematizing of the judicial administrative apparatus, beginning with public accountability and public review of the numbers and types of crimes committed in the city.[42] Lethargy in case resolution, along with improper use of police authority, occasionally caused delays of up to two years in the disposition of criminal cases. Hence the generalized frustration that pervaded the criticisms of a judicial system: "Nothing could excuse those who are responsible for such a scandal. There is no reason to hide within the obscurity of our laws, or the labyrinth of our procedures."[43] Before the 1860's, Argentina lacked civil and criminal codes; the execution of the law rested, instead, on a combination of Iberian principles and improvised judgments. Arbitrariness in the treatment of the accused was, therefore, a necessary feature of apprehension, prosecution, and sentencing.

Administration of Justice

The administrative hierarchy and the responsibilities of the various arms of the judicial system varied little during the period between 1810 and 1860. The city of Buenos Aires and the various towns growing in its hinterland were divided into sections in each of which a resident of the neighborhood was appointed general overseer. Each of these *alcaldes* or *jueces de sección* or *barrio* acted as a sort of keeper of his neighbors' behavior. These and other officials responsible for the management of the legal system derived their duties from inherited practices that amalgamated Roman, Gothic, and Iberian traditions. The *alcalde de barrio*, for example, was a nineteenth-century combination of two Roman officials, the praetor and the iudex, laymen who were entrusted with judicial functions on the basis of their high rank among citizens. Like their classical predecessors, *alcaldes* or *jueces de barrio* were problem solvers rather than jurisprudential theorists, and thus tended to avoid abstract formulations of general principle; instead, they reasoned case by case.[44]

A number of historical factors combined to provide these local officials with considerable power. Here the heritage of a dual Roman law system in Spain and its possessions was particularly important. Despite the general impression that it emanated from a purely Roman background, Spanish legal custom also incorporated other remnants, from pre-Roman Celtic and Iberian practices to post-Roman Gothic superimpositions. Yet the revived primacy and study of idealized Roman law, beginning in the eleventh century, provided the pattern of legal dualism by maintaining the coexistence of Justinian rigidity with the flexibility of regional and customary practices. This dualism—law as an ideal and law as a practical system—characterized the inconsistencies of porteños with judicial powers. In addition, the multiplicity of legal instruments that accumulated and shared legal importance—the *Fuero Juzgo*, the *Fuero Real*, the *Siete Partidas* (derived from Justinian's *Corpus Juris*), the various *recopilaciones*, the many *cédulas*, and the *fueros* regarding special privileges—provided lay and professional judges with such a wide array of both codified custom and written reason (*ratio scripta*) that inconsistency and arbitrariness became necessary consequences. Finally, Spanish legal doctrine had not evolved much since the early modern period; even such a recent exercise in legal updating as the 1805 *Novísima Recopilación* was performed with the same criteria as the New Laws of 1542.[45]

Thus, even though his power was localized, the *juez de sección* had wide latitude of action and interpretation of the law on each case before him. He had the power to call on the policemen assigned to his ward to intervene in matters he could not or would not solve himself; he had the power to subpoena witnesses to or participants in an offense and have them brought before him for private questioning; and he had the power to charge the accused formally as well as to bring contending parties to an amicable resolution of a case, thereby making formal charges unnecessary. The *juez de sección* also acted as arbiter of disputes among his neighbors, often among family members, before such disagreements could disintegrate into violent acts. In this respect, *jueces* can be seen as the secular counterparts of parish priests: confidants, problem solvers, advisers, and appeasers; in fact, their task of peacekeeping is best illustrated by the change of their title to *jueces de paz*, beginning with the Rosas period.

These *jueces* also responded to the political dictates of the times, reflecting the government's attitudes toward friends and enemies and the kind of moral order envisioned by the heads of state. After all, the *jueces* were selected by the highest political authorities on the recommendations made by their own supporters and influential members of the community. The applicants' qualifications included the correct combination of personal attributes, financial solidity, some military experience, and the appropriate political affiliation. The names submitted to Rosas to fill judicial vacancies are typical of the kinds of men who could be trusted with the stewardship of their respective neighborhoods: they would keep them socially peaceful and politically stable. The candidates were invariably white men of means, although not necessarily well born. The criteria and selection processes meant that these local judicial overseers would be whites of greatly superior social standing in neighborhoods where the non-white population prevailed, despite the exceptionally good relationship between Rosas and the Afro-Argentine community.[46] In 1839, the names of Don Simón Pereyra, Don Ynosencio Escalada, and Don José María García y Arguibel were proposed. Their personal attributes were sufficient proof that they would fulfill their duties: "Pereyra, of great fortune, highest honesty, and a decided federalist. . . . Escalada combines the same [personal] qualities, in addition to his decision to support the Holy Cause of the Federation. . . . In García y Arguibel's case, the same circumstances speak in his favor."[47] In 1846, the designees to serve in the sections within the parish of San Miguel provided more ample evidence of their qualifications. "Dn Nicholás Marino, native of Buenos Ayres, 36 years of age, married, aide-de-camp of His Excellency, Vice-President of the night-watchmen corps, commandant in the same group, and current Juez de Paz—reelected. Dn Pedro Vela, native of Buenos Ayres, 48 years of age, married, owner of his own estate, Federalist, good abilities. Dn Mariano Vivar, native of Buenos Ayres, 35 years of age, married, owner-merchant, Captain in the First *Patricio* Batallion, great aptitude, and a Federalist."[48]

Most often, the nominees were already serving as *jueces*, so their reelection provided a mechanism of continuity and stability. Not surprisingly, the entire group of judges whose terms came to an end in 1846 were retained in their posts. Each *juez* was served by assistants, called *tenientes alcaldes*, whose numbers depended on the population more than on the territory of each barrio or *cuartel*; for example, fifteen *tenientes alcaldes* assisted the *juez* of the populous cuartel number 3, while only nine served the *juez* of the extensive but rural cuartel number 50.[49]

Whether residents sought the post of *juez* for its potential economic benefit is impossible to determine; those who held the post already had considerable financial sources of support. Indeed, participation in law enforcement tasks was not popular in the barrios of Buenos Aires. When the corps of *serenos* (nightwatchmen) was formed anew in February of 1854, it was an experiment in participatory and communal involvement. Unfortunately, the results fell short of expectations. Approximately 120 *serenos* served during the years 1854–1857, representing a 20 percent shortfall in staffing; the regulations called for approximately 150 people to cover each block of the city (*Comisiones de Sección* and *Comisionados de Manzana*). The executive committee in charge of the nightwatchmen's corps reported that it had not found "the cooperation so indispensable in the face of such an increase in population. The very same citizens who so recently risked danger in defense of the country now evade their responsibility to participate in the modest service of forming part of the blocks' corps, to collect the share of monthly costs, and, perhaps, even to turn in the names of those people who are reluctant to pay [their fines] to an alcalde. Since this service is free and since there have been many difficulties encountered in order to have the citizens agree to volunteer," the committee had found itself forced to delay the fulfillment of its obligations.[50]

This was a particularly serious problem made worse by the increase in the population through natural increments among the native porteños and through the increase in migrants from the interior and Europe who hoped to benefit from the city's economic opportunities. In addition, the winter season would strain jail facilities further as the number of arrests increased in proportion to the rise in drunkenness. The authorities were aware that winter was a more dangerous period, as evidenced by their printed warnings about escapees: "On the 5th day of this month [May, 1827], Pedro Villagra, a habitual criminal and one of the most famous robbers, escaped from the provincial prison. This man is very dangerous, particularly

TABLE 2

Arrests in Buenos Aires, January–December 1857

Month	No.	Month	No.	Month	No.
Jan.	n.a.	May	45	Sept.	47
Feb.	28	June	60	Oct.	n.a.
Mar.	29	July	46	Nov.	40
Apr.	38	Aug.	43	Dec.	n.a.

SOURCE: AGN X-43-7-5, Serenos.
NOTE: n.a. = not available.

in light of the forthcoming winter season. Anyone who can give his whereabouts would be performing a most commendable service on behalf of peace and tranquillity, and for the well-being of the citizenry."[51] Persons concerned about safety called on the police to improve lighting, especially in the period of greatest darkness and rains: "To the Police," read the terse headline of a Buenos Aires weekly publication in 1817, "Autumn and Winter will soon be here, and this signifies the inconveniences and the dangers that they will bring, if we do not take care to avoid the darkness and the mud in the streets. . . . Paving some streets, . . . [and] adding many more streetlights are matters of absolute necessity."[52] Arrests by night-watchmen alone in the cold month of June were more than double those in March. The number of monthly arrests by the *serenos* of Buenos Aires in 1857, a typical year to judge by police records, is given in Table 2.[53]

From the moment of their arrests through the disposition of their cases, lawbreakers were handled by a judicial system in which judges were often preempted from ruling on cases because of decisions made a priori by police officials. The responsibilities charged to policemen tended to be only vaguely interpreted; thus, the use of their power moved in ad hoc and irregular patterns. Under such circumstances, policemen and officers of the court routinely exceeded the prescribed limits of force in making arrests. The arbitrary nature of police and juridical disposition is typified by the conviction of accused criminals despite lack of proof of their deeds: 30-year-old Lino Arce was summarily dispatched to serve two years with the First Cavalry Regiment simply for being, according to the police, "a well-known thief, even though it is impossible to bring evidence [to prove it]."[54] Although the practice of impressment into military service (*leva*) was supposed to be governed by specific regulations, local officials periodically went beyond them on their own initiative. Thus, it was not unknown for policemen—motivated by their own desires, or under the orders of a local *alcalde*—to raid pulperías and press into service men who were gainfully employed and who had broken no laws, even though the regulations subjected only vagrants and evildoers (*malentretenidos*) to the dreaded *leva*.[55]

Local police and judicial authorities acted on behalf of locally powerful men by condoning their excesses and by aiding in the punishment of their dependents. Illustrative of the self-empowered flexibility of local magistrates and police is a letter sent anonymously to the chief of police of Buenos Aires by a resident of the outlying parish of San Vicente, accusing one Casimiro Fálquez of the brutal treatment of a slave. The letter's prefatory statement, while respectful of the notions related to civic responsibility and voluntarist efforts, stands in sharp contrast to the arbitrary self-indulgence— aided by official complicity—that Fálquez enjoyed. "If it is the duty of a magistrate to make use of the means with which the laws empower him to maintain order, so it is the duty of a simple citizen to inform the authorities of all events that—by their gravity and importance—challenge moral tenets or upset the established order." Fálquez had allegedly whipped his slave for over an hour, then had poured salt and alcohol over the open wounds. "These atrocities," wrote the informant, "can be compared only to those which were perpetrated by Caligula and Nero on the Romans." In desperation, the slave had appealed to the local justice of the peace, who provided the slave master Fálquez with "enormous" chains to further punish the beaten slave for his insolence. At the time of writing, the unfortunate slave was being kept outdoors day and night chained to a post in a way that permitted him to lie face down only, and with virtually no freedom of movement. Fálquez, who had also been accused of the corporal punishment of a *liberto*, a freedman, was never indicted.[56]

In the wide array of possible confrontations between the citizenry and the legal authorities, appeals to higher officers were not uncommon. Yet the prevailing tendency was to respect local decisions, even when they had no basis in law. Until the process of penal codification began in 1865, and until the concept of action responsive to communal and, ultimately, national norms was internalized by the citizenry, the leaders of Buenos Aires acted on the federalist principle of local option. By the standards of the time, the Buenos Aires bureaucracy was the region's largest and most adept at intervening in local decisions, yet it usually rejected appeals that threatened to challenge local authority. Indeed, a motive of all governments during the period studied was to impress the public with the need to respect the local representatives of law and order. The distinctive quality of the Rosas period was that the political leanings—real or imagined—of the accused were brought in as further evidence of his presumed antisocial character. The combination of all these tendencies—required respect for local authority, arbitrary punishment of the accused without formal proceedings, and inclusion of political affiliations as part of the evidence—is obvious in a number of cases processed during the 1830's. In 1832, two Buenos Aires policemen filed complaints against Francisco Sayos for injurious language. Sayos had allegedly slandered the police loudly in the middle of the street while a neighbor's house was on fire. Even while policemen were battling the flames, Sayos insisted on making the time-honored complaint that the police were never around when needed, and on uttering "several expressions of the same sort, denigrating the current authorities." The two policemen stressed that such a deed, which outraged the honor of the police department, should not go unpunished. Pointing to the fundamental principle involved in the case, one of the police officers described Sayos' act as indecorous and as responsible for fostering the "agitation and public opinion against the employees of the [police department]." The chief of police, concurring with his men's complaints and demands for punitive measures, forwarded the case's documentation to the minister of government with a political addendum: "The Minister must be aware of the object and venom with which these harangues were shouted by a fellow known so well to be an enemy of the current administration, and who played such a large role in the disasters that afflicted the Republic at the time of the disorganizers [followers of Rosas' enemy, the Unitarian leader, Lavalle]."[57] Similarly, the overtness with which the judicial system was politicized during the Rosas era can be gleaned from the following arrest file from Police Precinct No. 2, dated July 2, 1835: "Juan Guajado for having beaten María Isabel Seballos and her mother; the former may lose an eye as a result of the injuries. This man is one of those who, in the year '33, joined up under the command of Dn Manuel Felicián Fernández, and became therefore one of the enemies of [Rosas], the Restorer of the Laws."[58]

Manuel Pariente was summarily sent in 1832 to serve two years with an artillery regiment for "fighting with a knife and for having been a Unitarian in Lavalle's time."[59] Men were also drafted for military service for disturbing the peace even if little or no physical violence was involved. Service in frontier garrisons was usually to be for a period of two years for crimes such as vagrancy, gambling, uttering public obscenities, and abandonment of a wife, among other offenses; the level of physical harm involved in the crime meant little. Not only was indiscriminate exile to the dangerous frontier territories a typical punishment in Rosas' period, but so it was among the authorities who later replaced him. Thus, when in 1854 a military officer named Vicente Ferré insulted a local civilian official in the town of Morón, outside Buenos Aires, the government authorities in the capital arrested the army officer and dispatched him to frontier garrison duty for three years, one more than the normal period of servitude.[60] Indeed, a feature of the disorder of the times rested on two sets of rivalries: one between military officers and local civilian authorities, and the other between the uniformed men serving in the military and those serving as policemen.

The strain between civilian and military authorities began to show early in the national period. The heightened status given first to the city's militia and then to the regular army gave military officers a sense of superiority that sometimes extended into outright abuse of political and even ecclesiastical administrators. By 1815, these acts were occurring regularly, and it had become well known among the gente decente that there was no sense in complaining to the government authorities: "No citizen is free from these acts of insult and vexation," wrote a chronicler, "since these abuses go unpunished and the government looks the other way."[61] The impunity of some military men crossed the lines from the officer corps to recruits. If Colonel Miguel Soler could reputedly knock down a priest and throw him out of his house for failing to take off his hat, recruits of the Eighth Regiment could collar a man named José Tartas as he was walking past their headquarters and force him to suffer hours of dangerous pranks. "These scandalous events and many others that are occurring generally," lamented Juan Manuel Beruti, "are taking place within our revolution, and nothing can be done about them in the circumstances of our times; because, to tell the truth, each colonel wants to be [the revolution's] director, and covets that power."[62]

The high incidence of complaints by local policemen and justices of the peace against military commanders and their men symbolized the caprice of a political system that contained few guidelines for distinguishing between military and communal needs. The absence of institutionalized policies served to maintain the uncertainty that governed these relationships; in the absence of practical regulations, national leadership was expected to side with one party or the other, even though the principle of local supremacy was upheld more often than not. This meant that military commanders were usually restrained or removed in the face of confrontations with local authorities. Furthermore, the principle of local autonomy, upheld under Rosas, interfered with the building up of a national or provincial body of law. By favoring local officials, practices in Buenos Aires (as elsewhere) obstructed the path toward the accumulation of legal principles that would tend to codification. Local police and other officers in charge of communal order continued to insist on the right of local option in the dispensation of justice.

An example of the rivalry attendant on the federalization of judicial policy was a case in 1835 that involved the chief of police of the city of Buenos Aires and the province's Tribunal of Justice (*Tribunal de Justicia*), the highest court of appeals. The case involved the financial state of Don Diego Martínez. Convicted and sent to debtors' prison by the judge of the lower court (*Juez de Primera Instancia*), Martínez was then ordered released by the justices of the higher court. The chief of police, considering himself a party to the proceedings, appealed directly to the attorney general (*fiscal*) and to the government's general counsel (*asesor general*). In so doing, the chief of police was contravening the superior court's ruling on the basis of his own opinion that the high court had no jurisdiction over the case; moreover, he asserted that the superior court had no right to communicate "with the police, which answers solely to the *Juez de Primera Instancia*." In his argument before the government's officials, the chief of police noted that "he was hesitating to heed the [tribunal's] order until he received the resolution of the case from the higher authorities."[63] In agreeing with the police, the *fiscal* and the *asesor general* were reminding the citizenry that the powers of officers of the law extended beyond the initial apprehension to the shaping of the disposition of the case by personal involvements that exceeded their normal activities.

The lack of consensus among political and judicial authorities

stemmed not only from the absence of uniform codes governing the
criminal justice system, but also from perceptions of rampant lawlessness in the city. Community spokesmen bemoaned both the lack
of administrative coherence and the breakdown of civility in their
urban reality by decrying the ineptitude of authorities who made it
impossible for an "honest man to walk the streets of Buenos Aires
in safety . . . [requiring] him to be unarmed in the face of a thousand criminals waiting for an opportunity to rob and kill."[64] The provincial legislature had passed a law in November 1821 that prohibited the use of bladed weapons (*armas blancas*). It was one of several
measures taken to stem the proliferation of weapons in the hands of
a population affected by a decade of mobilization for internal war.
Yet this law, too, was variously interpreted by local *alcaldes de barrio*.
In a vain attempt to control public disturbances, *alcaldes* instructed
policemen to arrest anyone carrying any type of weapon, including
firearms. Such measures had the unforeseen results of placing under
arrest a number of members of the gente decente. Although there
were exceptions, it was rare for criminals—other than renegade soldiers—to carry firearms; knives, daggers, and other more affordable
types of bladed weapons were customarily used by the poor, the social stratum most responsible for criminality. The city's gentry accused the *alcaldes* of exceeding their authority to the benefit of the
lawless elements. Yet nearly a decade after the 1821 legislation on
weapons, the problems caused by an armed and faction-ridden population continued to preoccupy authorities of ideological tendencies
quite different from those of the liberals of 1821. The semiofficial
El Lucero, speaking for Rosas and employing his authoritarian
tones, clamored in September 1829 for the continued proscription of
all weapons in the hands of civilians:

The language of reason is still impotent in the face of excited passions. It
was therefore urgent to prohibit the use of weapons, and now the current
state of peace renders them needless. It is essential that the citizens lose, if
at all possible, even the memory of having held them. The measures taken
by this government are the same as those found in every civilized nation,
where pistols, daggers, and rapiers are considered to be assassins' weapons:
an honest man does not think in terms of hiding his means of defense. We
know that the customs of this country are less strict in this regard; yet the
consequences of such relaxation demand reforms that have never before
been more necessary.[65]

Concern over public security was occasionally exacerbated by police measures taken to assure safety. Until the evolution of the police as a body composed entirely of regulars in the Rosas era, the citizenry was obligated to be available in an emergency called by the neighborhood's patrolman. Organized by city blocks, porteños were to render service as members of posses or defense committees. However, the custom, begun during the wars of independence, of sending a slave in one's stead for military or police duty was continued. When slaves were unavailable, lower-class surrogates could still be found; as a last resort, one could simply pay the barrio's *alcalde*, who, on receiving the money "with great relish," would find a substitute.[66] Since the law prohibited the private use of arms, the police equipped civilians with weapons; unfortunately, they were often antiquated, even useless. Such a state of affairs was not conducive to public confidence. The respectable classes felt themselves to be trapped, the prey of the *chusma*, the rabble, who so often composed the posses that, although organized for the public welfare, could turn instead on the gente decente with all the impunity afforded them by the equipment—however antiquated—donated by the authorities.[67] The fear of an armed mob gone wild was well founded: distribution of weapons to the citizenry carried with it dangers to the public order. For such order to be maintained, the distribution of weapons had to be as efficient as the control over their return. If the firearms that were handed out in times of crises suffered in quality, the system for their recovery suffered in its planning and execution. General Viamonte's warning of September 1829 illustrates the problems: "Whereas, the government considers that of the numerous weapons distributed to the population only one-half have been returned, despite the definite order given in this matter, and considering the harm therefrom, everyone must turn in his muskets, carbines, pistols, and sabers . . . to his section's policemen within three days or face fines and confiscations."[68]

Viamonte's concerns for public safety and for the racial tensions that underlay public worries were not unfounded. The militarization that began with the retaking of Buenos Aires from English invaders in 1806 had provided many of the city's blacks with weaponry, uniforms, and heightened status as defenders of the revolutionary order. They had also been heavily recruited into the frontline infantry regiments. Toward the end of the revolutionary decade of the 1810's few able-bodied men remained in the city, and the home guard comprised a large contingent of armed blacks. In February 1819, *alcaldes* Manuel de Luzurriaga and Manuel Arroyo y Pinedo called for the black regiment of the home guard to meet "unarmed" at the Plaza Monserrat, conveniently located in the ward with the largest concentration of freedmen. The order notwithstanding, over 300 of these men came to the open-air meeting "all armed with their rifles." Despite the tension of the moment, the authorities proceeded to announce to them that, having sent so many men to fight on the various fronts, the city had been left virtually without any troops to defend it in case of an emergency. The black regiment was therefore being asked to assume full-time duties in the barracks; anyone not wishing to do so would be forced to retire. The troops were thus faced with an unfortunate choice: either to be added to the rolls of men who faced the danger of being sent to fight at any moment, or to lose the benefits and privileges of their military status. Under such unendurable circumstances, they proceeded to riot, firing their weapons and wounding some people. During the evening, the government sent loyal forces and civilian residents to surround an area where it was suspected the dissidents would plan their next moves. Arrests of suspected blacks took place throughout that night and during the next two days. The government also posted an edict throughout the city announcing the penalty of life imprisonment for any black who failed to turn in his rifle, or who was caught with such weapons.[69]

Concerns arising from racial and social tensions—from "the impunity [of] a black or any other knave"—formed the single greatest preoccupation of the urban white middle and upper sectors of Buenos Aires.[70] To judge from editorials, letters by the citizenry, and police reports, the absence of nocturnal public activity had much to do with a generalized sense of fear of both criminals and security officers. It was said, in fact, that the high attendance of cultured porteños at the theater was actually a function of the lack of other forms of public amusement.[71] The paucity of nighttime events left much of the city to the night stalkers and the policemen who, it was hoped, would hunt them down. Combining elements of apprehension and prosecution, local representatives of order—police officers, *jueces de paz*, *sección*, and *barrio*, and nightwatchmen—wielded against the accused the disproportionately large amount of power accorded to them. And there were many such accused; indeed, Buenos Aires may have been only a village, a *gran aldea*, measured in terms of European material development, but that in no way implied that it was a sleepy, peaceful town. The absence of nighttime activities and an inadequate urban street lighting system made it very dangerous to walk outdoors at night. One could fall victim to an unmarked hole in the sidewalk or to an obstacle in one's path as easily as to an armed robber. The municipal lighting system, barely adequate at its best, depended almost entirely on the collection of a tax levied on the residents who wished to have their streets lit.[72] Yet a police survey taken in 1834 showed that virtually no one had paid the tax of two pesos. Darkness fell heavily on both the central and the peripheral areas of Buenos Aires despite the existence of over 1,800 lampposts. The replacement costs of grease and wicks alone were estimated at between 320 and 500 pesos. Since to keep the streets lit cost 5,450 pesos yearly, the 5,060 pesos owed by over 2,500 delinquent residents would have provided minimal lighting of the urban center only and haphazard maintenance of the posts.[73] The lack of payment of the lighting tax by so many porteños shows a general tendency—observed in other ways as well—to consider being outdoors an unnecessary display of vanity, and in the case of youths and females, a source of idleness and corruption. Being outdoors in the dark would not likely be the sort of activity willingly funded by taxpayers.

Arrests and Punishments

Neither the cases requiring police intervention nor the composition of arrests in the city of Buenos Aires show a "civilizing" trend, as the members of the liberal, anti-Rosas "Generation of 37" would have hoped; another way of saying it is that the populist regime generated no greater disrespect for the law than any subsequent liberal, elitist administration. Federalist or Unitarian, nationalist or internationalist, liberal or conservative, the governing circles of the capital continued to wrestle with endemic lawlessness. The available police records show arrest data spottily, and we must still wait for a systematically longitudinal study, but the available evidence complements other police documentation to indicate that most crime involved bodily harm, although death was rare.[74]

Under the Rivadavian interregnum of economic growth and political stability in the 1820's, the nature of crime had been similar to the criminality during the second liberal rule in the 1850's. The monthly report of the police commissioner in the rural town of San

TABLE 3
Arrests in San Antonio de Areco, December 1825
(N = 12)

Crime	Percent	Crime	Percent
Robbery	14.3%	Homicide	0.0%
Fighting and		Drunkenness and	
aggravated assault	35.7	vagrancy	42.9
Insult and		Suspicious behavior	7.1
insubordination	0.0	TOTAL	100.0%

SOURCE: AGN X-31-9-4, Policía, 1825-31.

Antonio de Areco, outside Buenos Aires, points to a pattern that was qualitatively similar to subsequent periods. To be sure, the much larger city of Buenos Aires was rowdier, but the ledger of arrests found for the quiet month of December 1825 (see Table 3) is comparable to the 1857 breakdown given above.[75]

The population of 158 men serving their sentences in the provincial penitentiary (*presidio*) in 1825 displays certain characteristics of both the criminal element and the dispensation of punishment. The majority of inmates were single men (60 percent) of color (65 percent), who held menial and semiskilled jobs (85 percent). This evident racial bias reflected an Ibero-American disposition among judicial systems to sentence men of color, along with men of the lower classes, with greater frequency, and occasionally with greater severity. The relative absence of clearly stated racial determinants in the secondary literature of Argentine historiography cannot hide the force of the archival evidence: it locates the Argentine case within the practices of judicial systems, such as Brazil's, that were more conscious of racial considerations.[76] Widespread apprehension over the dangers posed by armed blacks led the city's authorities in 1819 to impose the term of life imprisonment as the only and automatic sentence for freedmen and slaves arrested for possession of weapons.[77]

In 1825, the youngest inmate in the Buenos Aires penitentiary, aged 14, was sentenced to 6 years in prison for homicide and the oldest, aged 60, was serving a 5-year prison term for the same crime; the average age of the inmates was 31. The legal limit on prison terms until the late 1880's was 10 years, and while only 6 percent of the prisoners received this maximum, the wide latitude of power in the hands of the judiciary is illustrated by the great variety of offenses for which they dispensed this stiffest of sentences: if murderers and deserters were sentenced to 10 years in the penitentiary, so, too, were thieves and bigamists. Harsh measures of social control were evidently applied to criminal and immoral acts alike. Within this apparent arbitrariness, however, judges tended to alternate the length of prison terms: sentences handed down before mid-1825 were much stiffer. Prison terms of 6 to 10 years were being served by 28 percent of the inmates; 39 percent were serving terms of 1 to 5 years; and 29 percent were serving an undefined sentence (*sin tiempo*) at the pleasure of the authorities.[78] Capital punishment for crimes not directly associated with political plots remained rare.

In addition to racial considerations, the severity of punishment and the incidence of arrests were conditioned, in part, by the degree of political stability of a given historical moment. By late 1811, for example, the executive and judicial authorities had become aware that the traditional rule of law had begun to break down as the city experienced some of the consequences of revolutionary change. The officials' responses were centered on the regimen of penalty. The colonial penalties for illegal entry and assault, which included 200 lashes given publicly while the prisoner was paraded through the city's streets, followed by ten years of hard labor, had been abolished by the liberal revolutionaries, who considered them to be unenlightened and excessively harsh treatments—symbols of antiquated imperial aggression against citizens' rights. But within a short time, as the sense of disorder heightened, new regulations were decreed that included capital punishment as a remedy. The *considerandos* of the 1811 decree were utterly clear: the new regimen of punishment was the "result of the many thefts and robberies that are currently being witnessed in this city, [where] there has been such concern that no citizen feels safe in his own home; bands of twenty or more men with firearms are forcing their way into private homes, and under the guise of representing the forces of justice, assault the owners and steal their possessions." Instead of the old penalties for these infractions, the new leaders instituted the following drastic guidelines to deal with lawbreakers:

Every individual found with picklocks, master keys, and other similar types of instruments will immediately receive the death penalty by hanging.

Every robber who is captured and who has stolen more than one hundred pesos will be punished by hanging.

Every robber who is captured and who has stolen less than one hundred pesos will be punished by serving ten years in prison.[79]

However, no evidence was found of people who were actually executed for crimes other than those involving attempted mutinies, coups, or other political offenses. The related tempos of political crises and criminal justice measures can be seen in other crucial occasions. For example, in late 1829, when Rosas began eliminating his political enemies, arrests in the city of Buenos Aires increased dramatically: the 129 arrests carried out in October 1829 far exceeded the number of men and women arrested in any month in the stable year of 1857. These events suggest that social control was linked closely to political control, although not for protracted periods. The tensions generated during politically uncertain times meant that the police would be temporarily on the lookout for "suspicious characters," and that, in general, the number of arrests for failing to carry proper documentation would rise.

The aggregation of the available arrest records and the collapsing of individual arrests into discrete categories permit general comparisons over time. The data in Table 4 indicate that urban disorder seldom decayed into homicide. The pattern is consistent with the low homicide rates found in nineteenth-century urban France and Germany.[80] The unusually low incidence of murder in Buenos Aires can be inferred from the very high level of preoccupation that it caused on the part of the police on the rare occasions it was committed.[81] The link between political control and social control was not based on the arrest and elimination of political enemies only. Rather, the tensions and rumors about possible coups and actual armed confrontations between pickets in and around the city enhanced the possibilities for disturbances and disorderly conduct, including robbery and drunkenness. As an example of this phenomenon, note the much higher rates of arrest for both robbery and drunkenness in the turbulent month of October 1829 than in the tense but tranquil month of January 1830. Vigilance was essential in politically discordant times, as expressed by the high proportions of arrests in January 1830 for suspicious behavior, a charge closely related to drunkenness and vagrancy, which in 1829–30 represented a similarly high proportion of 24.4 percent.

Despite the greater vigilance by the police, however, cases heard before criminal judges did not result in greater severity of punish-

TABLE 4
Arrests for Selected Offenses and Periods, Buenos Aires

Period	Percent of period's offenses	Period	Percent of period's offenses
Robbery		*Homicide*	
Oct. 1829	22.5%	Oct. 1829	1.6%
Jan. 1830	12.5	Jan. 1830	5.0
Mar. 1857	10.3	Mar. 1857	0.0
June 1857	10.0	June 1857	0.0
Fighting and Aggravated Assault		*Drunkenness and Vagrancy*	
Oct. 1829	13.2%	Oct. 1829	19.4%
Jan. 1830	15.0	Jan. 1830	5.0
Mar. 1857	37.9	Mar. 1857	24.1
June 1857	45.0	June 1857	10.0
Insult and Insubordination		*Suspicious Behavior*	
Oct. 1829	5.4%	Oct. 1829	0.0%
Jan. 1830	5.0	Jan. 1830	32.5
Mar. 1857	6.9	Mar. 1857	17.2
June 1857	23.3	June 1857	3.3

SOURCES: *El Lucero*, Nov. 4, 1829, Jan. 18, 1830; AGN X-43-7-5.
   NOTE: The number of offenses for each period is 129 (Oct. 1829), 80 (Jan. 1830), 29 (Mar. 1857), and 60 (June 1857).

TABLE 5
Disposition of Criminal Cases, August 1829 to January 1830

Disposition	No.	Pct.
Sentenced to lashings	4	3.5%
Sentenced to prison	2	1.7
Sent to serve in the military	10	8.6
Sentenced to the city's jail	2	1.7
Turned over to military authorities	25	21.7
Set free	61	52.6
Pending	121	0.3
TOTAL	116	100.0%

SOURCE: *El Lucero*, Jan. 18, 1830.

ment. For example, Bernardo Vélez, who in 1830 was one of the two *jueces ordinarios* in the city, heard 116 cases in the course of approximately five months, and disposed of them in the manner outlined in Table 5.

Judge Vélez's findings reveal quantitatively some characteristics generally known about the relationship in Argentina between social control and the military in the nineteenth century. Approximately one-fifth of the cases heard before Vélez's court involved military men, whom the criminal justice system seldom took it upon itself to punish; instead, military men were usually turned over to their superiors. In addition, military ranks gained from criminals whom the courts punished by drafting them into the army.[82] Barely 7 percent of the criminal cases resulted in punishment by civil means, divided evenly between lashings and imprisonment.

Notably, over half of the cases resulted in freedom for the accused (52.6 percent). This indicates that, even in the midst of a periodically anarchic political situation and an arbitrary judicial system, punishment was not the primary goal. Indeed, one of the early decrees of the revolutionary authorities contained the principle, explicitly worded, that "the jails are meant to provide security, not punishment."[83] Seldom can one discern calls for increasing the severity of penalties; and no periods of harsh treatment by the criminal justice system were noted. There is no evidence, for example, that the capital punishment ordered by the revolutionary government for persons caught with equipment used to pick locks was ever put into effect. The ultimate goal of social control in Buenos Aires was, therefore, not punishment but the circumscription of the public misbehavior of marginal social groups. Not even the most reactionary ideologue among the elites of Buenos Aires would argue that terror should characterize the system of criminal law, that "if we diminish the terror of housebreakers, the terror of the innocent inhabitants must be increased, and the comforts of domestic life must be greatly destroyed," as did an English justice, Justice Christian of Ely, in 1819.[84] Nor did the number of capital statutes increase much, as they did dramatically in England over the course of the eighteenth and part of the nineteenth centuries. In this sense, the dynamics of penalty in the Río de la Plata resembled more the case of France, where, by the close of the eighteenth century, penalty was held to have "humanity" as its fundamental consideration, not punishment only.[85] Indeed, dismissal rates were high not only in Argentina during the nineteenth century, but also in France, Germany, and Brazil. In France, the dismissal rate for cases of theft and fraud stood at 53.5 percent at midcentury and rose to nearly 75 percent by 1900. Bavaria registered a 64 percent rate of dismissal in cases involving bodily harm and death during the 1860's, and 55 percent for theft.[86] Similarly high rates of acquittals and dismissals can be found in the region of Taubaté, in the state of São Paulo, where more than half of the accused criminals were set free between 1885 and 1944.[87]

In sum, the dispensation of punishment and the authorities' reactions to the various offenses remained largely unvaried throughout the period from 1810 to 1860, despite the radical changes in political leadership. However, the infusion of political preferences into the question of the maintenance of law and order meant that punishment of the accused took on greater certainty during the Rosas regime than during preceding or subsequent administrations. From the reports found in the police archives there does not appear to have been preferential treatment accorded to men serving under Rosas; nor was there inattention to the excesses of the lower classes—supporters and beneficiaries of the *rosista* machine, it was held by the opposition. Nonetheless, the vaguely articulated class antagonism that divided porteño society between the gente de pueblo—the plebeian underpinning of Rosas—and the gente decente—the "civilized" elements looking for a much different sort of social control—became a feature of the political treatises and romantic novels written by members of the Generation of 37.

Racial overtones appear clearly in Esteban Echeverría's *El Matadero*, the first Argentine short story, written between 1838 and 1840. Echeverría founded La Joven Argentina, a social club in which gathered the young intellectuals, the Generation of 37, who would rule Argentina after Rosas' fall in 1852. *El Matadero*, a classically romantic story, depicts the humiliation and death of a dapper young man at the hands of a working-class mob presided over by a municipal official who supported Rosas.[88] In Echeverría's story, this rabble represented a self-serving underworld of mestizos and the unruly lumpenproletariat whose libertinage was countenanced by the government authorities; after all, for Echeverría and his colleagues, the military and civil servants up to and including Rosas himself were of much the same mind as the rabble, only more polished in their material exteriors and more stylized in their manner. Echeverría painted a picture of a city paralyzed by religious superstitions that remained unchallenged by the politically servile clergy. In the midst of torrential rains, "the devout frequently moaned as they uttered novenas and continuous supplications. The preachers thundered in the temple where the pulpit creaked under the blows of their fists. 'It is the day of judgment!,' they said, 'the end of the world is at hand! . . . Your impiety, your heresies, your blasphemies, your horrendous crimes have brought the Lord's plagues upon our land. The justice of the God of the Federation declares you damned!' The poor ladies, short of breath and greatly humbled, exited from the church casting the blame for this calamity—naturally—on the Unitarians."[89]

Echeverría also depicted the supporters of Rosas as the lowest scum of Buenos Aires and related these people literally to the city's filth and backwardness by locating them amid the carcasses and the run-down structures in the sea of mud surrounding the slaughterhouse. The description of the setting for the story was a transparent metaphor that incorporated every important element of the lower-class order or *rosismo*, seen through the eyes of the gente decente, including its style of leadership and the quality of its supporters.

The slaughterhouse of the Convalencia . . . is on a large, rectangular lot. This lot, located on a southern slope, is cut by a canal formed by the current of the rainwaters, and on its banks innumerable rats' nests can be seen, while in the rainy season, its bed gathers all the blood that is produced by the slaughterhouse. . . .

In the winter, the stockyards are a veritable sea of mud into which the animals sink and remain as if stuck, and rest almost without movement. There is a booth where the corral taxes are collected, the fines for violations of ordinances are paid, and the judge of the slaughterhouse [*juez del matadero*] sits—important character, caudillo of the butchers, the fellow who exercises the totality of power in that small republic, as delegated by the Restorer [Rosas]. It is easy to figure out what kind of a man is needed to carry out the duties of such a position. At the same time, the booth is such a wretched and small structure that nobody would notice it among the stockyards save for its nominal relationship to the terrible judge who wears across his white waist the following scarlet signs: "Long Live the Federation," "Long Live the Restorer," "Death to the Savage Unitarians." These were very significant signs, symbolic of the political and religious faith of the people of the slaughterhouse. . . .

The appearance of the slaughterhouse from a distance was grotesque and full of bustle. Forty-nine [slaughtered] steers were spread out for their hides, and close to two hundred persons trampled that muddy soil sprayed with blood. Round about each steer stood a group of human figures of different complexion and races. The most prominent figure in each group was the butcher, knife in hand, bare-chested, hair long and rumpled shirt, leg cover-ups [chiripá], and face daubed in blood. Behind him was a carnival-like procession—stirring, snaking behind him and following his movements—composed of young lads, negresses, and mulatto women vendors of entrails, whose hideousness was reminiscent of the mythical shrews; and intermingled with these women, several enormous mastiffs sniffed, snarled, and bit at the air searching for prey.[90]

The class and racial consciousness of this passage was shared by others in Buenos Aires, including foreigners, who depicted the apprehension felt when walking the city's streets and meeting up with groups of frightening lower-class men poorly clad in their traditional garb. A visiting Frenchman urges caution in walking past a pulpería where patrons, hiding from patrolmen who may be passing by, are gambling at cards: "It would be very fortunate and unusual for these games to end up without fights, because whenever fights occur differences among the parties are settled with the long knife that each one carries. Use the opportunity of their preoccupation with the game to walk past without being noticed, otherwise you will be subjected to demeaning epithets, such as *gringo*, 'worthless foreigner,' or 'dandy.' "[91]

Echeverría's story line, as it relates to the confrontation between the rabble and the Unitarian, actually occupies only a few pages toward the end of the tale. Clearly, Echeverría's intent is to use the short story as a medium to criticize the squalid society that his Generation of 37 and successive generations of liberals accused of forming the mainstay of nineteenth-century authoritarianism. In the end, the nameless 25-year-old gentleman "of graceful and elegant personage" is forced down from his horse, tied, stripped, and about to be whipped when he wills his own death as his victorious negation of the rabble's tawdry joy. No objective reason is given for the young man's misfortune—ruffianism required no explanation; before his forced dismount, the characterizations hurled at him by the crowd served as the only reason for the eventual tragedy: "Here comes a Unitarian! Don't you see his sideburns in the shape of a U? He's a dandy. Look how he sits on his [English] saddle like a foreigner!" The real-life warning of the Frenchman noted above was unheeded in Echeverría's fictional setting.

But not all the literati among Rosas' opponents felt equally about the nonwhites. In fact, in José Mármol's novel *Amalia*, written in 1851, one year before the fall of Rosas, one can observe a more self-critical analysis of class conflict and the dangerous classes. In a scene in which Daniel, Amalia's cousin, is in her home hiding from Rosas' police, he instructs her to dismiss nearly all her servants, both white and nonwhite. He explains that in the current state of affairs in Buenos Aires, one's servant could easily be turned into one's enemy. But, asserts Daniel in genetic explanations of society typical of the era, "there is only one exception found among the lower classes, and it is the mulattoes; blacks have become haughty, whites have prostituted themselves, but the mulattoes, because of the tendency that exists within each hybrid race to rise and become dignified, are almost all enemies of Rosas, because they know that the Unitarians are the cultivated and illustrious people, and thus they always take them as their models."[92] Mármol's positive valuation of mulattoes over both blacks and whites was shared by others, including one who wrote that "the intelligence of mulattoes is superior not only to that of blacks, but also to that of white creoles."[93]

In either case—that of Echeverría or of Mármol—the physiological framework of social Darwinists was clearly present. Antipathies toward the gente de pueblo, the lower classes, were informed by the physical characteristics employed by the gente decente. It was a process fundamentally coincident with that Louis Chevalier chronicled in Paris for the same historical period. These were judgments that, on the basis of morphological foundations, went beyond racial characteristics to signify moral qualities.[94] In the case of porteños, such attributions may have been fueled initially by political uncertainty, but they were by no means limited to troubled times; indeed, the racial principles of Positivism gained strength in the second half of the nineteenth century during a period of political stability and wide-ranging economic progress.[95] Thus, to Rosas' opponents and later to liberals in general, the entire development of the nation rested on the victory by the enlightened groups in the fundamental struggle that Domingo Sarmiento named on behalf of all Latin American liberals: the battle of civilization against barbarism.[96]

From the standpoint of the maintenance of order, however, few analysts have recognized that it was only the form and extent of intemperance in the exercise of judicial power that distinguished one government from another. At no time in the history of Buenos Aires did the barbarism of either the turbulent period between the Revolution of 1810 and the *pax rivadaviana* of the 1820's, or of the Rosas oppression of the 1830's and 1840's, dissolve the importance of norm and legal procedure. Even Echeverría sensed this; he wrote in *El Matadero* that, on witnessing the young man's fatal transfiguration, the *juez del matadero*, the *rosista* municipal official who had overseen the Dantesque drama, noted: "Poor devil, we only wanted to have fun with him and he took the whole thing too seriously. It is necessary to report it [to the authorities]."[97]

Continuities, such as the continuity of official reporting and legal procedure, are seen not only through Echeverría's writing, but also through the contemporary documentation. Moreover, the records indicate an insistence on social control of the population and on punishment of criminals by Rosas' security officials—independent of the political questions of loyalty. The city's arrest records for the 1830's and 1840's demonstrate a very busy police force indeed; nor did superior officials countenance inappropriate behavior by their own security personnel. Despite the accusations of Echeverría and his like-minded liberal colleagues of sanctioned police crime under Rosas' government—depicted in the romantic novel, the political pamphlet, the newspaper article written in exile, and other instruments of political propaganda—policemen were, in fact, also subject to conviction and punishment. In 1832, for example, the *Juez de Primera Instancia* for criminal cases sentenced Lorenzo Ruiz Díaz, a police officer, to serve four months without pay in the General Hospital for Men under severe food rationing. The judge also sentenced Tomás Cáceres, another employee of the police department, to serve in the garrisons guarding the Indian frontier for two years and to pay court costs. Both men had been convicted of "grave improprieties in the discharge of their duties."[98] Similarly, Bruno Gutiérrez, a foot patrolman, was arrested in July 1835 for fighting with a mounted policeman named Mariano Royas. Policemen were also arrested often for brawling, one of the most frequent offenses. Among males, barroom brawls originating in pulperías typically arose from drunken behavior, accusations of cheating in card games—despite the illegality of gambling—and the preponderance of challenges based on the assertion of one's own prowess and a denigration of another's.[99] This competitive ritual, so typical of frontier society everywhere in the Americas, was one of the characteristics of porteño social life: it represented the coexistence of rustic norms and European etiquette, and its very presence within the urban confines of the principal city continued to astound observers.[100] Frustrated with the slow process of eradicating disreputable public behavior, critics continued to call for the containment of the rabble, which they considered to form the region's *classes dangereuses.* "Just as a country's political civilization is represented by the guarantees enjoyed by its inhabitants," wrote Alberdi, "so it is true that its barbarism consists in the lack of security [for its citizens]."[101]

Circumvention and Clientelism

Well before the implantation of the Rosas machine and the ensuing accusations of its selective inefficiency, the police and judicial system of Buenos Aires had been the object of criticism. In the words of an editorial written in 1827, something had to be done about a judicial apparatus that permitted so much civil and criminal disturbance.

Upon reading [reports of crimes] one feels himself being transported to Constantinople. A son whose only request is to be permitted to dwell within his paternal home, but who has yet to receive a reply after waiting for six months! Misplacing and losing writs in a court of law among a cultured people! The violation of an Argentine citizen's abode by a patrolman pointing a pistol at him! Two judges hearing and understanding the same case and yet arriving at opposite findings! Soldiers, rifles, threats of violence against an innocent man who had not violated the laws of his country! . . .

These are the ways by which what we have said previously is shown to be true: that there is no security for those who resort to the courts; that the appeal process of the superior court, the only check [on the power] of lower officials, ameliorates only a small portion of the harm that their judgments have caused; lastly, that for truly free men, it is not enough to be granted inviolable political rights in the cases where prerogatives of private [individual] rights are evidently not protected from arbitrariness.[102]

Matters of internal security were alternately handled by armies and municipal police forces, neither of which was staffed by men always responsive to institutional ideals. Fights and jealousies among policemen were not unknown, reflecting among the rank and file the same absence of consensus noted earlier among the superior officers of the judicial system. The periodic accusations leveled by some elements of the press against the arbitrariness of the police were generally shared by the public: children feared being whipped on the streets by patrolmen; others observed that the police interfered with the free and smooth operation of their private businesses by harassing their employees.[103] Porteños had learned to fear a regular constabulary, but unlike English gentlemen, they did not argue against it.[104]

The virtually reflexive distrust of policemen was indicated by the citizenry's doubts about such basic matters as the veracity of arrest reports. Distrust required popular and informal antidotes to perceived arbitrariness; porteños' measures stood halfway between the French model of rigorous state prosecution and the observed English tendency to initiate and conduct prosecution at the discretion of private persons and in accordance with their wishes. In the final analysis, the actual Argentine—and, it can be argued, the Spanish American—process of informal, ex camera resolution of social control cases fits within a rigid superstructure of nominally rigid legal form. The coexistence of rigid theory and informal practice appears to be an essential feature of Iberian continuity. Concretely, the perception of arbitrariness encouraged the public to try to influence superior officers in an informal, personal, and implicitly reciprocal manner. Influence-peddling in this patrimonial society was the result, and it was not at all limited to the benefit of the elite: the poor also circumvented lower authorities and appealed to the top of the police hierarchy, though in such cases the meeting of social unequals transformed reciprocality into clientelism. The degree of success in the process of extrajudicial appeal depended on a variety of factors, principally the extent of solidarity felt by the chief of police with a petitioner. For their part, the petitioners acted on their estimation of the effectiveness of their relations with the police chief, based on three types of links: familial, kinship (real or fictive), and friendship. The following letter, sent by Serafina Brom de Hidalgo in 1848 to the police chief Juan Moreno, illustrates these various considerations.

My dear relative, the object of this letter is to arouse your interest on behalf of Domingo Espires, who was taken to jail on Sunday . . . , according to my information, for having a dispute—they say—with an assistant *alcalde*. Who knows if the policeman's report follows truthfully what in fact occurred; I cannot give assurances. But I venture to take this step, having taken pity on his poor wife, entreating you to see if it is within the realm of the possible to have you set him free, in which case I shall eternally remain indebted to you; his wife commits herself to pay the fine that may be imposed. By way of this motive, I have the pleasure of greeting you, Cousin Umbilina, and the rest of your laudable family with my customary appreciation. I am, Sir, your humble servant . . .[105]

Similarly, the police chief Don Pedro Romero received from his friend Manuel T. Langenheim the following note in 1849:

Respectable Sir and my Dear Friend: The bearer is the mother of a mulatto carpenter named Pablo Liniers, who has been detained since Tuesday. I do not know, Sir, what really went on, but I resort to your friendship with the objective of having you intercede to the extent possible on behalf of that poor man.[106]

The large amount of correspondence received by the various men who held the office of chief of police of Buenos Aires from citizens seeking their personal intervention in judicial matters attests to the success of this procedure. In addition, one must assume that at least as many individual requests to circumvent the normal processes of arrest and incarceration were made also of arresting officers, although there is no known way to measure their success.

Another reason that impelled individuals to resort to the personal approach in seeking justice was the value given to the notion of *carácter*, the moral position that each member of society was held to have. *Carácter* added moral authority and practical importance to testimony given in a particular case. The validity of testimony as legal argument was important to the extent that its veracity was directly dependent on the social position of the witness. Numerous examples exist of this convention: for instance, in an attempt to bring to public awareness the problem of banditry on the roads traveled by the stagecoach line linking the cities of Buenos Aires and Salado, a newspaper reported that "respectable" passengers on the line declared that they had been insulted and threatened by vagrants feigning drunkenness. "If these excesses are true," the newspaper reported, "as indeed we cannot doubt *in view of the character of the person who informed us*, we think it a public service to so alert the authorities" (emphasis added).[107]

Obviously, a little-known person—typical of most of the population—had less credibility, so that, in practice, the judicial system conspired a priori against lower-status groups. This left the thorny problem of conflict resolution among peers, but it did serve to alert those men and women deemed socially inferior to the folly of criminal activity against the "naturally" more credible gentry. Indeed, much of the concern shown by both the civil and military authorities and by the literate public over the establishment of law and order was motivated by the colonial imperative of subordinating lower-status groups. Beyond this, the colonial legacy was given contemporary urgency in the wake of the breakdown in the consensus among elites, politicized first by the independence process and then by the debate over the centrality of national political authority. In the event, the interest that brought together elites of diverse and otherwise inimical positions was the subordination of individual social action to their requirement of civility. Incivility, unlike political tendencies, permitted elitist consensual definitions not only in Argentina but also elsewhere in the parts of Spanish America torn apart by the political uncertainties of the first half of the nineteenth century.[108]

Petitioners could be motivated to ask for the intervention of their contacts in the superior ranks of the bureaucratic hierarchy either to seek special dispensations and release the accused or to exact their extrajudicial punishment. The arguments for special dispensations were called *disimulos*: few words in the porteño language related to criminal justice are more subtle. The term and its application evoke an image of decorous and gracefully demulcent argumentation aimed at soothing the apparent ire of an official already disposed to be mollified. But if these special dispensations were generated by an aesthetic ritual of circumlocution, they moved out to wreak havoc on a system of criminal justice that already tended toward harsh punitive measures in principle more than in fact. The result was a public perception that the judicial system was accessible to the artifices of those members of society well enough connected to the politically influential. As early as the 1820's, the perception of a corrupt system had become public; a distraught porteño wrote in a local newspaper that he was "convinced that the *disimulo* amounts to a consenting agreement to crime; and that the leniency with which crimes are treated is one of the principal causes responsible for backwardness and for systematic disorganization."[109]

Examples of the use of the *disimulo* abound, and although each one bore its own distinctive stamp, certain characteristics were common to virtually all of them: the kinship or familial bond of the

accused to a respected figure of local society; the accidental presence
of the accused at the scene of the crime serving to preclude any accusation of premeditation; the minimization of physical injuries, if
any; and the appeal to the kindheartedness assumed of the authorities. The following abbreviated plea, sent to the chief of police by
Rufina Días, is illustrative.

Respectable Sir: Certain as I am of your willingness to be charitable, I am
moved to make the following request of you. For the last eight days a young
man named Juan Rua has been jailed; he is a person I hold in great esteem
because of his probity and because he is the nephew of the Father Chaplain.
Rua defended himself [in the act of separating two men who were fight-
ing]; there are no seriously wounded men in the hospital . . . and nothing
serious has happened. Thus, I beg and implore you to . . . secure his freedom. I make this plea in the name of the Child Jesus into whose hands I
have placed this entire matter; and since I am presently engaged in spiritual
retreat at home, I noticed that today's prayers call for the adoration of the
Child. And while engaged in this Mystery, I have felt encouraged enough
to overcome the sense of embarrassment for my effrontery that results in
this imposition on you. In view of this, I hope you will forgive me [*estimaré
me disimule*].[110]

The practice of informal and direct appeals to mercy was not simply an expression of anguish and desperation; rather, it responded
to well-founded hopes of success and to a general awareness that the
informality of the pretrial process was at least as important for the
ultimate disposition of the case as it would be should it come to formal judicial proceedings. It effectively resulted in a dual criminal
justice system; it also promoted the public's calculated definition of
police officials as a corps of parallel judicial authorities who served
to free the judges for more prestigious civil and commercial cases.
Finally, and most importantly, the tactic worked on behalf of the
appellants often enough to encourage the continuation of the practice throughout the period covered by this book and beyond. Thus,
as late as the mid-1860's, well after the modernizing stages of national organization and legal codification had begun, the tradition
continued: letters from private citizens seeking special dispensations
were still arriving at the office of the Buenos Aires police department. As had been the case with his predecessors, whose arbitrariness during the Rosas era resulted in the so-called period of "inor-

ganic democracy," police chief Cayetano Cazón freed men in the 1860's on the strength of his own authority and out of the goodness of his own heart.[111] For example, he freed Francisco Carballo, who had a lengthy record of previous arrests and who had been arrested once again in 1864 for fighting and disorderly conduct. His sentence of fifteen days in jail was reprieved by Chief Cazón on the same day that he received a plea from the jailed man's wife, who was heavily burdened with their four children and her aged mother. Despite his previous arrests, she asserted, Francisco was a good man whose offense of disorderly conduct was not, in her words, "such a grave crime."[112]

Personal mediation and clientelistic interference in the smooth operation of the criminal justice system does not suggest that the organized terror experienced during the Rosas era continued beyond the end of the caudillos' rule in 1852. To be sure, the variegated strains of liberals who occupied executive offices between 1810 and 1829 and after 1852 did allow a much greater degree of expression than was permitted during Rosas' "restoration of the laws." Moreover, the feverish activity that during the 1850's and 1860's began to codify legal and political formulations and to institutionalize bureaucratic procedures went far toward establishing a theoretical framework of judicial operations. Yet the differences in the precepts before, during, and after the authoritarian rule of the caudillos stand in sharp contrast to the continuities in absolutist and arbitrary practices among the political and judicial personnel. Rather than signifying a drastic change from the past, or a style never again repeated, criminal justice under Rosas was not a "vast system of accusations unequaled in the history of tyrannies," as portrayed by the historian José Manuel Estrada.[113] Instead, it was the politicization of historical practice that, albeit informally, had served to maintain social control through the device of popular observations and accusations. Nor was the execution of the system of private accusations limited to the lower classes and women of color, as the philosopher José Ingeneiros stated in 1918: "Mulatto women obeyed . . . blindly, taking to [Rosas' residence] all the news they would gather in the alcoves, the patios, and the kitchens; hybrids in their souls as well as in their blood lines, they felt the pleasure of the lie and the accusation, thereby avenging their humiliating native inferiority at the cost of their white masters."[114] Indeed, political support for Rosas held strong among Buenos Aires' men of color, but neither this allegiance nor the practice of delation was restricted to the nonwhite population and lower classes.[115]

In the large cache of private correspondence of the city's chiefs of police, examples abound of accusations penned by the gente decente after Rosas' fall asking that punitive measures be taken in order to teach the accused some lessons in civility and morality, and that they be done as special favors on the part of the police authorities. In other words, the system that permitted the freeing of a jailed criminal upon private intervention also served to punish prisoners at the request of a private citizen with the agreement of the police official. Thus, the successful control of public behavior required the same balance of toughness and mercy on the part of police officials as was required of judges at court. In 1860, Don Mateo Antonio Miranda demanded that a young mulatto (*pardo*) be severely dealt with for his act of aggression against Miranda's house. Miranda's use of hyperbole exemplifies the intolerance the gente decente displayed in their disagreements with those whose incivility offended them and who were felt to delay the progress that the governing Generation of 37 was then trying to establish. The unnamed pardo had been throwing "rubble against my window, and one of those rocks hit with such force that it shattered the glass and hit [an interior] wall, flying very close to the temple of my grandson, a child of two-and-a-half years of age, and who—without overstressing the case—can be said to have been born again; and I can see that he is now sickened with fear, [while] my daughter suffered a fainting fit as a result of the loud crash. The nature of the event as I have described it demands that this pardo be treated by law as guilty of infanticide and aggravated assault."[116]

By the same token, private citizens who were friends of the police chief would use him as a harsh tutor of those who were considered socially maladjusted. This practice used public officials to shape private behavior and values. The familiarity with which petitioners occasionally made their wishes known to officials is noteworthy, including the use of the familiar second person—a highly unusual form of address for the period, especially in the written language.[117] A similar example of temporary wardship and punishment by the police at the request of a private citizen is evident in the case of a black minor, who in 1858 was handed over to police authorities. In his note of explanation to the precinct chief, the plaintiff writes,

Yesterday I sent to [your] Department a black minor [*negrillo menor de edad*] named Justo Guzmán (alias "Carioca") for being one of the many little rascals who are growing up without any useful and profitable occupation: always in the streets, always *looking for trouble* with the other boys of his age. He has forced me to give him a good scare to serve as a corrective, and this interest that I take in moderating their habits has also been instrumental in my sending him to jail. Since my objective is that he suffer no more than eight days cooling his heels to see how it suits him, I did not consider it necessary to address myself to the Chief [of Police], but rather to you in order to have him held for the suggested length of time, and later—if you deem it to be sufficient—to set him free.[118]

The same plaintiff, following the informal practice of private intervention, returned the day after filing his complaint to request that the youngster be put in the custody of his brother, who promised to shelter him and make him a useful citizen either by apprenticing him to some artisan or by contracting him to someone else as a *conchabo*. Thus, the ultimate goal of social control for porteño elites—the circumscription of the public behavior of socially marginal groups and not necessarily their lengthy incarceration—was achieved. That police authorities as late as the 1860's could satisfy private requests by assuming for themselves the right of corporal punishment of the young men arrested but not yet convicted is an important feature. It suggests one common thread that joined together liberals and conservatives on the issue of subordinating commoners to the needs sensed by political elites: xenophilous liberals who ruled after 1852 through apparently civil means could dismantle the official machine of terror wielded previously by xenophobic conservatives without at the same time disposing of authoritarian extralegalities.[119]

Another thread that bound together widely different political groups over time was the continued deference on the part of officials to local barrio sentiments. For example, *alcaldes de barrios* were given a free hand during the era of war to collect charitable donations in their wards, and to mount public affairs to raise community spirits.[120] As late as 1856, the tradition of barrio and *alcalde* autonomy persisted as undesirable elements of the population were driven out of the areas where residents complained of criminal activities; that is, troublemakers were not run out of town by the authorities, but out of the barrio. This served to mollify the neighbors while keeping troublemakers out of jail whenever possible. French authorities dealt with undesirables in a similar but harsher manner by means of so-called "forbidden places," sometimes encompassing entire cities, where former convicts were barred from residence.[121] Occasionally, however, the practice failed, as is shown by the case involving Don Nicolás Frucio, set free on the orders of the chief of police; this official was subsequently informed in a letter sent to him that even though Frucio had been freed "under the condition that he would move out of the Section, he had remained in it, thereby alarming the neighborhood. I wish you would do me the pleasure," the writer went on, "to remind [Don Frucio] of the obligation he contracted."[122] In any event, the practice of involuntary banishment from neighborhoods had its origins at least as far back as the Rosas period.[123]

Despite the preponderance of public complaints about the overly liberal treatment given to criminals through the intervention on their behalf by influential private parties, the reality was that special dispensations for mercy represented only one edge of the double-edged sword of clientelism. The difficulties faced by apprehended criminals were often made worse by individuals who informally requested especially severe punishments for the culprits. Moreover, the political leanings of the lawbreaker continued to be employed past the Rosas era to cast him in an ever more injurious light. The south side of the city, observed a correspondent to the chief of police about a criminal investigation in 1854, "is well infiltrated and worked up by Urquiza's followers."[124] This schema prolonged the popularization of prosecutorial responsibilities to the extent that literate groups served effectively as advocates against the accused, usually without the benefit of a balancing defense.

Reform and Reaction

Advocates of reform suggested trial by jury, an element not present in Iberian judicial practice, as a means of publicizing the dynamics of the criminal justice system and of increasing the public's political consciousness and social responsibilities.[125] Advocates of the status quo, however, accused the reformers of casuistry, and they argued that the participation of an ill-prepared populace would deprive Argentine society of the opportunity to become civilized—a slow and deliberate process requiring patience and programmed training. In despair, reformers insisted that the change they espoused "would have to be the very worst before it would exceed the imperfections of the current system."[126] To believe that Argentina was unprepared for the jury system, argued these liberals, "would be one of the most dismal mistakes the public could ever make."[127] Yet nothing ever came of the proposed jury system: a general distrust of the public was one of the common denominators among the different generations of rulers in Buenos Aires.

Their doubts were echoed by outside observers as well, like the English chronicler Alexander Caldeclaugh, who doubted the availability of a sufficient pool of men in Buenos Aires equipped to serve on a jury.[128] Others, like Juan Ignacio de Gorriti, the distinguished creole from the northern province of Salta, cautioned against the jury system by reminding his readers in 1836 that Napoleon had accepted Cottu's advice that the bad habits of Frenchmen would have to be altered first if the jury system of France was to function properly.[129] The Argentine legislature in 1888 excluded the jury system when it approved, without debate, the bill that codified criminal procedure. The code's author was Manuel Obarrio, professor of criminal law at the University of Buenos Aires. In the note he attached to his proposed code, Obarrio's sentiments on juries echoed those of both his governing contemporaries and their predecessors in the previous three-quarters of a century of nationhood: "In a country like ours, in which the citizens see [jury service] not only with indifference, but also with aversion, it would not be possible to give the institution a stable, profitable, and efficient life."[130] As in other matters dealing with judicial reform, the rejection of the jury system was a triumph of the right over elite liberals accused of parroting European ideas and customs.[131] Indeed, sometimes the same voices that argued in favor of instituting the jury system, which was historically alien to the Spanish American heritage, warned against the adoption of imported legal practices, advising judicial and political leaders to "forget what is done by other peoples in different parts of the world, whose needs and whose institutions do not resemble ours at all."[132]

Reformers also tried, without success, to ensure the independence of the judiciary branch by altering the system of judicial terms of office on the basis of ideas borrowed from the French Enlightenment and the contemporary British Utilitarians. Judgeships—appointive offices—were usually as durable as the official responsible for the appointment; hence the natural subservience of the judicial system to the prevailing political leadership. Reformers insisted, instead, on the need for an independent judiciary branch with judges appointed for lengthy terms.[133] "In general," wrote a critic in the mid-1850's, "I have witnessed in despair this institution of the *Juez de Paz* suffer from annual changes. They should be appointed for life, assuming their correct official conduct; otherwise, we open ourselves up to having new apprentices every time, with no practical experience or knowledge of the law, and they will thus always act as uncaring outsiders, perpetrating scandals and injustices that will fall, after all is said and done, on the Government that appoints them."[134] By specifically calling on Jeremy Bentham's tenets of civic responsibilities, Argentine reformers gave some of the earliest indications of acceptance of the modern concept of officials whose inherent charge is the promotion of "the greatest good for the greatest number."[135] Bentham's analysis of the growing importance of interdependent relationships within the membership of an increasingly complex society did not escape these reformers; the customary current most in their way, however, was the continued use of the patriarchal principles of power and deference transferred from Iberian corporatism.[136] The Utilitarian principle of maximizing the well-being of the greatest number in the society was frustrated—in the judicial arena, at least—by the vagaries inherent in the region's clientelist politics. While in England the Utilitarians' principle had been an objective of the political order as early as 1725 and had taken on practical meaning by the early nineteenth century, it remained limited in the Argentina of the 1800's to the rhetorical expressions of a few political ideologues.[137] Even prominent liberals like Alberdi and Manuel J. Quiroga de la Rosa were opposed to Benthamite tenets. In his 1837 thesis for the law degree, Ortega de la Rosa sided instead with Kantian metaphysics and precepts of natural law: "No legislator exists other than God," he wrote, and went on to attack Benthamism bitterly.[138] For his part, Alberdi followed his usual principles of pragmatism and cultural inapplicability of customs imported to Argentina from other cultures: laws and procedures must follow from the national character.[139]

The clash between partisan interests and the general community welfare was an early source of ideological battles among literary participants. "Let it be noted: that [some voices] confuse the well-being of the many with the common welfare," chastised a critic; "this, however, is a mistake. The common welfare is composed of the sum of the well-being of all, [but] the promotion of the well-being of the majority destroys the wealth of some to the benefit of others. Never should the general welfare be labeled as such when it is formed on the basis of destroying individual well-being. Whatever the nature of the organism may be, what is harmful to one of its parts is harmful to it all and vice versa."[140] These positions were analogous to the situation of the physical laws governing irresistible forces and immovable objects, with the expected societal results. The failure of progressive reform in Argentina contrasts sharply with the changes in European theory and practice that began to appear by the early nineteenth century. This contrast, in turn, is an expression of the differences in attitudes and concerns of the revolutionaries of each area. The first wave of French penal reform, which took place from 1790 through the 1820's, responded in part to the social welfare program of the Revolution and to the growth of central authority.[141] In Argentina, as elsewhere in Spanish America, the revolutionaries had little of the social welfare consciousness of the French revolutionaries, and few regions succeeded in concentrating sufficient power to impose their central authority.[142]

Conclusions

Almost as soon as the earliest heady expectations of republican bliss gave way to the brusque realities of political instability early in the independence period, the attention of porteño authorities turned to the reestablishment of the civil order by police and judiciary methods. The goal was to counter the generalized sense that "not a day passes by without the police having to face disorderliness and criminal behavior."[143] A systematic investigation of the public's and the officials' reaction to criminality during the half-century after independence leads to the following set of conclusions.

Localism. Porteños of the period covered in this book witnessed the implementation of a wide array of politically diverse philosophies. Despite their inherent differences and indeed the virulent enmity among their various spokesmen, they all displayed very similar traits and attitudes toward the problem of social control. One of the basic tenets of liberalism—that the rule of caudillos such as Rosas necessitated the support of the rabble and thus prevented their containment—is not supported by the evidence provided by the criminal justice system. Indeed, Rosas' strongarm tactics fell no less heavily on lawbreaking gauchos and military men than on his political enemies.[144] Banishment to the Indian frontier as forced military recruits, a typical form of punishment, was as real and as lethal under caudillo rule as it was under the liberals who followed. Rarely did *rosista* authorities excuse the civil disorder of the rustic plebeians normally associated with the mainstay of the caudillos' power. To be sure, criminals who were accused of political opposition to Rosas fared worse than others, but such accusations in reverse were not unknown after his fall. Moreover, the perennial nineteenth-century schism within the political elites, between those advocating federalism (usually equated with *rosismo*) and those favoring a centralized administration (the unitarians, liberals for the most part), did not appear to affect the tradition of local decision making on the subject of criminality. Throughout this period, at least, the neighborhood— the barrio—seldom suffered interference by national or provincial authorities, except to uphold the notion of local option in dispensing judgments. Furthermore, the criminal justice system failed to provide an integrative mechanism of community building, and ultimately of nation building, because of its adherence to the philosophy of barrio autonomy, and because of the discontinuous bureaucratic structure in charge of judicial matters.

Clientelism. The continued acceptance of the barrio signified the survival of direct influence by certain types of individuals on the state's bureaucratic processes. It expressed the continued importance of traditional clientelism in the wake of increasing bureaucratization. If growth of state functions and expansion of public personnel—such as occurred during this period, albeit at a slower pace than at the close of the century—implies an attendant impersonality in social exchange and a loss of influence by the individual in society, these consequences were not evident in the city of Buenos Aires. What did occur was the opposite: certain growth and diversity in the number and social attributes of advocates of punishment and clemency. The society of Buenos Aires, as was the case in other secondary areas of the Spanish Empire, had not contained an aristocracy with virtually monopolistic access to and influence over public power. Elites did, however, possess undue influence over the colonial authorities. They were joined by the gente decente, a sort of gentry and lower gentry, in the ranks of the influential; and toward the end of the period covered by this book, the gente de pueblo, the urban poor and even mestizos who composed the lumpenproletariat, had made considerable inroads in getting access—even if sometimes by proxies—to the criminal justice system. Yet rather than signifying a modernization in value systems, the evolving heterogeneity of claimants to influence required only adjustments to the preexisting model of clientelism.

Since the bureaucracy was indeed growing, especially under the hands of the political figures of the Generation of 37 who governed after Rosas, the relatively narrow scope of the individual clientelism of the eighteenth century grew into a bureaucratized variant by the middle of the nineteenth. Seen from this perspective, the clientelism inherent in the highly bureaucratized Latin American states like Argentina had little to do with the modernization attendant on the industrial capitalism of the late 1880's, but rested, rather, on colonial traditions adapted to independent republics. Here the conclusions of Lawrence Stone may be as appropriate to Argentina as they are to England: "The logic of a sociological theory based on an overarching concept of modernization marching relentlessly through the centuries appears less than convincing. It is merely one more example of the many pitfalls of any unilinear theory of history, which ignores the ups and downs of social and intellectual change, the lack of uniformity of the direction of the trends, and the failure of the various trends to synchronize in the way they ought to if the paradigm is to fit."[145]

Cultural stratification. Are we left, therefore, bereft of grand theory to explain social development in Argentina, indeed in Latin America? Clearly, certain components of modernization theory provide suitable ways of analyzing change: the secularization of belief systems, the reification of well-being through market mechanisms, geographic mobility, particularly of Latin America's population, and its consequent alterations in goal orientations; all of these and more are expressions of modern tendencies. What the theory lacks, however, is the context of contradictions through which it can be amended. If the study of social control provides any lesson, it is that societies can aspire to modernization as an ideal while adapting to it norms based on traditional practices. Tradition and modernity, far from being antagonistic, work together in ways that—over the long run—can cause changes through the absorption of modern values and principles variously by layers of class and status groups.

This notion of stratified cultural diffusion has been known to anthropologists such as Clifford Geertz.[146] Historians and other social scientists who observe the Latin American scene have been caught in the neo-Aristotelian quagmire they create when they assert that development and modernization are immanent and unilinear and then find themselves needing to explain the failures of development in modernizing behaviors. It is evident, however, that, at least in matters of law and order, the absorption of modern values did not take place in a broad stroke that covered all social surfaces. Moreover, even while the definition of what is held to be modern in the realm of social relations is in a state of slow, historical change, the absorptive capabilities of certain class and status groups, together with the retentive predilections of others, conspire against the establishment of a consensus of cultural patterns.

If this is, after all, the natural order of things, it nevertheless takes on serious political and economic dimensions in Latin America, where Sarmiento's duality of civilization or barbarism took such fast hold of philosophers and political actors in the nineteenth and twentieth centuries. In Argentina, this construction took on the practical expressions of a socioeconomic imperative: to bring to the country millions of Europeans who would establish a law-abiding and hardworking community to replace the rustic individualistic community engendered by Spanish colonial rule and resuscitated by Rosas and other xenophobic traditionalists. Thus, following from Sarmiento's dictates that the city represented civilization and the countryside barbarism, the liberals' campaign to eradicate lawlessness concentrated on the rural sector; rural pacification, largely through the persecution of gauchos and the extermination of Indians and *montoneras*, became an economic imperative that would pave the way for the importation of European human and financial capital.[147] In this fashion, an equation was made that linked high cultural attainment to modern values, to the detriment of the mass of the creole population. In the meantime, the dramatic rise in exports of cereal and beef and the alterations in the agricultural production system continued relentlessly.[148] The human dynamic that resulted from these currents of economic expansion included the channeling of increasing numbers of marginal men and women from the Argentine interior and from Europe to the city of Buenos Aires, where social control mechanisms became much more difficult to establish than ever before.[149]

3

Growing Up in the City

Children and Labor

Population mobility, a feature of the society of the Río de la Plata since the start of its full-fledged participation in the expanding commercial capitalism of eighteenth-century Europe, resulted in a youthful urban work force during peaceful times. As a result of the wars for independence and the political turbulence that followed, a new and unforeseen demographic feature began to characterize Buenos Aires: a growing proportion of children in the population, including an increasing number of orphaned and abandoned infants. In this chapter, I shall consider these children and the conditions under which they labored. Furthermore, I shall examine the nature of the decisions that brought them into the world, the political conditions that affected them, and the prevailing religious formulations that framed the mental states of their parents.

Male-preponderant migration, coupled with steadily available youngsters, meant that the laboring class would be abundant, given stable conditions. This resulted in a large contingent of unbound laborers for the artisans, casual helpers for the merchants, and cheap unskilled peasants for the agriculturalists of the city's greenbelt. Generally, then, overhead costs of employment for the propertied classes tended to stay modest. Indeed, surplus adult labor would remain a historical feature of Buenos Aires province: as late as 1908, 42 percent of the permanent work force in the countryside was composed of women and children, while among adult males, only 42 percent could find steady employment.[1] Surplus wage labor also meant that the middle and lower levels of the urban entrepreneurs had few economic incentives to have large families. This segment of porteños included the petty merchants not linked to the Atlantic trade, the streetcorner pulperos, the artisans, and the *chacareros* who owned family agricultural plots in the outlying city wards. Unlike their social superiors, such as the wholesale merchants, these men held on to their precarious positions as petty proprietors or dependents, and they had to include the objective terms of economic rationality and maximization of personal resources in their calculations regarding the procreation of offspring.

In Buenos Aires and elsewhere, family formation strategies followed, to a large extent, from economic positions. Thus, among the middle classes, wholesale merchants in Buenos Aires, like wholesale merchants in other important ports of trade, characteristically had the largest families. In the late eighteenth and early nineteenth centuries, the wholesale merchants of Buenos Aires fathered an average of 7.38 children, not much different from their contemporaries in the port of Salem, Massachusetts, who averaged 7.06 children per family; the median number of offspring was 8.[2] Among the elites of Buenos Aires during the same period, the median number of children was 11.[3] The lower median number of offspring among wholesale merchants of the same era manifested one of the consequences of the deferred marriage practices among the city's Spaniards, who represented the single most prominent group of merchants. This difference between the elites and the well-to-do merchants exemplified the complex relationships that linked occupation with family and household formation.

By contrast, lower social groups practiced considerably different family formation strategies. The data collected here do not permit precise comparisons with the mean number of children ever born among the merchants, but the statistical data for this book and others show that the social strata beneath merchants and elites in port cities tended to have fewer children. For example, artisans in early nineteenth-century Salem averaged 5.69 children while laborers had 4.27 children.[4] Salem's merchants, who represented the city's elite, had an average of 42 percent more children than the families positioned on the lower rungs of the social ladder. For Buenos Aires the indications of much smaller numbers of children ever born among the lower classes come from the age-standardized marital fertility data collected for 1810, according to the methods described in the

Appendix. These data show that families of merchants and professionals averaged fertility rates one-third higher than lower social groups. Wives of merchants and professionals had a fertility rate of 865 per 1,000, 48 percent higher than the figure of 583 per 1,000 registered among the wives in the lower-status occupational groups. Evidently, birth control was not a privilege reserved for the well-to-do; it was exercised, instead, widely and differentially by a broad spectrum of the same society. It thus appears that even in an Ibero-American Catholic society such as that of Buenos Aires, socio-occupational conditions determined birth control practices at least as much if not more than traditional principles of morality or religion. The practice of family limitation among Argentines of the 1800's is not implausible; knowledge of birth control was widespread in the West, and it was actually practiced in France as early as the latter part of the eighteenth century.[5]

By the standards of modernization theory, early nineteenth-century Argentina did not possess the structural conditions that caused the decline in fertility elsewhere in the West. Argentina was characterized by a relatively low urban concentration, it had virtually no manufacturing industry, and its population displayed high levels of illiteracy. However, we know that in significant regions of the West, basic structural changes in society, such as increased levels of urbanization, industrialization, and literacy—"the *dei ex machina* of the theory of the demographic transition"—were not necessary in shaping the demographic transition toward reduced fertility. Such was the French situation, for example; despite the relative absence of such structural changes, the population experienced low birth rates and high mortality rates exceptionally early.[6] Clearly, something more than technological innovation and industrial capitalism must have been at work to create the contradictions between relatively low levels of modernization indices and modern fertility rates in parts of Europe and of Spanish America. To the extent that economic rationality prevailed in determining a relatively smaller family among the middle groups in nineteenth-century Buenos Aires and elsewhere, it was, in part, the consequence of the ample supplies of unskilled and semiskilled wage labor that made hiring young people rather than fathering them economically sound. These laborers existed as the result of the mobility of unbound populations and the high numbers of illegitimate infants who grew up and roamed the countryside and the cities without the protective mantle of their families.

The city's slave force was in only limited, indeed decreasing, competition with this abundant salaried working-class population. Although the slave population of the 1810's was considerable, the formal end of the institution of slavery was known to be close at hand: moreover, their narrow distribution among few masters and extremely low natural reproduction rates served to limit the number of masters to a modest proportion of the city's petty proprietors of businesses and farms. Finally, slaves commanded a very high price, too high for most members of the city's middle groups to use them extensively. A decade after the formal abolition of the slave trade and of slavery—the so-called "free-womb law" of 1813—the awareness of the impending demise of the system had settled in among the slave-owning classes. The decreasing reliability of slavery promoted a type of competition for slave laborers that produced verbal and legal battles among their employers; for example, captured young runaway slaves were kept by their new de facto masters, who refused to return them to their legitimate owners. After making several fruitless public appeals for the return of a young runaway slave girl, a porteño slaveowner published in 1829 the following note in one of the city's dailies: "The person who has a small Black girl of about 8 to 10 years of age, who ran away on November 28, is hereby advised please to return her. If so, he will be rewarded as announced in the newspapers on previous occasions; otherwise, however, the culprits will be subjected to all sorts of repercussions, because her masters are certain that a slave girl of such tender age, and who has no skills—since she is from the countryside—has no value, were it not for the reception given to such youngsters in certain homes. Therefore, it is expected that whoever is responsible will deliver her to Piedad Street, number 306."[7] The allusion to what occurred in "certain homes" did not suggest any ideological motivations, for this was not a society with a significant grass-roots abolition movement. The "reception" referred to by the frustrated slave master represented merely a target of opportunity for the illegal acquisition of urban labor.

General awareness of the unreliability of slavery as a source of labor was expressed by the many advertisements offering menial positions that, as early as the 1820's, invariably included the promise of freedom, usually at the end of ten years of contracted service. Working conditions, more than salaries, became the new incentives offered to prospective applicants for menial jobs. In an advertisement published in 1823, the seeker of a slave promised to "offer the favor of providing [him] with advantageous conditions for his freedom."[8] In an advertisement that reveals the increasing tendency toward negotiated labor relationships even within the framework of slavery, the owners of a 25-year-old female slave announced her sale and the reasons for it: she preferred not to join her masters as they moved to an outlying *estancia*. Moreover, the young slave herself would speak on her own behalf about her qualities and aptitudes: "*Las habilidades que sabe, ella las dirá.*"[9]

The transition toward contracted labor was facilitated by the more relaxed Iberian treatment of urban slaves, a tradition expressed by the relative independence of action given to slaves, whether artisans or female domestic servants. By the start of the nineteenth century, female domestic slaves were entering into agreements with their masters that were designed to change bosses and displayed the conjunction of "the patriarchal spirit and the slave's will."[10] An example of this type of agreement appeared in the pages of the *Telégrafo Mercantil* in 1801: "For Sale: A Black girl named María Luisa de Sola, slave of Doña Francisca Xaviera de Sola, for 350 pesos. She is between 18 and 20 years of age, and is being sold because the girl wishes it so."[11] Contract labor also followed the course set by both legal and environmental conditions. Thus, as noted by Lyman Johnson, manumission in Buenos Aires depended much less on religious and humanitarian values inherent in the Iberian system than has been suggested.[12] Manumission and contracted labor were the results, in part, of the increasing awareness that the mortality rate of blacks was so much higher than their ability to replenish their numbers that, in time, they would effectively cease to be a reliable work force.[13] And Pampean Indians had never provided the draft labor that whites had been enjoying for centuries in the neighboring Andean regions. As it turned out, the available palliative was the presence of a large and growing contingent of free wage laborers, which continued to be a feature of urban Buenos Aires.

The availability of relatively inexpensive labor, in turn, bore different consequences for the formation of families, depending on economic position. The declining reliability of the slave system and the steady supply of unbound labor within the city, supported by a reserve force of circulating pampean migrants from the interior, meant that the competition for urban wages among the semiskilled and casual laborers accrued to the benefit of the city's middle group of employers. Menial workers took out advertisements offering their services under conchabo contracts; they were often destitute women who were trying to keep their children rather than abandon them to private or institutional care.[14] The following example is typical: "Healthy wet-nurse with a well-fed and well-cared-for six-month-old baby wishes to find someone to offer her a conchabo contract to care for another infant, being in fine condition to do so. Details can be found at 254 Peru Street."[15] In the end, the nature of the occupational schema left its stamp on the size and structure of the families of unskilled and semiskilled workers, as critics took note of the "familial disorganization" taking place around them.[16]

The conchabo system was the Platine version of the mechanism found elsewhere in America and in Europe of putting excess populations from needy families into the homes where their labor was needed and their maintenance would be provided.[17] Illegitimacy, child abandonment, and population mobility also affected the composition of many households as the conchabo system accommodated the professional needs of artisans, petty merchants, and greenbelt operators to the needs of youngsters who had been left without the sustenance of their own families. The mediator, whenever private parties were not in charge of arranging the placement of young workers, was the *defensor de menores*, a public office dating from the colonial period. The changes in the organizational framework of the municipal government enacted in late 1821 specified the appointment of a lawyer to oversee the welfare of minors and the indigent. The same person would also hold the office of solicitor general for the province of Buenos Aires.[18] The preamble to a series of new regulations updated his responsibilities and now specified the socioeconomic requirements for the post: "The office of *Defensor de Menores* is one of those destined for honor that should satisfy the philanthropic sentiments of any good citizen; the principal aim is to care for the fortunes of the members of an interesting social class, to save them from either the greediness of bad tutors, or from legal and complicated suits that are always ruinous. A property owner with a reputation for zealousness will find great satisfaction in exercising these paternal functions and will earn the blessings of the relevant families and the respect of society."[19] In principle, the *defensor* was responsible for the welfare of public charges, such as abandoned or troublesome children and the indigent; in practice, however, he tried to minimize the extent to which these unfortunate cases burdened the state's finances by acting as a labor agent and putting youngsters to work in either private homes or in institutions that, in any event, received relatively little financial support from the authorities.[20] The protector system turned out to be an inexpensive but also an inefficient way of eliminating unsupervised youngsters from the streets. At the end of the 1850's, municipal plans were drafted to create a home for the indigent in order to contain the "alarming spectacle witnessed throughout our streets, where one can see beggars, composed of individuals of both sexes and children, imploring for the public's charity."[21]

The increases in parentless children roaming the city's streets occasioned a deepening involvement by the government in their management. The added responsibility for their care given to the *defensor de menores y naturales* was one example of this expanded role; another was the new charge given to the *juez de paz* of each of the city's barrios. State, church, and the neighborhood's population were now combined in a governmental attempt, through a *circular* of December 29, 1829, to solve the problems caused by these homeless youngsters. The *juez de paz* would now gather information about these youths from the parish priest and the neighbors of his district and forward it to the ministry of government. This information included the number and the quality of tutors provided for the children, the amount of personal property owned by the children, and the persons held accountable for the safety of those belongings. The importance of these measures was deemed by the authorities as "excessively self-evident."[22] Thus, infant mobility depended on the personal exchanges between parental or official authorities and small-scale producers. Argentines responded to the availability of children who were deemed economically superfluous by their own families in ways similar to the European societies undergoing the technical and organizational changes brought about by the factory system. Yet these responses among porteños preceded the very dynamic socio-economic alterations associated with the European Industrial Revolution and their consequences in Buenos Aires late in the nineteenth century.

Although no empirical data yet exist to illustrate the nature of the relationship between the putting-out system and its demographic aftereffects, the concern by the authorities over the gangs of unsupervised children in the streets and the loose public behavior of lower-class young men and women, often *conchabos*, suggests that the norms of morality and sexuality were changing to the dismay of the elites. In fact, these changes were not the province only of the lower classes: any discord displayed publicly was subject to especially sharp criticism. This was particularly true in the case of street fights, which even among the gentry involved civilians and military men— a consequence of the contradictions inherent in an economy sustained by civilian elites and a political system borne on the shoulders of a military machine.[23] Most alarming to contemporary observers was the sight of children who sought satisfaction outside the boundaries of home and beyond the control of family.[24] Not surprisingly, social critics decried the concentrations of youngsters on the streets, particularly during holidays and special events like Carnival and bullfights. At the same time, the perceived erosion of moral traditions caused by youths was illustrated by the continued use of an antiquated civil code that defined male adulthood as commencing at the age of 25, while in England it began at 21.[25]

From the perspective of sexuality, the putting-out system served to loosen the moral and especially the material bonds that had restricted indigent youngsters living at home. The new security provided to the young on the basis of the rights and obligations specified in the labor agreements—the *contratas*—translated into a kind of increased moral and material freedom for boys and girls to act: the master's authority lacked the imperative of moral force normally associated with a parent, while the guarantee of food and shelter, sometimes in combination with opportunities for collecting wages, provided youngsters with greater freedom to acquire the material prerequisites for marriage or consensual unions. The following *contrata*, signed in March 1841, illustrates how parents transferred the daily responsibilities for their children to strangers; it also demonstrates the transformation of the youngsters' rights and obligations from affectively based motivations to contractually based deference. And the sanctioning authority—intent on controlling the movement of youth, especially of young men—was the state in the form of the police.

LONG LIVE THE FEDERATION!

General Department of Police

CONTRACT

Buenos Aires, March 1841,

Year 32 of Liberty, 25 of Independence, and 12 of the Argentine Confederation

We, the undersigned, in accordance with the Law of November 17, 1821, agree upon the following articles:

Art. 1. We, the principals of Bourgan, Funge, and Co., declare that, in accordance with the proposal made to us by Da. Juana María Olivera to accept her son, Benjamín Montes, as apprentice in our factory, and receiving her promises of his good conduct, have agreed to do so for a term of three years, beginning at such time as we commence his training in the making of plush and silk hats at the level of perfection at which they are currently produced.

Art. 2. We commit ourselves to his maintenance and to give him shelter and thirty-five pesos monthly during the agreed-upon term of three years.

Art. 3. Benjamín Montes commits himself to perform all duties customary in the factory on Sundays and holidays, as required of him. He will maintain his cleanliness, he will be punctual in his working hours, and with his obligations away from the factory during such days when there is no work, and he will comply with his religious obligations.

Art. 4. Benjamín Montes, apprentice, will be obligated to maintain good order and harmony with the other members of the house during the agreed-upon term of three years, and to obey without hesitation whatever we or the foreman may ask of him (which will be only those things related to the factory or to its good order), and in the event that Benjamín should flee from the factory, it is the obligation of his mother to find him and to bring him back, and two days will be added to the contracted period of service for every day that he remains a fugitive.

Art. 5. I, Benjamín Montes, fully cognizant of everything contained in the previous four articles, and with the approval of My Lady Mother, declare that from this day forth I enter into apprenticeship for the agreed-upon term of three years in the hat factory of Messrs. Bourgan Bunge [sic] and Co. under the conditions and obligations herein expressed, and as proof of our [agreement] they add their signatures to the one of My Lady Mother . . . and to the same effect it is all hereby authorized by the Chief of Police.[26]

The conchabo system followed the norms of the Iberian legal traditions instilled in Argentina: witnesses were present, the acts were notarized and registered, and the contracts were signed by those who were literate. Moreover, contracts with illiterate youngsters were made without the benefit of having parents or guardians present to oversee the drafting of the terms. Such was the case of a young immigrant woman named Sebastiana Batista o Coita, who, in 1844, agreed by oral consent and without parental or proxy supervision to serve the needs of Don Leonardo Gonsales. This conchabo contract typifies the vague wording and open-ended nature of these versions of the agreements, which clearly accrued to the benefit of the new masters. "I, Sebastiana Batista o Coita, hereby attest that I commit myself to serve Dn Leonardo Gonsales *in everything I am charged to do related to the service of his house*, by virtue of the payment of one thousand and fifteen hundred pesos . . . made by said gentleman to the consignee of the ship *Gran Canaria* for my passage and passport; Dn Gonsales is responsible for paying eighty pesos monthly for my services, from which forty are to be used toward the refund of his advance [to the consignee], and he will use the remaining forty to help pay for my needs. As parties unto this agreement, we hereby sign."[27]

The practice of putting in service was common enough that, as early as the mid-1840's, the police and even private parties had forms already printed that needed simply to be filled in with the details relevant to each agreement. This was the practice at the port of Buenos Aires, where authorities supervised the transportation and delivery of laborers put in service. Ship owners, such as D. Ramón Francisco Piñeyro, had their own forms printed. Piñeyro, owner and outfitter of the "Unión Compostelana" and in partnership with various captains, ferried indentured laborers to the port of Buenos Aires from interior towns upriver. The contracts spell out the time in service and the indebtedness, which began early with the advance payment for transportation. In the interior village of Camal, the agree-

ment signed in March 1845 for the transportation of Francisco
Muñíz to the city of Buenos Aires highlights the contractual nature
of youthful labor.

Condition 1: Upon arrival, the said Muñíz will be put in service in the
home or with the person that the ship's Captain or Consignment agent de-
termines. Muñíz will pay to the said home or person the sum of one hundred gold pesos as compensation for his transport; in no way will he be able
to leave service for one year, nor will he be able to absolve himself from this
contract until he provides a full year of labor, since the sum of one hundred
gold pesos will be considered an advance provided by the home or person
to facilitate his transportation, and since that person pays the ship's Captain
or Consignment agent, obliging such officers to verify this obligation.
Condition 2: If said Muñíz should need any money during the year of
service, the contracting house or person will so provide, obliging Muñíz to
return the sums, thereby extending the length of service in relevant proportions until such a time as the debt is liquidated."[28]

The contracts also provided opportunities for the indentured servant to get out of service either by paying the captain 75 gold pesos
before docking or by guaranteeing the payment of 80 gold pesos
within two months. In effect, Muñíz became, as did other indigent
workers seeking greater opportunities in Buenos Aires, a debt peon.
On July 1, 1845, D. Miguel Ferreyra arranged for a reduced fee of
80 gold pesos as payment for transport to the captain, and Muñíz
began to serve his new master, who would "discount by way of his
labor a monthly assessment in gold pesos until the liquidation of the
eighty gold pesos, in addition to whatever other sums his expenditures may occasion."[29]
The obligations of conchabos and the stipulations of their contracts did not mean, however, a lack of independence or leisure time.
To be sure, workers were obliged to provide their labor under conditions not of their own making, but they were also the beneficiaries
of the greater freedom and possibilities for social and sexual intercourse provided by the city. Their growing self-realization was made
possible by the very same uprooting from home and village that had
placed them in service. Premarital pregnancies occurred frequently
as material considerations—for those men and women in service—
were eased by their patrons. Opportunities for sexual intercourse in-

creased; one could easily yield to the attraction of the other sex during labor holidays, after hours, or during unauthorized absences, to
judge by the higher birth rates reported for freedmen, the likeliest
candidates for the conchabo system.[30]

In Argentina, economic and employment conditions played their
part in affecting sexual unions and offspring among the lower classes;
and in the end, the putting-out system served the needs of producers
while it intensified the problems caused by surplus children among
poor families. In addition, it exacerbated the difficulties in maintaining social control in light of so many families without adult
males present.[31] This was not limited to the contracted slave or free
Afro-Argentine populations: whites and mestizas also contributed
to the problem considerably, as was the case in other nineteenth-
century Latin American regions.[32]

Social Structures and Marital Fertility

So little work has been done on the history of the family in Argentina, including its structure, composition, and determinants of
fertility, that we must begin at the stage of aggregating empirical
evidence. I intend to provide data at this basic level, but I also wish
to illustrate how such data may be used at new levels of conceptualization. Thus, this book may be viewed as a modest step along the
road to the ultimate goal of formulating what Kuhn described as the
community's paradigm, in this case, that of family historians of
Ibero-American societies.[33] Furthermore, the paradigm will be
sought, in part, with the aid of statistical evidence, but without losing
sight of the fact that improvement in historical techniques is largely
incidental in the context of historiographical progress.[34]

The composition of the porteño household, and in particular the
number of children ever born, was determined principally by political, economic, and legal factors: the turbulence of the civil wars; the
urban economic realities of nineteenth-century Platine society; and
the inheritance system. The political environment and the civil wars
will be analyzed in a separate chapter in terms of the effects wrought
on the porteño household. The changes in household structures in
the first half of the nineteenth century, it will be argued, resulted
particularly from the loss of young men, victims of the political and
military turbulence of the period that affected the city's entire social

and racial landscape. Still, the incidences of young men absent from their homes, of young widows, and of family extensions as survival strategies designed to overcome the loss of young male heads of households all registered their highest levels among the humble ✓ classes and the population of color. For now, however, this chapter *hw* will address issues that concern the rates and the determinants of marital fertility in Buenos Aires. Fertility and childhood have been issues of scholarly interest in Europe and the United States; it is time we extended this scholarship to a major South American city.

The data yielded by the manuscript census schedules elaborated in this book can be compared with recently revised observations about the size of conjugal family units in the past. The image of the preindustrial household swarming with children close in age is now recognized as an idealized version of historical reality that has not stood up well to empirical investigation.[35] In the United States, the theses that link industrialization and urbanization to the decline in fertility underwent a serious challenge beginning with Yasuba's research on birth rates from 1800. The cause of decline in fertility, he argued, had little to do with industrialization or urbanization, since the decline preceded the rise of the North American industrial, urban-based economy.[36] Fertility was principally affected, instead, by the availability of cheap or free land. Other studies indicate that land availability, more than any other single cause, was found to be responsible for the timing of both marriage and the formation of families in colonial New England; again, neither industrialization nor urban growth appear to have been positively related to family size or to its composition.[37] More recent research on nineteenth-century fertility behavior in the United States indicates that the fertility indices declined in both rural and urban areas after 1810. On this subject, Richard Easterlin has employed economic theories of fertility to suggest that the optimal number of children is the result of a complex equation that incorporates personal preferences, prices, and income. The extent to which actual births exceeded optimal births depended on considerations related to birth control practices: the extent of information about such practices, the attitude toward them, and the available means.[38]

For its part, the European family was often caught in the incompatibilities that arose from its attempts to provide for its younger children while retaining the familial patrimony.[39] John Habakkuk

studied the extreme difficulties of disentangling the effects of the
rules of succession from other considerations in the evolution of European family structures. He was able to observe general tendencies
only within the agricultural populations, where, in areas of equal
partibility—such as France, Portugal, or Spain—the typical rural
family tended to consist of parents living together with a relatively
small number of children who, normally, were also married. By contrast, families in rural areas where succession rules permitted property transmission to only one heir tended to include a large number
of unmarried children, and were "surrounded by a penumbra of celibate uncles and aunts, younger brothers and sisters."[40]

In porteño society, the nuclear family was found to prevail by far
over all other family structures from at least 1810 until approximately 1860. Only at about the middle of the century do the data
show an incipience of complex household formation. The nuclear
family was small in absolute terms, and unexpectedly small considering that we are dealing with an Iberian Catholic society.[41] Indeed,
the average nuclear family in Buenos Aires during the first half of
the nineteenth century comprised barely four people. The average
sizes of nuclear and extended families, based on a "city sample" (a
random sample of the entire urban population from each census year
shown) of 1,149 people, were:

Family type	1810	1827	1855
Nuclear	4.2	3.7	3.9
Extended	5.0	4.2	5.1

The sample data show that in approximately one-third of all
households in Buenos Aires children were altogether absent. Moreover, when children were present, they were not very numerous, as
shown in Table 6: approximately 16 percent of all married couples
had only one child living at home, and another 15 percent had two
children. The socialization of children among their peers thus took
place largely outside of their domestic environments. The home
tended to provide a very limited opportunity, which generally precluded possibilities of learning from other children; instead, schools
for the gente decente, and markets and streets for the gente de
pueblo, offered opportunities for children to learn from other
children.

Although the average porteño family had few offspring, the city

TABLE 6

Married Couples by Number of Children Living at Home,
City Sample, 1810, 1827, and 1855

(N = 755 couples)

Number of children	1810		1827		1855	
	No.	Pct.	No.	Pct.	No.	Pct.
0	45	16.3%	60	25.2%	50	20.7%
1	56	20.3	38	16.0	46	19.1
2	50	18.1	38	16.0	38	19.1
3	32	11.6	34	14.3	29	12.0
4	48	17.4	31	13.0	24	10.0
5	17	6.2	17	7.1	22	9.1
6	17	6.2	8	3.4	13	5.4
7+	11	4.0	12	5.0	19	7.9
TOTAL	276	100.0%	238	100.0%	241	100.0%

SOURCE: The source of this table and, unless otherwise indicated, of subsequent tables is the sample data described in the Methodological Appendix.

took on an increasingly youthful character, particularly after 1830. Between 1810 and 1855, a sample of all the residents in 64 city blocks, labeled the "selective universe," shows the following variations in the ratio of general population to children aged 14 and younger:

Period	Decline	Increase	No change	Unknown
1810–27	20	10	3	31
1827–55	44	16	2	2

Subsequently, this youth index showed a much faster geographical spread as the rate of increase in the population of youngsters continued to climb in relation to the total population. Thus, more couples were having children after the 1820's, although each couple continued the pattern of limiting the number of offspring.

Infant mortality, which was normally high in an era of poor sanitation and limited medical resources, surely had an important role in determining the number of children per family, but average marital fertility—shown in Table 7—which had also been relatively low at the beginning of the century, declined consistently thereafter at least until the 1850's. In 1810, the average marital fertility rate in Buenos Aires stood at 616 per 1,000 women; it declined by 13 percent, to 536 per 1,000, by 1855. Although precise comparisons with other Latin American regions are not possible, the average fertility

TABLE 7
Marital Fertility of Women Aged 15–49, City Sample, 1810, 1827, and 1855
(N = 764 women)

Age group	No.	Pct.	Marital fertility per 1,000
		1810	
15–19	7	3%	286
20–24	35	14	714
25–29	39	15	641
30–34	62	24	566
35–39	39	15	641
40–44	52	20	654
45–49	22	9	545
15–49[a]	256	100%	616
		1827	
15–19	10	4%	500
20–24	31	12	677
25–29	49	19	592
30–34	62	24	565
35–39	33	13	576
40–44	48	19	521
45–49	20	8	600
15–49[a]	253	100%	571
		1855	
15–19	8	3%	375
20–24	32	12	719
25–29	43	17	605
30–34	53	21	547
35–39	55	22	455
40–44	42	16	500
45–49	22	9	455
15–49[a]	100	100%	536

[a]Age-standardized fertility.

rates of women in Buenos Aires appear to have been lower than those of their contemporaries elsewhere in the Americas. For example, in a fertility study of Erie County and the city of Buffalo, women who had migrated from New England to Buffalo had an average fertility rate in 1855 of 940 children per 1,000, while Irish Catholic immigrant women reported a fertility rate of 926 per 1,000.[42] Elsewhere in the Americas, the Brazilian city of Ouro Preto reported an average of four children per married woman in the early to mid-nineteenth century, compared to the fewer than two in Buenos Aires.[43]

Yet the relatively low average marital fertility rate of nineteenth-century women in Buenos Aires masks what must have been high illegitimate fertility indices and considerable differences in fertility behavior among the city's social classes and ethnic groups. A comparison between the fertility behavior of the lower and upper strata of porteños shows two secular trends headed in opposite directions and on the point of converging at midcentury, according to the data in Table 8.

The age-standardized fertility rate registered among the low-status population of laborers in 1810 stood at 583 and was on the ascent; it rose to 709 in 1827 and to 749 in 1855. A contrary trend was developing among members of the high-status group, composed of merchants, professionals, and rentiers. In 1810, these well-to-do porteños had a very high age-standardized fertility ratio of 865, but the decline from then on was continuous, to 822 in 1827 and to 766 in 1855. The poorer residents were evidently increasing their birth rates, while the more comfortable classes were sharply reducing theirs. Moreover, the data indicate that the lower strata maintained their historical preference for bearing children when they were between 25 and 29 years of age. Wealthier women, however, helped to lower their overall fertility rates by deferring procreation as the century progressed from the age interval of 20 to 24—the prevailing age interval of motherhood in 1810—to the age interval of 25 to 29.

The indications that the poorer classes were more apt to increase their birth rates over time are reinforced by the reported increase of 38 percent in the marital birth rates among women in cuartel 19, the ward that contained one of the city's densest concentrations of Africans and their descendants. According to the sample data, from an age-standardized fertility rate of 529 in 1810, women in this cuartel reported a rise to 662 in 1827 and to 727 in 1855. Although illegitimacy rates are not available, it is very likely that the working-class women of Buenos Aires behaved like their peers in other parts of Latin America where illegitimacy levels were high.[44] Furthermore, the potential for even greater illegitimacy rates can be inferred from the following data (selective universe, N=8,372), which show the longitudinal increase in the percentage of single women as heads of household:

Year	Single women heads of household	Total single women	Heads of household as percent of total
1810	332	1,667	19.9%
1827	650	2,788	23.3
1855	882	3,917	22.5

The proportion of unmarried women who headed households within the selective universe rose from barely 20 percent in 1810 to 23.3 percent in 1827, then dropped slightly to 22.5 percent in 1855. The rise in 1827 coincided with the period of greatest military activity, the conditions of which raised the potential for "hit-and-run" sexual affairs and the consequent rise in illegitimacy. "Hit-and-run," the term given by Edward Shorter to a certain type of illegitimacy in Europe, is appropriately evocative for this period of Argentine history. These were the children of young people succumbing to romance in "a social landscape of disorder and flux. There was much intercourse, but people were stepping out of their old places en route to new ones, and temporary cohabitations often failed to turn into permanent concubinages. This combination of circumstances raised illegitimacy to historic heights, for the years 1790–1860 were, in virtually every society or community we know about, the peak period of illegitimacy."[45]

Disorder and flux were very much the symptoms of this Argentine society that forcibly drafted disproportionately large numbers of its powerless members and continually faced the consequent desertions. Numerous instances can be found in the documentation of masters who "donated" the services of their slaves to the government's military needs; the involuntary military service forced on black slaves, moreover, was not limited to periods of heavy fighting. In the early 1840's, an era that registered the lowest military expenditures of Buenos Aires since 1821, slaveowners continued to provide manpower to the state, which still had an unusually high number of men in uniform.[46] For example, Mariano Lahitte, slave of Don Eduardo Lahitte, was "donated" in February of 1841 to serve in the navy for one year, the normal term for such recruits. The official in charge of the transfer sounded a note of warning to the naval officers that this slave "suffers from the bad habit of fleeing constantly, which he will undoubtedly try to do the moment he steps back on land."[47] Not surprisingly, desertion was rampant in Argentine armies beginning with the wars

TABLE 8

Marital Fertility of Women Aged 15–49 by Occupational Status,
Selective Universe, 1810, 1827, and 1855

(N = 2,287 women)

Age group	Low status		High status	
	No.	Marital fertility per 1,000	No.	Marital fertility per 1,000
		1810		
15–19	11	273	11	818
20–24	33	818	33	1,269
25–29	39	1,282	38	1,105
30–34	34	206	35	428
35–39	22	545	24	1,042
40–44	34	235	22	773
45–49	15	67	9	0
15–49[a]	188	574	172	779
15–49[b]	—	583	—	865
		1827		
15–19	19	368	15	267
20–24	52	750	67	1,149
25–29	71	1,338	90	1,433
30–34	63	476	57	421
35–39	44	682	51	706
40–44	34	265	41	244
45–49	17	118	22	227
15–49[a]	300	706	343	831
15–49[b]	—	709	—	822
		1855		
15–19	34	676	18	333
20–24	133	797	95	989
25–29	174	1,287	103	1,621
30–34	154	500	131	435
35–39	101	733	96	865
40–44	79	405	82	390
45–49	27	259	57	123
15–49[a]	702	773	582	766
15–49[b]	—	775	—	766

[a]Average fertility.   [b]Age-standardized fertility.

for independence, notwithstanding the severe punishments it carried, including death; in fact, cash rewards were paid to anyone who shot military escapees. "In this respect," notes John Lynch, "there was little difference between federal and unitarian armies: neither were 'popular' forces and both were decimated by desertions."[48]

TABLE 9
*Marital Fertility of White and Non-White Married Women, Aged 15–49,
Selective Universe, 1810 and 1827*

Age group	White married women			Non-white married women		
	No.	Pct.	Marital fertility per 1,000	No.	Pct.	Marital fertility per 1,000
1810						
15–49	24	7%	542	2	5%	500
20–24	63	18	794	7	17	429
25–29	73	21	1,123	10	24	458
30–34	69	20	290	10	24	200
35–39	46	13	761	3	7	667
40–44	53	15	434	8	19	250
45–49	25	7	0	2	5	500
15–49[a]	353	100%	632	42	100%	524
15–49[b]	—	—	639	—	—	376
1827						
15–19	41	5%	293	3	5%	0
20–24	150	19	813	15	24	133
25–29	202	25	1,163	18	29	556
30–34	154	19	344	12	19	250
35–39	115	14	591	5	8	200
40–44	93	12	204	7	11	286
45–49	43	5	163	2	3	0
15–49[a]	798	100%	647	62	100%	290
15–49[b]	—	—	640	—	—	288

[a] Average fertility.   [b] Age-standardized fertility.

Increases in illegitimacy among the poor can be gleaned from two types of statistical indications. The first can be found in the variations in marital fertility indices that distinguished the populations of whites from nonwhites. The investigation of marital fertility rates based on racial categories is possible only for the years 1810 and 1827; afterward, racial references disappear from census records. The marital fertility rates for white women held steady, according to the data in Table 9. Nonwhite women, however, showed a precipitous decline of 23 percent. Yet the nonwhite component of the urban population fell only 2 percent between 1810 and 1822.[49] Such a minor decrease in population compared to the striking decline in marital fertility among nonwhites points in the direction of significant illegitimacy rates, probably aided by the higher incidence of single women in the population.

The second indication of high illegitimacy rates comes from frag- mentary baptismal records for various urban and suburban parishes. The spotty available evidence suggests that porteñas of low socio- economic positions were forced to cope with numbers of children beyond their ability to feed and maintain them by the drastic mea- sure of child abandonment. Indeed, physicians in Buenos Aires were dismayed throughout the nineteenth century at the high rates of abandonment.[50] The practice was institutionalized in the form of the Casa de Expósitos, run by the city's Sociedad de Beneficencia. How- ever, as discussed earlier, infants continued to be abandoned regu- larly at the doorsteps of churches and private homes. Between 1826 and 1831, the urban parishes experienced illegitimacy rates of 33 per- cent for whites and 88 percent for people of color.[51] These figures, culled from the baptismal information that registered children born from consensual marriages as *naturales*, show the underside of a so- ciety led by morally conservative elites frustrated in their attempts to legislate morality. Of course, not every unplanned baby was aban- doned, nor was illegitimacy a fact of life only to the poor. The prev- alence of illegitimacy even among women who were not mired in the lowest socioeconomic levels is indicated by advertisements in the local press taken out by wet-nurses in search of employment by women who could afford their clandestine services. This feature of family life among porteños is clearly illustrated in the following ex- ample of elliptical wording in a classified advertisement published in 1830 in one of the city's dailies: "Wet-nurse seeks concealed child [*niño oculto*] for rearing services. Interested parties may inquire at 1890 Paraguay Street."[52]

In addition to matters of race, socioeconomic position, and war, national origin likewise affected the fertility behavior of married couples living in Buenos Aires. Creole, English, and Spanish groups were selected for comparisons on the basis of their numerical and cultural contributions to the city. The fertility rates of all three groups, shown in Table 10, were quite different, perhaps not a sur- prising fact in the case of the English population of Buenos Aires, but curious in the case of the Spaniards—cast supposedly from the same cultural and religious mold as the creoles.

The English fertility curve was significantly lower than the Ar- gentine or Spanish, but it headed in the same upward direction over time as the Argentine curve. The Spanish, in contrast, showed a rate that declined steadily, although it had started from a significantly

TABLE 10

Marital Fertility by Nationality, City Sample, 1810, 1827, and 1855

Age group	Argentine				British				Spanish			
	No. of children	No.	Pct. of total	Marital fertility per 1,000	No. of children	No.	Pct. of total	Marital fertility per 1,000	No. of children	No.	Pct. of total	Marital fertility per 1,000
1810												
15–19	6	9	6%	667	—	0	0%	0	4	10	6%	400
20–24	13	28	18%	464	—	0	0	0	35	31	19	1,129
25–29	36	37	24	973	2	1	100	—	42	32	19	1,313
30–34	9	30	20	300	—	0	0	0	12	31	19	387
35–39	13	22	14	591	—	0	0	0	23	19	11	1,210
40–44	7	19	12	368	—	0	0	0	14	29	17	483
45–49	1	8	5	125	—	0	0	0	0	14	8	0
15–49[a]	85	153	100%	556	2	1	100%	—	130	166	100%	783
15–49[b]	—	—	—	527	—	—	—	—	—	—	—	777
1827												
15–19	4	15	5%	267	2	5	10%	400	1	2	1%	500
20–24	62	56	19	1,107	4	7	14	571	24	21	14	1,143
25–29	117	78	27	1,500	16	18	35	889	41	25	17	1,640
30–34	23	55	19	418	6	9	18	667	7	25	17	280
35–39	26	41	14	634	2	8	16	250	27	23	16	1,174
40–44	8	30	10	267	0	3	6	0	6	28	19	214
45–49	1	13	5	77	0	1	2	0	5	21	14	238
15–49[a]	241	288	100%	836	30	51	100%	588	111	145	100%	766
15–49[b]	—	—	—	827	—	—	—	591	—	—	—	753
1855												
15–19	3	9	3%	333	1	1	1%	1,000	6	7	4%	857
20–24	63	64	21	984	10	8	9	1,250	12	17	14	706
25–29	108	53	17	2,038	39	21	24	1,857	35	36	23	972
30–34	26	73	23	356	9	24	27	375	23	36	23	639
35–39	56	52	17	1,077	13	15	17	867	20	26	16	769
40–44	18	34	11	529	3	15	17	200	9	24	15	375
45–49	4	27	9	148	0	4	5	0	5	12	8	417
15–49[a]	278	312	100%	891	75	88	100%	852	110	158	100%	696
15–49[b]	—	—	—	900	—	—	—	728	—	—	—	695

higher base in 1810 than that of their Argentine counterparts. The speed of decline in fertility demonstrated by the Spanish is not unusual: for example, Italian women who migrated to the United States reduced their fertility significantly in a relatively short period between 1910 and 1940.[53] Furthermore, it is possible that the steep decline in fertility among Spaniards in the Río de la Plata was in fact the reconstitution of Iberian procreation strategies that had become ingrained decades earlier.

The rate of population increase that the Spaniards had experienced in Iberia since the eighteenth century had not resulted from any reduction in mortality, in contrast to the rest of Western Europe. Indeed, Spain's population increase was relatively modest, implying a balance between birth and death rates.[54] The marital fertility rates in Spain declined steadily between 1768 and 1860 and precipitously afterward. By 1910, the Spanish birth rates were three-quarters of what they had been in 1768, and historically much lower than other Western European countries during the nineteenth century.[55] Of particular relevance to Buenos Aires was the fact that the sharpest and earliest declines in birth rates appeared in regions from which many Spaniards had traditionally emigrated to the Río de la Plata, such as Aragón and Catalonia. Massimo Livi-Bacci, in a brief seminal study of Spanish fertility, is not convinced of the early adoption of voluntary fertility controls in Spain, where the secularization of values, the diffusion of education, and the indices of industrialization and urbanization were at much lower levels than in the rest of Europe. With the exception of Catalonia, basic transformations in attitudes regarding procreation, Livi-Bacci notes, remained weak at least through the first part of the nineteenth century.[56]

Economic conditions combined with the rules of primogeniture to create pressure for changes, beginning with the nobility. The *mayorazgo*, an unbarrable entail of land or other property, had posed such severe limits to marriage that the celibacy rate among Spanish men was significantly high. Moreover, despite the weakening of antiquated customs and social biases in the course of the nineteenth century, thanks to the contact with more modern European ways, the Spanish birth rates remained low. In sum, it appears that Spanish society had internalized the practice of restricted fertility, for the elimination of many obstacles to marriage gave smoothly to an era of "neo-Malthusian" checks, or voluntary controls of fertility within marriage.[57] Such a change in attitude to procreation may have been transportable to the Indies and may thus have been responsible for the decreasing rates of fertility among Spaniards in Buenos Aires. If so, the changed, and presumably improved, economic opportunities experienced by Spanish immigrants did not alter their values on procreation. What became the Peninsular norm had spread from Catalonia southward to the Mediterranean and then westward to Argentina. At any rate, neither Spaniards nor Argentines could hope to establish entailed estates, as they were outlawed in 1813 by the revolutionary authorities.[58]

Two features of the findings on fertility for Buenos Aires strike a surprising note. First, it was unusual that the socioeconomically superior groups should have marital fertility rates so much higher than their lower-scale counterparts so early in the nineteenth century. Second, although the decline in the rates was similar to the European case in that it was registered first among the upper strata, the poorer cohorts in Buenos Aires, unlike those in Europe, were heading in the opposite direction, their rates rising steeply. Did the diffusion of birth control techniques, particularly coitus interruptus, fail to filter down from the Argentine elites to their subordinates? For the moment, any precise answer must await further studies, but in the meantime, two possible explanations may be advanced here. One is that the wastage of the revolutionary and civil wars in the first part of the century drove the poor, the group that suffered the greatest casualties, to compensate for its losses with accelerated rates of procreation. Ironically, such a regimen of high mortality and high fertility rates would represent a reversion to premodern demographic features.

The second, related possibility is that the higher fertility rate among the poor contained a significantly higher fertility rate for blacks, whose infant mortality indices in the first part of the nineteenth century were virtually two-thirds higher than those of whites.[59] The higher fertility rates and much higher incidence of illegitimacy among Afro-Argentines were not sufficient to overcome their losses, so that by the second half of the century, blacks and mulattoes were being characterized as relics—residuals of an Iberian-vintage Buenos Aires.[60] Poor dependents in general, and blacks in particular, were encouraged in their higher fertility rates through the patronage afforded them by patriarchal traditions. The argument here is similar to the one made for England, where parish-based welfare arrangements promoted young marriage and thereby contributed to the population boom that took place among the indigent from the mid-eighteenth to the mid-nineteenth century.[61] By contrast, the parish in Buenos Aires was not the most important mediating element in helping the poor with their offspring; rather, the slave masters and, later on, employers made up for the lack of an institutional and effective welfare system in a society where altruism and the economic self-interest of the gente decente were deeply intertwined: "You may add one more to the number of slaves," announced Victoria de Pesoa to her husband in 1754, "since the negress happily gave birth (may God grant us the fruits of their presence for many years)."[62]

Although the study of family and household structures in the Latin American past is still in its infancy, the few glimpses it gives us show a very complex set of structures. The traditional view holds that there is a "Latin American family." This notion of the existence of a homogeneous familial structure among Spanish Americans emanates from compelling logic, derived from the apparent uniformity in Iberian legal and theological applications. The legal formulations that were transported across the Atlantic from Court indeed covered uniformly the colonial possessions. This monolithic aspect of legalism still allowed for the existence of many corporate privileges—the *fueros*—and the special dispensations given to exceptional groups; indeed, these legal indulgences were intrinsic features of Iberian legalism, but they were often granted after the enactment of ordinances that originally contained no exceptions.[63] In summary, the prevailing political and theological conditions strongly suggest a historical evolution in the direction of commonly shared patterns of reproduction among the Western (or Westernized) societies of Spanish America. And yet the few available historical studies of family formation suggest that market, socioeconomic, ecological, and—I would add—political conditions affected family size and structure variously. Thus, as early as the eighteenth century, flexible and adaptive strategies appear to have been as common for the elites as for the plebeians of Buenos Aires.

The historical formation of families in Latin America on the basis of variable and conscious responses to environmental conditions—in contrast to the ideal of uniform and culturally habituated practices of fertility—informs this analysis of the data gathered for the city of Buenos Aires. Indeed, the consideration of variability in the porteño family size is important enough to warrant calling on the precious few studies of other Latin American regions for support. The population of the city of São Paulo, for example, displayed such flexibility in the late eighteenth and early nineteenth centuries. Families from different socioeconomic layers adapted their organization, size, and composition in response to changes in economic conditions, even those of short duration. As production increasingly took place within the urban household during the nineteenth century, family size grew; furthermore, familial composition became more complex in a relationship between economic growth and family structure that was the opposite of what modernization theory predicts.[64] The linear, almost teleological aspects of modernization theory do not apply; indeed, persistently "traditional" family behaviors have remained among Brazilians who participated in the historical processes of economic growth and integration into the European marketplace.[65] Moreover, in contrast to the tenets contained in the paradigm of the "culture of poverty," the secular trend was for elite households in São Paulo to increase their size, while the poor, who had fewer children, diminished their household size in general.[66]

Similar flexibility existed in early and mid-nineteenth-century Chile, when rural families adapted their size and composition in reaction to the market forces that were affecting land values and use. Here size of family and number of coresident children were determined variably within different regions of Chile. By 1860, a smaller number of children were remaining at home in areas of subsistence agriculture than in territories where large estates prevailed. The modern hacienda was intensifying land use as it employed more sophisticated production techniques and as it guarded its landed resources.[67] The summary conclusion on the subject of Chilean nineteenth-century family formation is that no single type of household structure could be considered typical; the complex household was, in fact, the conscious result of population pressures occasioned by transformations in the uses of land and labor as Chile deepened its participation in the international capitalist network. This was not the behavioral expression of cultural determinants: in the end, pragmatism and rational calculation determined that the complex household would serve as a mechanism for survival.[68] Finally, as the number of children leaving poverty-stricken homes increased so did the incidence of premarital intercourse and bridal pregnancy.[69]

The antinomies in Buenos Aires can be reduced to three, but they are strikingly problematical: a homogeneously Catholic society in which family sizes appear to vary over time and space, suggesting variable birth control practices; indications of increases in nuclear family size as one ascends the social ladder, contrary to what we would expect on the basis of the narrow spread of knowledge about contraception among the poor and the expansion of secular values among the wealthy; and an evident increase in the incidence of complex households in the course of time, in contradiction to the tenets of modernization theory.

To arrive at a resolution of these contradictions is very difficult because of the complex relationships of the processes attendant on family strategies, including economic calculations, value systems, religious belief, impersonal market forces, and the legal regimen of transmission. Moreover, the difficulties in disassembling these various components are greater in nineteenth-century Latin America because the empirical findings are relatively few. For the moment, however, let us speculate—aided by the plausibility structure of argumentation and the limited available illustrations—about the extent to which intent and norms of procreation were mediated by intervening constructs and intellectual currents seldom considered for Latin America. Three mediating factors played a role in family formation: patriarchy and its governance over family resources; the Catholic church's stand on procreation and marital sexual practices; and the dislocations caused by revolutionary and postrevolutionary periods. The last factor, political turbulence, will be treated separately in the chapter dealing with household structures; the relationship between patriarchy and inheritance and the evolution of the church's ideas on procreation are discussed below.

Patriarchy and Transmission

Reforms in the rules of inheritance made matters difficult for patriarchs. The system of primogeniture had vested the Ibero-American father with advantages intrinsic to the well-being of the household as a recognizable unit of social and economic power. The patriarch's moral leverage over his children was enhanced by his political leverage: the shares of the patrimony to be given to children who came after the firstborn male could be arranged to the benefit of some at the cost of the others. Moreover, there was always the possibility that the primogenital order could be altered by the accidental death of the senior son or a falling-out between parent and child. These were certainly inescapable considerations held by members of the nuclear family. Beyond this was the opportunity for the patriarch to place the family in key social, political, and economic locations within public life through the appointive power he had over the rest of his children. Thus, the family would be represented by children and kin in political, financial, and clerical posts, a process that would position both the family as a unit and its members as individuals in strategically important loci for consolidation and further advancement.

By contrast, equal partibility, an eighteenth-century innovation, threatened to undermine the autocracy of the patriarch, whose moral authority now depended more than ever on his parental and affective qualities; patrimonial shares to the offspring were guaranteed by the monarchical state and upheld by the courts. Political power based on patriarchal supremacy within the familial estate was seriously undermined—at least, the financial basis for patriarchal supremacy was largely eliminated. In contrast to the waning power of parental elites, the children of couples who belonged to the laboring classes and petty merchants benefited increasingly from their independence of parental authority. Their parents' accumulated capital would probably not amount to very much, and in any event, the lifestyles of the urban masses would not have been altered by an inheritance. Elite children, however, were placed at risk by the rules of equal partibility. Much depended on factors beyond their control, particularly the number of siblings and the size of their parents' fortunes. In sum, was there enough in each share of the patrimony to maintain the children of the elite in the style of their upbringing? In Spain, the effects of primogeniture on personal finances and family formation had created a few fabulous entails and a large number of celibate men: at the close of the eighteenth century, approximately 13 percent of all males of about 50 years of age were single. This demographic crisis within the Spanish nobility was the result of the entailed estate, the *mayorazgo*, which, according to Gaspar Jovellanos, caused the "worst of all evils." "Nothing is more repugnant," he wrote of the young aristocrats looking for place before considering marriage, "than seeing the cadet sons of noble families, with no position and no career, condemned to poverty, celibacy, and idleness."[70]

The decline in parental power threatened by equal partibility was tempered in Spanish America by the pressures that patriarchs brought to bear on individual family members by way of informal negotiations that took place within the family fold. Early nineteenth-century aristocratic patriarchs in Mexico, for example, had succeeded in weaving together and maintaining vast empires despite the existence of a rule of equal partibility. The Crown bestowed on a favored few the right to entail virtually one-half of their most important financial base, which took the form of real property. In time, the most important empires would be built through a superstructure composed of just a few clans overseeing many more families subordinated to a handful of patriarchs.[71]

The irresistible power of these family lords was shown by the absence of females as heads of these clans, even though no legal barriers prevented financial matriarchy. In large measure, this was the result of the relentless pressures that any given clan's principal brought to bear on all potential matriarchs to marry, even against their wishes. The interests of the clans were seen to be at risk should matriarchy develop: Mexican society was evidently not ready to defer to the strategies of women, no matter how great their wealth. Marriage, by which the family's assets were turned over to the husband, remained the prescription. The efficacy of the private negotiations carried on within families is demonstrated by the extremely high rate of marriage—over 90 percent—among women of the Mexican nobility.[72]

In matters related to inheritance, American application altered Iberian ideals as they had evolved in the Peninsula. This was true in other considerations, such as the reinforcement of the concept of nobility with its attendant privileges on the basis of the racial context of the Indies; thus, the Iberian tradition of racial purity was retained and reinforced in the multiracial American arena. The virtual impossibility of women inheriting mayorazgos provides another example of the ways in which Iberian familial practices were altered in the setting of the Indies with consequent further restrictions of females in matters of succession. Regular succession of mayorazgos in Spain had excluded females only until the mid-sixteenth century.[73] Thereafter, females of the elite were not at all marginalized by the Castilian inheritance practices. In fact, the founders of mayorazgos chose their own forms of succession, which usually favored females before remote males; indeed, many founders of mayorazgos explicitly included females in the transmission contracts.[74] Additionally, by the seventeenth century, the Crown had come to the explicit defense of female inheritance of mayorazgos.

The Royal Pragmatic of 1615 attempted to clarify the accumulated inconsistencies in the laws governing mayorazgo succession; it
provided that females should be favored over remoter males, "unless
the founder had expressly, clearly and literally excluded them [which
was seldom done]. Even where females were excluded they ought to
have portions charged to the mayorazgo." Moreover, unlike the English situation, which required division among coheiresses, the Castilian mayorazgo provided the entirety to the eldest daughter. The
effects of female inheritance, notes J. P. Cooper, were more profound
in Castile than in England. In Castile, the practices behind mayorazgo inheritances "ensured a supply of heiresses," contrary to the
professed purpose of perpetuating the name and memory of the
founder.[75] The extent to which Castilian noblewomen inherited
mayorazgos is illustrated by the incidence of litigious disputes begun
by contentious males. The solution to these disputes frequently
rested on the internal solidarity of the family and on charging the
eldest with the responsibility for providing fair shares to the youngest. To be sure, the Castilian female remained a subordinate heiress,
yet she apparently enjoyed much higher levels of actual succession
than her American counterpart, aided by the stronger leverage she
derived from both parental and monarchical support. In areas of
Spanish America, the era following independence brought further
restrictions on females while males who came of age increased their
leverage in matters of patrimony and familial power. This was the
case in Chile, for example, where the civil code increased the husbands' patrimony over their wives' property and goods from what
had been the norm under the colonial regimen.[76]

In both Spain and her American possessions, the central and controlling factors in the politics of wealth transmission was the Crown.
From the late Middle Ages, the monarchy had served as the legiti-
mator of mayorazgos in a manner that consistently overrode common and customary law pertaining to succession. Court influence
and royal prerogative, not judicial or parliamentary procedures,
were the primary means of determining succession among the nobility; in the process, the great nobles came to depend increasingly
on court favors for their economic survival. Revolution and independence in the Americas untied the historical knot that had linked
royal patronage, family wealth, and number of children among the
Spanish American elites.

For instance, the independence movement cut short what would surely have been a successful procreative career on the part of the Mexican nobility, despite the regimen of equal partibility. A systematic investigation of the processes by which Argentine families maintained the coherence of parental wealth is still to be done, but in general we know that patriarchs employed the device of internal negotiations with success.[77] Furthermore, elite families in Buenos Aires also clustered their resources into units that gained control over the nation's politics and economy; in Argentina, as in Chile, wealthy families succeeded in weaving their intricate networks through the political fabric within the span of two generations. Marriage within the aristocratic circle was as important a key to successful clansmanship during the national period in the Southern Cone as it had been in late colonial Mexico.[78] "Marry only for love" was the advice that old General Lucio Mansilla gave to young Miguel Angel Cárcano from melancholy self-imposed exile in Paris at the close of the nineteenth century. "But do not marry a woman, however attractive she may be, if she does not belong to your own circle or possess your own culture."[79]

Wealth, as both a material and a social asset, was sufficiently ample for the Argentine aristocracy to permit relatively little practice of contraception for much of the nineteenth century. The median number of children among the aristocrats, consistently the highest of all social groups in the country, was eleven in the first generation of the Argentine elite.[80] Among the wives of the city's wholesale merchants of the late eighteenth and early nineteenth centuries, the fertility rates were also very high; here, the average family contained slightly more than seven children.[81] Indeed, success among the merchants correlated highly with a large number of offspring. The wealthiest merchants fathered up to sixteen children, which on the average left nine or ten successors to inherit considerable sums equally divided.[82] The devolved wealth of these merchant families stood precariously in the absence of recombining strategies by the surviving siblings; not surprisingly, kinship affinities were fundamental in maintaining the cohesion of the mercantile group.[83] Thus, patriarchy's ability to orchestrate the destinies of children—both males and females—remained strong after independence.

Still, patriarchal power survived the regimen of equal partibility better and longer principally in the uppermost social circle of Spanish American society. The strength of such power diminished rapidly, however, as one descended the social scale. For example, the strong patriarchal power experienced in the colonial period by Jalisco's tenant farmers had been radically diminished by mid-nineteenth century as the shift to village residence and actual ownership made estate partibility equal between sons and daughters.[84] In Chile, the growing numbers of young men and women leaving their poverty-stricken homes also meant the loss of parental authority. In Buenos Aires, infant vagrancy and abandonment gave rise to similar consequences and posed serious problems for the authorities.

Catholic Ideals and Norms

The role played by the Catholic church in shaping strategies of family formation in the Latin American past has not been the subject of much historical research; one is thus reduced to speculation. However, the variations in fertility indices already noted lead the historian to consider the existence of contraceptive practices of some sort: how else can we explain the abrupt changes, and the distinctly opposite trends in the number of children ever born for families of the upper- and lower-status groups?[85]

Family planning has been reasonably well established as a conscious mental construct of European populations from as early as the eighteenth century. In France, for example, ecclesiastical authorities of the first half of the nineteenth century were alarmed by the well-known use of contraception among their parishioners.[86] Jean-Louis Flandrin has suggested the controversial argument that there had existed a theological loophole that an increasing number of people at court had been exploiting since the late sixteenth century, and that, in the long run, had led to the popular use of contraceptive methods within marriage—particularly coitus interruptus.[87] Flandrin made much of certain theological treatises covered by John Noonan in his comprehensive work on the views held by Catholic theologians on contraception. Specifically, argued Flandrin, the Jesuit casuist Tomás Sánchez's *Holy Sacrament of Matrimony*, which appeared in 1602, contained an exception to the church's ban on contraception in the case of pre- or extramarital intercourse. To be sure, the act was not without sin, but it was an evil lesser in scale than the consequences of offspring from such a union; coitus interruptus was thus permitted, in Sánchez's scholarly view, "so that fornicatory intercourse not be consummated to the serious disadvantage of raising the child."[88] Flandrin suggests that accepting the idea of coitus interruptus in illegitimate relations was very close to accepting it within marriage. No major change in mentality was required, therefore, for couples, at least of the bourgeoisie, to engage in contraceptive practices: "The innovation was to behave in marriage as one did outside of marriage. . . . The sin lay in believing this a century too soon."[89]

However speculative Flandrin's proposition may appear, Sánchez's respectability as a church authority on sexual relations is undeniable. In speculating on the possibility of contraceptive practices in Buenos Aires, one cannot but note that Spaniards figured heavily among the most important moral theologians who drew a descending scale of sin in the distinction between marital and nonmarital contraception; these men included Juan Azor, Domínico Soto, and Tomás Sánchez. Moreover, Azor and Sánchez were members of the Society of Jesus, the most powerful and culturally influential order in the Río de la Plata, despite their brief absence between their expulsion in 1767 and their recall by Rosas in the 1830's.[90] That sixteenth- and seventeenth-century treatises on contraception published by Jesuits and other orders had come to the attention of clerics in Spanish America by the late eighteenth and nineteenth centuries becomes plausible in the face of the descending fertility curve registered by the middle and upper sectors of Buenos Aires society.

Finally, it has been well established that St. Augustine's rejection of amorous love as sinful—"I do not see what other help woman would be to man if the purpose of generating was eliminated," he wrote tersely—had been seriously undermined as the idea of limiting intercourse for the purpose of limiting population received theological approval, and as the laity began to differentiate between emotive and physical rewards, between adult sexual love and parenting.[91] This distinction had simply become too widespread among both Europeans and their descendants in the Americas to allow us to consider seriously that Augustinian principles were important to nineteenth-century porteños. Among the literate groups, and especially among the young liberal men, the practices of residing for periods in romantic-era France and reading the epoch's literature meant that these men circulated within the secular and humanist network that possessed the most modern values related to men, women, and family. In sum, it is most unlikely that the majority of nineteenth-century porteños were moved to consider marital sexual relations and procreation on the basis of antiquated religious ideals.

Conclusion

Perhaps the element that weighed most heavily in the minds of the men and women of Buenos Aires in considering their families was the extent of political turbulence and the costs they would incur from it. The consequences of the period's disturbances on the women and the young have already been noted: increases in the rates of widowhood; the unfortunately premature adulthood that was forced on young boys as they, too, were drafted into military service; the economic burdens created by the lack of laborers; and the generalized apprehension of a society gripped by periodic crises. On the poor fell the heaviest demographic burdens: the increases in their fertility, their vagabondage, and the presences of "street urchins" paralleled the taste for political activity cultivated by the young bourgeoisie in the heady days of the Argentine "reconquest" from the English and the early years of independence. These were all symptoms of the tempestuous course of nation building in the Río de la Plata. But if these symptoms originated in the utopian ideals of the revolutionary Enlightenment that had been imported from Paris and Philadelphia, they were perpetuated by political authorities who, in their desire to rescue order from the politico-military maelstrom, made it all the more difficult for families to have faith in the principles of republicanism and equality. This reaction was brought to bear on the young by a state that insisted on policing the daily schedules of the privileged minority that attended schools and increased its punitive and restrictive regulations on the laboring majority. It was bound to fail as a policy of security as long as relative peace was missing. In the meantime, the increased presence of young boys and girls, particularly in the period following the 1820's—a feature of Buenos Aires that represented growth in the formation of families by desolate, often single women—fueled the antagonisms between the gente decente and the gente de pueblo.

Ultimately, liberals provided these antipathies with ideological form, as their political formulations made special note of the plebeian support given to caudillos. On the basis of their explanations, the historical problem of conservative autocracy would find its cor-

rective during the subsequent era of misapplied scientific rationalism, when Social Darwinists and Positivists promised to redeem the
political darkness of the past with the brilliance of a future carried
on the shoulders of whites imported from Europe and perpetuated
through the reformed Argentine family.[92]

4

Youth and the Challenges to the Moral Order

Under the colonial order, people knew their place, or so the gentry came to feel after years of war. In the eyes of the gente decente, political independence had been understood by the masses as moral license. For their part, officials perceived these changes as the erosion of traditional morality, the spread of incivility in social relations and public deportment, and the adulteration of the historical notion of deference to superiors. As the turmoil generated by the independence movement spread, the confidence that had characterized the original revolutionaries was transformed into worry about social and moral decay; behind the asserted freedoms for the people and the growth of citizen armies, the gentry glimpsed social tensions that lay ahead. Their concerns were expressed in written opinions and in government ordinances, all aimed at the strict regulation and supervision of public morality and behavior. Without regulation, the authorities feared, popular misunderstandings about the nature and extent of individual freedoms could easily lead to libertinage.

Thus, over the course of the nineteenth century, the antagonisms that developed between the two major Argentine social groups—one representing rustic or rural values, and the other urban bourgeois aspirations—began to take on an Argentine variant of class distinctions. The opinion shared by members of the Generation of 37, for example, was that the problem of controlling the troublesome plebeians was complicated by the shortcomings of their parental habits, which were rooted in their "lack of home and law" and in their having been born of "obscure mothers."[1] Accordingly, for the urban bourgeoisie, the solution to the problems of loose public behavior, vagrancy, and social disorder centered on families, beginning with the children, on whom the possibilities for a brighter society depended.

Concerns for the maintenance of moral standards were regularly expressed by political and judicial authorities of various ideological leanings, the conservatives merely applying greater rhetorical urgency.[2] A porteño social critic noted in the late 1820's that the Argentine public must receive lessons in detesting crime and in fearing the law, all of which would result in "the shaping of [public] morality."[3] For his part, Juan Alberdi considered a nation's civil code to be the reflection of its people's customs, habits, and familial traditions: "The government of the home," he wrote, "has an immense connection with a country's political government." He followed the lead of Montesquieu's *Spirit of the Laws* in having a discriminating eye for formulating a civil code that would fit well with the society's historical and familial traditions.[4]

The attention to order and proper behavior normally paid by elites was further sharpened during politically turbulent periods. For example, the government enacted regulations in December 1829, at the time of the coup that brought Rosas to power, that forbade the playing of music in the streets without prior permission by the police. Once a permit was secured, musicians had to be escorted by one regular policeman and two *celadores*, or neighborhood monitors, in order to "prevent the exchange of words and insults that promote the arguments that upset the orderliness that the government wishes such events to possess."[5] In addition, the hours that pulperías and other recreational establishments could be open on holidays were sharply curtailed.[6] Similarly, regulations that limited public sale of foods prepared in the streets were periodically reinforced by government resolutions.[7] In a more praetorian style, the city's police reinstituted in September 1829 the siege-like regulations that the independence-era revolutionaries of 1813 had enacted during the civil wars. Stiff fines were imposed on anyone moving into, out of, or within the city without permission and valid documentation. Similar fines were imposed on anyone who failed to report such movements, and income was confiscated from landlords who rented rooms or homes without notifying the authorities.[8] Rhetorical styles may have differed among political antagonists, but attempts at suppressing potential trouble and at smoothing the rusticity of habits cut across time, space, and political ideologies.[9]

To the dismay of the urban patriciate, different social behaviors, representative of contradictory and antagonistic value systems, were being interwoven in postrevolutionary Buenos Aires. The fundamental intent of the many regulations and ordinances governing urban public life was to return as much activity to private quarters as the circumstances required (and allowed) in order to rid the streets of as much of the plebeian population, its rituals, and its expressions as decent society demanded. Not surprisingly, authorities devoted much attention to controlling activities related to the casual labor market, where the participants comprised a large proportion of the lower classes, including a good number of child laborers. Children typically worked as hawkers on the streets of Buenos Aires, distributing domestic products on behalf of local merchants. Such activities placed these children at risk when public authorities cracked down on merchants, either for disturbing the peace, as was periodically the case of pulperos, or for infractions of the commercial ordinances. Under these circumstances, children faced the difficult choice of heeding the authorities or obeying their bosses. A case was reported in 1823 in which a milkman claimed that his delivery boys were being run down by saber-wielding policemen on the orders of a judge, allegedly intent on preventing the raucous behavior of the children who gathered for work at the milkman's depot in the early mornings. Eyewitnesses corroborated the milkman's depiction of youngsters, fearful for their safety, being chased by policemen with swords unsheathed.[10] In the proceedings of this legal battle only two issues arose—the insistence on quiet by the well-to-do neighbors of the barrios, and the right of the merchants to carry on with their businesses—and neither party addressed the issue of the children's safety.

The militant style of monitoring public behavior fell with equal or greater force on bourgeois and elite families whose sons and daughters were privileged to receive formal education. Here, as in other cases governing children's behavior, no significant differences in attitudes between liberals and conservatives can be ascertained. Indeed, not even the differences that developed early on between the revolutionaries and the loyalist Spaniards appear to have affected the new officials' attitudes toward parental authority and the need to maintain the public peace. In 1810, D. Ventura de la Vega, a Spaniard who did not sympathize with the revolutionaries, ordered his young son to be sent to Spain in order to avoid the "contagion" of the new

ideas then percolating through porteño society. The young boy, un-
happy at the prospect of moving, pleaded with his father to no avail.
As he was forcibly being led by servants to the ship that was to take
him abroad, the child pulled himself away, wrapped his arms tightly
around a lamppost at the corner of Perú and Victoria streets, in the
very heart of the city, and cried out for help. A crowd quickly gathered to observe what would happen next; however, "the authorities
did not intervene to prevent the execution of the will of the paterfamilias," and the child was put on board, never to return to his native Buenos Aires.[11] In a similar vein, in 1830, eight years after the
liberal heyday of the Rivadavian ministry, Tomás Guido, on behalf
of Rosas, instructed the chief of police to enforce zealously the 1822
law enacted by the liberals concerning the public deportment of children. The preamble to his orders illustrates the connection that was
perceived between disorder and youth: "The Government considers," wrote Guido, "that a large share of the mischief that charac-
terizes young people today, comes from their disobedience of the decree of December 6, 1822, which carries penalties for youngsters who
are seen in public places during the hours designated for their studies; the Government wishes the strict and rigorous compliance with
this decree."[12] It has been argued recently that the characteristic of
conservatism generally attributed to the Rosas era is actually misplaced, and that Rosas and his ministers did not reject wholesale the
Rivadavian reforms.[13] "Rosas was a better liberal," argues David
Bushnell, "than either his admirers or his detractors generally admit."[14] If the political and economic considerations of Rosas and his
liberal predecessors had much in common, it is no less true that the
pre- and post-Rosas leaders shared with the caudillo a common concern for the maintenance of ethical values related to authority and
deference. And while differences existed in the style of execution of
such authority in the arena of politics, the similarities in the realms
of public and familial moralities were great. The Buenos Aires decree of 1822 required the police to place in debtors' prison for a 24-
hour period any student found in "the streets, *quintas*, cafés, or other
public places" during school hours. In addition, the police put itself
at the disposal of parents who called on the authorities to help them
"guard against and contain the misguided acts" of their children. In
fact, the police would arrest and place in debtors' prison any child
on the request of his mother or guardian. In the case of older youths
attending the University of Buenos Aires, the rector and the profes-

sors were requested to notify the authorities of any students absent from their classes. The police would "search for them in earnest" and take them wherever was necessary. Finally, the decree of 1822 prohibited even the flying of kites.[15]

A systematic review of the archival evidence and the journalistic literature of the nineteenth century leaves the observer with the impression that the values of all the elites and political authorities defined the street and virtually all public space as inappropriate environments for decent youth. For example, government authorities rushed to rectify a schedule in a public school in 1833 that had resulted in the students waiting outdoors for their classes to begin, an act considered by the minister of government to be "an evil thing."[16] These preoccupations expressed an equation that the elites had drawn between conspicuous behavior and the social practices asserted to be characteristic of the gente de pueblo. Public space was reserved for those men—and for certain types of women, mostly belonging to the lower classes—whose trades required them to be manifest. Children who worked were, of course, members of the lower social and racial groupings; children and young people who did not belong to the lower classes but were nevertheless seen in public excessively brought embarrassment to their families and retribution on their persons.

Accordingly, the regulations of the liberal era of the 1820's, which restricted the public presence of youths in the city's streets, were executed with even greater vigor in the subsequent conservative decades. School and university officials reported to the authorities the names of all students missing from their classrooms; and in an effort at pressuring decent families to channel their children's behavior properly, the grades of every student in the secondary and university levels were published in the city's newspapers.[17] Children's education had become a matter of public concern early in the republican era among the gente decente because their youths' training would become instruments by which to reconstitute their class's political rule. The learning that children undertook promised to redeem the nation: "It is undeniable that our ruinous defects proceed from no other beginning than the lack of an education that would result in a fraternal society [and] in inculcating man's obligation to his mother country," editorialized *El Censor* in 1816.[18]

In the end, restrictive measures appeared to have worked in the direction of restraining the public visibility of children, at least among the gente decente: observers in the second half of the century noted with great puzzlement the absence of children playing outdoors in the city's parks and plazas. "That the promenades were always empty," wrote a chronicler of Buenos Aires in the early 1880's, "caught my attention. I have frequented them at all hours, and never have I seen a child! 'Where are the children?' I asked myself. In the United States and in Europe, the public gardens are filled with children; their health requires it to be so. Youngsters need the festiveness of the landscape, the view of the flowers; they need to run under the shadow of the trees, they must leave their homes for the fresh air made possible by the vegetation outdoors. This is the only city where I have not seen children in the public walks. . . . In Buenos Aires one never finds people sitting on public benches."[19] The norms and even the written regulations prescribed the times when children and women of the gentry could be seen in public without incurring the judgmental gossip of peers. These included Sundays after mass and days of civic festivities, when families paraded in the city's parks and promenades, as had become fashionable in eighteenth-century urban society in Europe and in the Americas. But these were programmed, not spontaneous, rituals of public socialization.

The noted absence of children of the gentry in public implied a continued and, in a sense, a reinvigorated privatization of family activities, in particular those related to the young, that would not be relaxed until the heyday of the porteño *belle époque* at the turn of the century. Here Ariès' concept of "domain" is helpful in understanding the delay of public socialization among children and women in Buenos Aires.[20] The evolving division of space into areas assigned to work and areas assigned to living—a characteristic of all societies undergoing the modernizing effects of capitalism—was complicated in the Río de la Plata by the cultural attributes given to public spaces. In turn, this cultural tenet was strongly reinforced by the militarized political conflicts of the period and the fears they engendered among the city's patrician, middle, and lower classes. This interpretation is supported by Ariès' observation of the simultaneity of public and private domains in premodern societies as the roles of individuals were affected by both types of spaces: private space allowed self-awareness and inner being, while public space was a constant reminder of the individual's role in the community with all the rights and obligations thus incurred. For most of the period covered here, however, those rights were being restricted in practice, while the military obligations loomed large. It was not merely emulation of European social norms that accounted for the prevalence in turn-of-the-century Buenos Aires of cafés, with patrons of both sexes inside them and around tables set on the sidewalks; in fact, these images of European urban societies had been known for decades. However, the emulation of Parisian social practices among porteños of the middle and upper ranks could take place only after public space had been secured and made reliably peaceful. This peace would be instituted by means of different political and economic processes, including the arrival at a political consensus of the previously factionalized elites; the Europeanization of both material and human capital circulating within the city; and the disappearance of freely mobile men as the *estancia* modernized its operations and stabilized its workforce, and as the state improved its policing authority by monopolizing weaponry and military personnel. Until then, public spaces for the purpose of social interaction were few in Buenos Aires, according to contemporary observers.[21] In the meantime, the city's public social scene was marked by the pervasiveness of the infamous pulperías, not the kind of public space that would lead to a "shift of public life from closed spaces . . . to the linear, open space of the boulevard, the center of the city's night life," as was the case in Paris already by the 1830's.[22] No accurate figures exist to document the size of the clientele that the city's pulperías drew, but it was large, to judge by their ubiquity, especially on street corners, and by the officials' reports. One such notation by the police early in the national period estimated a population of "four to six thousand men . . . all of them evil, but who become worse still when they get inside these establishments."[23] Only loose women and uncared-for children were expected to patronize those taverns where "the owner resembled his rustic patrons in appearance" and social background.[24]

The youthful unruliness that porteño authorities were intent on quashing was neither new nor peculiar to the region of the Río de la Plata; nor can it be assumed to represent simply the pranksterism of children and adolescents that can be found in all places and in every era. Yet it symbolized a struggle between the ruling elite and its dependents that was given an adversarial militancy by the elite's insistence—regardless of its political leanings—that deference and obedience were synonymous with political and public stability. Respect was given wider meaning, which resulted in a narrowing of the limits of expression, a policy reinforced with ample instruments of punishment. As has been argued in the case of monarchical Europe, misrule had its own rigor and could help to decipher authority and state.[25] An example of the growing impatience with youthful misrule comes from 1827, when the vice-rector of the University of Buenos Aires reported to the police authorities the unexcused absences of several students from their classes. They were found at a tavern playing billiards.[26] The police investigation files on the matter characterized this tavern, along with similar "cafés" and pulperías of all types, as "provocative" establishments that incited disorder by luring young people away from their parental homes and from their classrooms "on a daily basis."[27] Manuel Bilbao, a chronicler of porteño customs, noted that the upper and older segments of the city's society looked on public establishments as places designed for "the young to be lost."[28]

Differences in values related to public propriety could already be discerned between the young men and the patriarchs at the dawn of the nineteenth century. Cafés in central regions of the city around the Plaza de Mayo became centers of "feverish agitation, [where] the frivolous and happy young men floated in the social circle: lawyers, officers of the courts, employees of businesses, and the unemployed sons of the comfortable classes gathered, in sum, the apex of creole society," noted Vicente Fidel López.[29] But these were the expressions of the youthful enthusiasm found at the very earliest stages of the revolution—the animated and publicly held political discussions that characterized the meliorism of the era—which would shortly thereafter be redefined as the unseemly excesses of republicanism. No wonder that political discourse subsequently became reprivatized among both supporters and opponents of the government; and as the home increasingly became the locus for such discussions, the centrality of the café diminished until after its resurgence in the late 1800's.

The private nature of social action was used to rechannel political discussions into cloistered, sometimes conspiratorial sessions in the bourgeois home.[30] This served to provide women and children with participant-observant opportunities denied or made difficult on the outside. The more judgmental observers of porteño traditions dismissed the role of women in such crucial activities for being excluded from public life in those patriarchal times.[31] However, even though public space had much more to offer men than women and youngsters of the gente decente, the sociocultural convention of privacy dovetailed with the dangers inherent in discussing certain subjects so that, together, tradition and pragmatism served to pull those discussions into private space. Here was the "pleasant environment" of the home, a place where women's contributions "can go much further, since they attract unto themselves a world forbidden to them, and where they sneak in like contraband, slipping into the discussions an opinion or a suggestion in between a cup of chocolate and a rigadoon."[32] The conduct of political or economic discussions, inherently public issues, within familial and private spaces suggests that the bourgeois porteño family can be defined as a private entity only territorially; it had a very real public character insofar as nondomestic concerns were pursued vigorously by the adults and witnessed by the children.[33]

Parents within the porteño gentry worried that their sons would be involved in the unfortunate consequences that could follow from open discussions of political events; these could produce incidents that resonated throughout the city because of the esteemed character—"quality," in the contemporary language—of the participants. For example, two such young men of quality, Don Juan Cruz Varela and Don Miguel Sánchez, were quickly arrested in 1828 by the chief of police, along with all who had been present in a café at the time of an alleged disturbance that arose from a political argument. The central point, that officials of otherwise divergent political ideologies all came to consider public debate on political matters intolerable, is demonstrated by one of the most significant aspects of this arrest: the chief of police, Don Juan del Pino, was the brother-in-law of the recently fallen unitarian Rivadavia and, in testimony to his political pragmatism, was now serving under his federalist replacement, Manuel Dorrego.[34]

Ironically, the concern of government authorities with the public conduct of children was in part caused by generations of public officials themselves. The roots of the problem that would eventually be known generically by the term "disorder" can be found in the zeal with which the earliest political and military elites had celebrated their victories. The city of Buenos Aires had always been quite dull even by the staid standards of small Iberian cities in the Indies.[35] Public processions were limited to the days of religious celebrations and important dates in the lives of monarchs or governors.

These celebrations were traditionally reserved affairs and officially sanctioned, and participation was generally limited to the narrow circle of religious and secular authorities. Other social affairs were private, and public celebrations were discouraged by civil norms that considered secular and nonpolitical festivities conspicuous, indecorous, and contrary to public peace.

All this changed with the English invasions of 1806 and 1807. After the reconquest of the city by the militia, Buenos Aires became the scene of constant celebrations, most of them now political (that is, secular), although clerical benediction and pomp were almost always required ingredients. In the heady days of the porteño *reconquista* a radical transformation of the role of the private individual took place. No longer was public life limited to affairs of the church and of the Caroline court; nor were the participants in public processions limited to the local notables. Now the militia—and the growing societal valuation given to military posture—made celebrations martial. Matters of arms and patriotic pride were now symbolized and defended by instruments of naked power, not merely by pedigree and vested economic interests. Here was a new form of popular entertainment, the martial celebration, which in 1806 few porteños suspected would soon be policed by officers, manipulated by authorities, and feared by the public.[36] Over the next several years, the city's residents heard the periodic resonance of church and cabildo carillons calling the urban multitudes to assemblies. The Plaza Mayor and other public spaces frequently became arenas for parades and drills, oratories, and public hangings of traitors.

In these exercises, where participants and victims now spanned virtually the entire social gamut, children were included, as the following event, chronicled by an observer, makes clear. From August through November 1806, entirely new militia battalions were formed, and with each occasion a public celebration was arranged. One of the most impressive of these rituals of newfound patriotism occurred on January 15, 1807, on a field immediately beyond the city's southeast fringe, near the Riachuelo. The general alarm was sounded at 2 A.M., the signal for all the various regiments to assemble and march toward the appointed place. By sunrise, nearly 8,000 men in full dress and gear were gathered in the field, ready for review by the new viceroy and hero of the *reconquista*, Santiago Liniers. After the mass, bands played, food and drink were served, and at 4 P.M.

Liniers read a proclamation appropriate to the spirit of the occasion. He then gave orders for a general fusillade. The account of this incident in Juan Manuel Beruti's diary serves well to illustrate how widespread was the pride generated by youthful participation, and how far down the age ladder this newly militarized pride had reached. His language, romantically naive in the context of the political and military misfortunes to follow, described the continuous paeans in honor of the city redeemed from the English infidels.

The artillery had all been placed to one side. It started to fire with such a powerful blare that it lasted about three-quarters of an hour, first one wing, then another, and so on. In all that time, 16 batteries fired four volleys, each one the equivalent of 250 rifle shots. At this point it was truly joyous to watch the children's company, composed of volunteers between the ages of 12 and 14, with their two cannon pieces . . . fire a volley of such thunderous power and with such precision that they easily matched the best and most seasoned veterans.[37]

Ironically, Liniers would be apprehended and shot by a firing squad three years later when an alert and politically conscious adolescent informed the authorities of his whereabouts.[38] Although no systematic study of war and childhood has been made for Spanish America, it would appear that the independence revolutions accelerated significantly the arrival of adulthood among male youngsters. Observers in revolutionary Chile, for example, commented on the military attire worn by elite children and on the martial ethos that had spread among the youth. "In a typical portrait," writes Mary Lowenthal Felstiner about Chilean creoles, "the twelve-year-old grandson of a colonel wears a miniature colonel's uniform, epaulettes and all." Furthermore, children would often terminate their schooling at the age of 12 or 14 to be given regimental assignments.[39]

The participation of Buenos Aires' children in organized military activity had its many counterparts in the private acts of young boys who executed their acquired sense of political duties within more traditional confines, such as the city's private schools. In one of Pastor Obligado's vignettes depicting life in old Buenos Aires appears the illustrative case of young Juan Bautista Peña y Lezica's tangle with the Spanish authorities in 1810.[40] The young boy was a student in the school headed by Francisco Argerich, one of the city's most notable personalities. Viceregal authorities in Peru had asked the of-

ficials in the Río de la Plata to discover the author of an inflamma-
tory pamphlet—known to have been penned in Buenos Aires—that
called for political independence. The investigative trail led to Juan
Bautista, who at first refused to cooperate. He was repeatedly
flogged until he broke down and identified the handwriting on the
pamphlet as his own. However, the school and his own teacher, Francisco Argerich, had been ultimately responsible for the crime. Juan's
pamphlet had been the result of an artifice; as an assignment in
handwriting, he had been given leaflets to copy that had been au-
thored by the more radical political activists at the time, including
Moreno and Belgrano.[41] Of course, in the wake of the Revolution of
1810, there was no longer a need for surreptitiousness in the political
behavior of schoolchildren. In September 1811, students in the secondary grades of Córdoba's School of Our Lady of Monserrat publicly offered their aid in "the defense of the just cause" and promised
to do battle against "the oppression brought by the enemies of the
fatherland." The students' offer and the governing junta's appreciation were prominently displayed in the pages of the *Gaceta de Buenos Aires*.[42]

There could be no turning back to civilian activities only. Nor
could anyone prevent further outlets for youthful and plebeian participation in military exercises and public displays, any more than
the Buenos Aires militia could be dissolved after its victories against
the British invaders. Ecclesiastical and secular authorities knew this,
and some lamented publicly the unwholesome effects that these activities and liberal nineteenth-century republican principles, imposed by an ever more intrusive government, would have on the
traditional regimen of familial rule and obligation. The liberals'
philosophy on the treatment of children ran contrary to the policies
urged by the traditionalists, who felt that children stayed within the
family circle only out of their naturally practical disposition to sur-
vive; if left to choose for themselves, "children would thus always
gravitate to where they sensed they would find the best care." Father
Francisco Castañeda, a member of the Buenos Aires cabildo briefly
in 1811 and a Franciscan noted for his sharply honed social criticism,
was alarmed at "all these nineteenth-century philosophers." He
grieved for the demise of parental power, now degenerated into parental negotiation. Once their children grew up, noted Castañeda,
parents paid the consequences of their lax childrearing practices.

They now had to "draw up *alliances and social pacts* with their children to avoid having their own offspring hit them and break their heads for lack of proper education and upbringing."

The encouragement of free will and the insistence on the notion of equality that included children had created "the generalized spirit of rebellion that has managed to change governments as easily as we change shirts, and that has encouraged the poor to persecute the rich, in the name of brotherly equality."[43] Father Castañeda was not alone, to judge by the advice given by one of his readers, who, in her worries about the future of porteño society, advised parents that "if we wish to be happier in the forthcoming decade, let us whip our children without pity whenever they fail to conduct themselves correctly and as good Christians."[44] School authorities shared much of this conservative philosophy, while liberal government officials would have none of it. Thus, corporal punishment of schoolchildren was alternately abolished and reinstituted by the authorities, depending on the political circumstances of the moment. In October 1813, the government forbade the use of corporal punishment in public schools. But the preconstitutional provisional statutes drafted in 1815 reflected the politically rightward turn of the intervening years by restoring the practice of whipping in educational institutions, "which was immediately adopted by the schools." Thereafter, the Argentine Congress of 1817 abolished corporal punishment once again, but school authorities apparently continued to whip children in disregard of the law and despite pressures from government officials to desist. In 1819, the government enacted yet another decree forbidding the use of the whip in schools: the government "cannot ignore," stated the new decree, "the transcendental aspects of this abuse, nor the influence it has in degrading the youth who ought to be educated for the service of the Fatherland with decency and with honor. The objections raised by the schools' principals against the just measures of the Government in this regard are so worthless as not to merit a response."[45]

A decade later, in contrast, Rosas' spokesmen demanded that something be done about the sorry state of the city's public places: "Not one street is without a gang of boys bothering the neighborhoods' residents with their fighting, shouting, and yelling obscenities to passersby. Parents are no longer able to contain these disorders, and the Police are only partly successful in avoiding them. What are we to do? Let the government give ample powers to all the citizens so they can deal directly with these gangs and punish these vagrants. Then let's see if they can continue to escape from their deserved discipline."[46]

The return to a youth-oriented philosophy of tighter restrictions and more punitive responses did not immediately disappear with the end of Rosas. Indeed, reactionary sentiments, coupled perhaps with class antagonisms, were recorded at midcentury, after his fall, about the sons of well-to-do families, who "consider themselves beyond the reach of a just and severe reprimand because of their distinguished position in society."[47] Liberal and conservative values related to the moral order continued to conflict with each other. Ramón Cárcano's first memories of school spoke clearly about the contradictions that shared the same space and time. He recounted that in 1867, when he was seven years of age, his parents sent him to school in the town of San Francisco, north of the city of Córdoba. His teacher, Doroteo Bustamante, came from a well-to-do landowning family of the same region. Within a week of young Cárcano's entry into the world of formal schooling, he ran into its authoritarian style. The children played one of those tricks that broke the order of silence that the teacher had imposed over the classroom and Bustamante, who had lost his patience, announced that each child would receive a blow on the palm of the hand with a hardwood stick. The seven-year-old Cárcano panicked and ran home without waiting for his turn before the "executioner." "My parents decided that I would never again receive lessons from the schoolmaster Doroteo," he wrote. "After deliberating for several days, my family decided that my grandfather would take charge of my primary instruction. . . . Within a few weeks I was reading freely and writing my big letters. The whipping stick is vanquished. Nothing is built on the basis of blows and pain. The galley's captain, Doroteo, has been deposed by my grandfather's school even if my grandfather never read Pestalozzi. Everything blossoms with love."[48]

Porteños of the nineteenth century experienced an increase in the challenges to the traditionalists' expectations of deference on the part of young people. The unseemly action of these upstarts, however, did not develop in a political vacuum; on the contrary, they were symptomatic of the era's general turmoil in social and political relations. Thus, neither militarization nor public activities by the young could be restricted any longer or successfully policed by executive authority, although much of Buenos Aires' subsequent history would be dedicated to just such futile attempts. Obstacles to the recreation of the domestic character of youthful action came from both the individual and the state. As individuals, caudillos attempted to perpetuate the principles of war in Argentina through their family lines, propelling militarized political conflicts into the next generation. Parental love and patriotic duty were inextricably bound, for example, in the value system of the liberal caudillo José María Paz: "For the present time," wrote General Paz to his very young son in the note attached to the sword he sent him as a gift, "you will not be able to understand the love that moves me to bequeath this to you, but when you become older you will know better how to appreciate it."[49] This was as real a transmission of property in an era of conflict as was land in the financial circles. Familial affinities to young boys and men killed in politico-military struggles were sure to prolong animosities in an era when emotional exploitation of these matters was a tool used by all antagonists.

In his description of Facundo Quiroga's assassination in 1835, Domingo Sarmiento made much of the unreasonable loss of young life. Two postilions were riding with Quiroga's party, including "a mere lad and nephew of one of the company that lay in wait for them." Santos Pérez, a "gaucho-outlaw," led the assassins, and once Quiroga and his associates were killed, "the young lad alone remained alive, and Pérez, upon seeing him, asked who he was. His sergeant replied, that the boy was his own nephew, and that he would answer for him with his life. Without uttering a word, Pérez walked up to the sergeant, shot him through the heart, and then seizing the boy by the arm, threw him on the ground and cut his throat in spite of his childish cries for mercy."[50] More formal examples of capital punishment of children were carried out by government authorities. In 1831, a 14-year-old boy named Agustín Montenegro was among the Unitarian prisoners of war who were executed in San Nicolás on the order of Rosas. Although the boy had apparently not participated in actual fighting, he was the son of one of the military prisoners: the lad's inclusion among the executioners' victims was not an oversight. Adolescents actually fought, however, on both sides of the period's political struggles. Thus, when it came time for executions, they, too, suffered the consequences.[51] The spending of children's lives was not peculiar to Rosas' followers. In July 1820, Manuel Dorrego launched an offensive against troops loyal to Estanislao López. Dorrego rallied his followers by pointing to the barbarian style of the enemy, describing them as a "gang of bandits and murderers who proclaim themselves to be defenders of the public welfare while at the same time they pillage and destroy everywhere they go, murder unarmed men, rape women, and even take the lives of innocent children."[52]

For its part, the state's contribution to the perpetuation of public and militant activity by—and consequent loss of—the young came by way of its increasing demand for more men destined to serve in the military. Children were not spared in the hour of need. By 1826, the regimen of conflict had undermined significantly the productive capabilities of the food-producing regions, while it had also ener- vated morale in the city. "Because of the indiscriminate conscription of people in the city and the countryside," lamented an observer, "without any concern for whether the men were vagrants or labor- ers, married or single, adults or even 12-year-old children, poor mothers and aged fathers have been left desolate in the absence of the protection that their sons had been providing them." The chil- dren were no longer available to sell milk or other goods through the streets, forcing mothers to do so instead, "provoking the sym- pathy" of onlookers.[53] The laments of 1826 were registered a scant few months before the fall of the government, then headed by Ber- nardino Rivadavia. Similar urban conditions obtained at the close of 1851, when Rosas was making preparations to defend himself against the threat posed by Entre Ríos' caudillo, Justo J. Urquiza. A contemporary noted once again the misfortune of having "all citi- zens of the city and the countryside under arms, running military drills as if they were regular soldiers, including . . . even 12- to 16- year-old children, the younger ones as drummer boys and the older ones as soldiers." Once again, women, old men, and children under the age of 12 were left in charge of homes, ranches, farms, and busi- nesses, all of which was "causing general ruin."[54] Just a few months later, this armed population failed completely in its military defense of Rosas, and he fell as had Rivadavia a generation earlier.

The concern for the welfare and the public conduct of children reflected the loosening of traditional moral behaviors and caused widespread alarm among the urban gente decente. But this was not an idiosyncrasy of Río de la Plata society; on the contrary, the cus- todians of traditional moral values in nineteenth-century Buenos Aires were not alone in their apprehensions. To an entire layer of Western society that felt responsible for ensuring propriety even among the lower classes, the tenets of chasteness, probity, and Christian virtues were being tested. The management and defense of conservative deportment was everywhere more difficult to achieve. Similar arguments were being made in Europe, as working-class men and women gravitated toward occupations away from their homes in the wake of an industrializing economy that offered employment opportunities in organized workplaces. These aspects of modernizing society provided the lower classes with newly found outlets of self-fulfillment and diversion, including sexual pleasure. In turn, it is argued, this resulted in considerable increases in criminal and disorderly behaviors and great leaps in the rates of illegitimacy.[55] The Platine littoral's version of this argument runs along similar lines, except that the occupations held by the sexual actors were qualitatively different and the economic changes were caused less by domestic industrial innovation than by commercial upsurges attendant on the Bourbon Reforms related to free trade. The dramatic increase of nearly 90 percent in the population of the city of Buenos Aires between 1778 and 1810 was intimately linked to the invigoration of the regional economy, the resumed output of silver from the mines in Potosí, and the trade advances in the newly legalized port. Although the population increases resulted from the many new immigrants from Europe, the economic opportunities of the region also pulled large numbers of in-migrants from the coast's hinterland and from the viceroyalty's interior. But instead of being attracted to the regularity of industrial labor, as was the case in much of Western Europe, these in-migrants were composed principally of young men who were linked to the irregular and migratory activities of the wagon trade and to the apprenticeships available in the city.

The considerable population mobility was aggravated by the nineteenth century's sociopolitical bane: roving men—organized in bands or travelling singly—whose sexual gratification in town and country was taken en passant, resulting in alarming rates of illegitimacy. An observer commented, "It is well known that even though roving love"—*venus vaga*, in the period's elliptical terminology—"is fecund at times, the upkeep of its unfortunate fruit is subjected to incalculable obstacles. Never did disorder produce well-being."[56] The "incalculable obstacles" to the upkeep of unplanned offspring resulted in the growing problem of infant abandonment. The few available figures on the rates of abandonment of children in several parishes of urban and rural Buenos Aires indicate that similar family limitation procedures were operating in the Río de la Plata.[57] In 1840, Buenos Aires' urban parishes recorded very high percentages of abandoned newborn babies, with considerable differences showing among various regions: in the parish of Monserrat, 6.1 percent of white children and 2.9 percent of children of color were abandoned; in the parish of Concepción, 19.2 percent of white baptized children; and in the parish of Catedral al Norte, 15.5 percent of whites and 31.3 percent of *pardos* and *morenos*, or blacks and mulattoes. The situation was worse in the outlying districts, such as the parish of Chascomús, south of the city, where nearly 46 percent of all children born were soon abandoned.[58] These rates of infant abandonment, though high, correspond to only a part of what certainly were high levels of illegitimacy. In this, Argentina was no exception; rather, it kept pace with the radical increase of illegitimacy in the West between 1750 and 1850, when the soaring incidence of premarital relations was especially evident in urban centers. Thus, while Buenos Aires experienced unprecedented increases in unwanted newborns, over one-third of all children born in Paris between 1815 and 1848 were born to unwed mothers.[59] In Buenos Aires the privileges accorded to the gente decente gave children a sense of physical safety that allowed them to postpone adulthood. Lower-class children, however, had to begin to struggle for their survival at a much earlier age, and were thereby forced into a precocious adulthood.

These problems did not easily disappear; porteño physicians throughout the nineteenth century continued to be dismayed by the high rates of infant abandonment.[60] The municipal facilities had long been inadequate in coping with the problem, and often called on the public to help with private donations, without which "the fortunes of the abandoned infants are necessarily dim, especially if persons of intelligence never remember these unfortunate infants."[61] Saturnino Segurola, appointed to head the Casa de Expósitos, the city's foundling hospital, reported at the end of 1817 on the unwholesome state of affairs that had historically been maintained by previous administrations. "I cannot adequately convey to Your Excellency," wrote Segurola to his superiors, "the feelings I had upon seeing the numbers of children who died in this institution, according to its ledgers. Of the one hundred forty who entered yearly, over ninety died."[62] Segurola's vigorous management of the foundling hospital improved conditions; by 1830, the annual mortality rate in his facility had dropped to 22.4 percent.[63] The improved chances for life motivated a contemporary traveler to note that mothers now allowed themselves the freedom to deposit their infants with confidence and "without any concern for their well-being."[64] This judgment turned out to be premature. In keeping with his measures to save costs and minimize the social functions of the state, Rosas closed down the Casa de Expósitos in 1838, placing at risk uncounted numbers of infants until it was reopened in 1852. In the meantine, "countless" infants were deposited at the doorsteps of private dwellings in the hopes that they would be taken in and brought up as servants; abandoned children were known to have died of exposure and bites inflicted by roaming dogs.[65] In terms of general consequences, the Río de la Plata appears to have shared in the contemporary relaxation of sexual behavior in the West to the extent that its lower classes experienced similar demographic processes of illegitimacy under similarly beneficial periods of economic growth.

But very different dynamics operated behind those similarities: layers of behavioral change were being draped over bases of economic tradition. The relaxation of sexual practices in the Río de la Plata did not coincide with the rise of domestic manufacturing industry, as was the case in Europe; indeed, no indications point to such an evolution coincident with the middle of the eighteenth century, the starting point of the increase in European illegitimacy, nor with changes in the economic infrastructure.[66] Behind the European relaxation in sexual values rested a fundamental change in mental states, which emanated largely from the urban lower classes' increased awareness of the conception of self in tandem with their economic function as free wageworkers in industrial cities. In Europe, parental bonds were weakened by economically impelled migrations. Young men and women, finding it increasingly difficult to rely on the traditional support of parental lands in an age of burgeoning population, turned to cityward migration as an economic solution; consequently, they found relatively greater freedom from the limits placed by family and guarded by village supervision. In virtually every community, youthful liaisons made and unmade during the European era of the nascent industrial order gave rise to increases in temporary relationships and cohabitation, and thus to the largest numbers of unwed mothers yet seen.[67] In the Río de la Plata, too, the government had to confront the problems caused by the relaxation of sexual mores. By 1813, the *residencia*—the city's facility for women lawbreakers, which had been closed since 1806—was opened

once again for the purpose of jailing prostitutes. Their numbers had
been growing over the previous years: "In the absence of [this facil-
ity], so many scandalous, bawdy, and lewd prostitutes now abound
that it has become necessary to reopen it in order to cleanse and rid
this infected city of the bad seed, which had been the cause of many
ills for the youth and the general public."[68] The rise in prostitution
coincided not with radically altered forms of production and laboring populations, but with the Argentine, and possibly the Spanish
American, syndrome of nineteenth-century loosening of bonds on
behavior. Indeed, women in general, not just prostitutes, were challenging tradition through different means, including their participation in political debates and rallies.[69] Pasquinades protested against
the impropriety of such women. One of these anonymous lampoons,
which appeared in the 1810's, was entitled "Petition on the Need to
Contain the Excessive and Prejudicial License Taken by Women in
Speaking." "It is shameful, and in every sense scandalous," wrote the
author, "the free manner in which a considerable number of patrician young women express themselves with attention to matters of
politics which the worthy sons of the fatherland have made possible
through their personal sacrifices."[70] In sum, this loosening of behavioral norms was the product of two generalized features of the period: the much greater geographic mobility, mostly of men, that resulted from the arming, training, and mobilization for war; and the
much greater breadth of participants, including women, in public
action.

The degree of precision of the data on illegitimacy in Europe is
not generally available for Spanish America, but indications of at
least the consequences of relaxation of sexual mores, if not of eman-
cipated ideas on the subject of amorous love, point to similar results.
Only the causes for these similar consequences cannot easily be attributed to economic modernization.[71]

The subjects of illegitimacy and child abandonment cannot easily
be found in the popular literature; "Public opinion! It does not exist!" the noted essayist and diplomat Vicente G. Quesada wrote in
the 1880's, complaining about the Argentine press, which tended to
avoid publicizing issues of social concern.[72] Alberdi shared this opinion. He disapproved of Sarmiento's use of the press for political attacks, and noted that it had been the press's "combative journalism
and the silence on the subject of war" that had facilitated Rosas' despotism. "The press of combat," he wrote in 1873, "has had nothing

to contribute to the subjects of social and institutional concerns. Rosas has left this evil legacy to the Argentine Republic. He has left the habit of combat. . . . The soldier, the writer, the merchant, all of whom made combat a feature of their normal lives, confront today a real crisis in the face of a life of peace and tranquility."[73] Whatever the root of the relative silence on the issues of illegitimacy and abandonment may have been, the gente de pueblo's conspicuous deviation from the elite's acceptable moral standards was too appalling to merit public comment directly. And yet the social problems of illegitimacy and child abandonment were known well enough by the public that the press made use of a rather traditional mechanism for calling attention to it: understatement spoke clearly in the form of the classified advertisement. Here the newspaper fashioned its own literary *disimulo*, a subtle—and sometimes graceful—pretense at tolerance: "NOTICE: In the home of Sr. D. Manuel de Bustillos, facing the café of the shanties, an infant of about two-and-a-half years of age can be found; no one knows to whom it belongs; any interested persons are hereby notified that they may pass by this establishment."[74] The deed had been done, and the abandonment cleared the way for interested individuals to claim the infant, give him shelter, and, in the end, enjoy the fruits of child labor. The system of private transfer of children from their natural parents to strangers posed a strong potential for the endangerment of the children. Perhaps the clearest example of this form of putting children at risk was found in 1855, when José María Rodríguez placed an advertisement in one of the city's dailies asking that someone with a "humanitarian heart" adopt two of his offspring. The children, a ten-year-old girl and a four-year-old boy, were eventually taken in by a prostitute, to the dismay and outrage of the press.[75] The father, a widower with five children, had recently moved to the city from the interior and claimed later that he had made a mistake in his ignorance of the big city's people and ways. He needed to dispose of some of his children because of his financial difficulties. He was unable to work because of wounds he had received while in the army, and his military pension was insufficient to feed and maintain his family.[76] These were some of the simple and basic ways in which the years of war and military service continued to leave their unfortunate imprint on both the individual and the urban society.

If the signs of public challenges to the established moral order were being observed with alarm among porteños from early on in the postcolonial era, conservative moralists were having it no easier at midcentury. The application of liberal principles by the Generation of '37, following the fall of Rosas, in the area of individual liberties was received with mixed emotions by anti-*rosistas* who felt the upright moral order was being sacrificed to the misapplied principle of freedom. In July 1855, the ministry of government of the state of Buenos Aires enacted a series of decrees governing public games and amusements. The political philosophies that moved these regulations were fundamentally libertarian, and were thus considered unwholesome by the intelligentsia's moderate wing. They perceived the decrees' *considerandos* to be allowing the surrender of the political state's responsibilities for the maintenance of high moral standards. The preamble included two considerations that were found obnoxious by moderates and conservatives. "1st. Given that the Constitution of the State has declared that it is the right of every one of its inhabitants to choose freely his labor or industry, as long as nothing that is done results in an offense against public morality, this includes the public amusement companies; 2nd. That, therefore, no one among the higher authorities, regardless of his own values or of the inconveniences that he may find in these matters, has the jurisdiction to prevent such activities." These considerations were taken by critics to be an abdication of political authority, which had previously included policing morality. One of the city's dailies wrote in an editorial: "Why not admit that, for the sake of tossing some popular amusement to the masses, the Government wished to mask immorality and thus renounce one of the principal responsibilities of the executive branch?"[77]

Clearly, consensus on the subject of public morality and proper behavior remained elusive; furthermore, the national authorities maintained the naive conviction—inherited from colonial practices, perhaps—that morality was part of the political patrimony and could thus be legislated. Indeed, the latter part of the century would provide still greater obstacles as hundreds of thousands of lower-class European immigrants flooded into Buenos Aires with their own cultural practices and behavior.[78] Until compulsory education became a reality, children of the poor had to struggle with the labor market and its conditions, while for the children of middle-class and wealthy families formal primary education was the norm. To the extent that the state continued to fail in its attempts at legislating proper behavior, the gente decente continued to fear and be frus-

trated by the excesses of the gente de pueblo. Rather than laws for
the public, it would be the process of children's socialization in
schools that offered the best oppportunities for the state to inculcate
in the family certain components of the notion of "civilization," the
term that midcentury liberals so often employed to denote the
achievement of progress.

Illustrations on pp. 123–32 by courtesy of the Pho-
tographic Division of the Archivo General de la
Nación.

Plaza Victoria (western half of the Plaza de Mayo), 1829.

The home of an elite family.

The interior of a modest home on Independencia Street.

The interior of a suburban shack.

The working classes. *Left:* The laundress. *Upper right:* The milkman.
Lower right: The street lights official.

The working classes. *Above:* The water vendor. *Below:* The butcher.

Pulpería activities.

Street corner scene, 1866 (note the disapproving look given by the black maid to the approaching street vendor).

Gaucho and woman (note the suggestive and sensuous pose given to this lower-class woman by the artist).

Gauchos and women dancing (outdoor dancing and festivities were associated with the *gente de pueblo*).

La Ranchería (The Cluster of Shacks), by an unknown artist.

Family at work in a *rancho* (shack).

Left: Mother and son, 1860's (note the doll-like attire on the boy). *Above:* Portrait of a young boy of the *gente decente*.

Young boys selling milk.

Husband and wife. By the 1850's, affectionate public contact was acceptable.

Porteño salon, 1830.

Priest and young man, 1795.

In Church, a painting by León Palliere.

5

Children, Politics, and Education

The study of childhood in Latin America has not been the province of historians. And yet the transfer of values to children is one of the clearest expressions of a society's historical processes and cultural norms: praise and admonitions frame the boundaries of acceptable public behavior for the citizenry and formulate limits on private activities. This is true of modern societies to the extent that the transfer of values is assumed to be part of a youngster's education, as determined by the state; in turn, the educability of youth is itself a principle of action held by political elites that distinguishes modern Western societies from their medieval predecessors.[1]

In societies where cultural and behavioral norms sharply differentiated socioeconomic groups, the elites found their ideals of acceptable behavior difficult to implant. This was the case in Buenos Aires, where only over the long term did childhood education provide the city's elites with the best chance for establishing the most efficacious mechanisms to control society. The infusion of a value system that was defined as worthy by the gente decente, insofar as it contained acceptable parameters of rights and obligations, was most efficiently done among the youth. To be sure, the political elites did not achieve this easily, and indeed many among them resisted the ideal of widespread education. But in the end, social control policies and education functioned as complementary elements aimed at the same goal, which, in the conjunction of penality and instruction, served to socialize a growing proportion of the porteño public according to the elites' desiderata. Moreover, educational politics served as one of the primary mechanisms by which the state actively and forcefully entered the realm of the neighborhood and the family in order to make its wishes and expectations known and have its demands satisfied.

The student of this era needs first to identify the conditions that mediated between elites' ascription of responsibilities to parents and to the state and the public's response. In the absence of the principle and practice of universal education, conflicts based on political traditions, cultural heritage, and economic constraints were not unusual and, indeed, formed an integral part of the problems inherent among the educational aspects of social control. This condition was especially true of Buenos Aires before the full implementation of compulsory education in the later 1800's. In addressing the nature of schooling in Buenos Aires, particularly for young children, this chapter will also analyze the educational system in the context of political elites trying to imprint their respective visions of order, morality, and loyalty on a growing proportion of the population by the teaching of the attendant ideals.

Education and Civic Consciousness

Government authorities and civic leaders in Buenos Aires were moved to train the city's youth by their appreciation of a long-standing Western tradition: that education was the fundamental instrument for reconstituting political leadership. Beyond this, the purpose of education had broadened in the republican dawn of the nineteenth century to include the public in its attendant considerations. Thus, the creation and reinforcement of moral and political ideals suitable to the general welfare—though still within the practical context of the gente decente's continued leadership—had been added as goals of education to the one of the political elite's reconstitution. The Enlightenment had paved the way for the execution of this more generalized purpose by replacing the traditional and authoritarian ideal of the loyal subject with the progressive ideal of the participatory citizen.[2] By the start of the nineteenth century, the Argentine school was meant to serve as the medium by which "to inspire in children the habit of order, the sentiments of honor, love of truth, the search for justice, [and] respect for their peers."[3] In the course of the postrevolutionary period in Buenos Aires, notions related to the education of youth were formulated within a pervasive apprehension over the general failure to achieve and maintain social and political stability. Thus, the need to strengthen the moral basis of the educational curriculum was felt with greater urgency by both the authorities and the gente decente, as expressed by the porteño social critic who asserted that "moral education is the first item of importance that should be considered." His logic carried its own imperative: the youth must be taught to love work, because "it is well known that every hard-working man is an excellent member of society; the man who works all day has very little time left to perpetrate crimes."[4] Thus, as the idea took hold that the establishment of order needed to begin with the children, and as the traditional hegemony of the church over educational institutions weakened, the roles played by schools took on greater dimensions.

The study of schooling in Buenos Aires is a very helpful vehicle for understanding the political and social values that compete for domination of the community. It allows the observer to note the delicate balance that existed between the political uniformity sought by the state and the local variants necessitated by the contingencies of families' finances and the tradition of barrios' autonomy, between administrative continuity and political change. The construct of schooling served to enhance competitive demands among communes and families, while it eventually succeeded in imposing on parents the disagreeable notion that the care of their children was no longer a monopoly of the family. In its own way, schooling in Buenos Aires came to form an institutional legacy of the revolution. In sum, the very idea that learning took place away from home, in a new environment, under the aegis of a virtual stranger, had considerable psychological and cultural implications.[5]

While the consideration that education was a mechanism for improving society in general figured prominently as part of the value system of the city's literate group after independence, it was still widely accepted that the effects of education on individuals would continue to be derived from the socioeconomic positions into which they had been born. This was the internalized value system of a widow left alone with six children who, in 1825, requested and received a government scholarship for her fourteen-year-old son to "be accorded the education to which he is entitled by his distinguished social origin, even if he [now] figures among the poor."[6] Similarly, the people who applied for one of twelve government-sponsored scholarships in support of their sons in 1826 showed high social positions and respectability, even if they were undergoing financial difficulties. They included men such as Mariano Vico, the army's surgeon general, who had served in Paraguay, Uruguay, and Peru, and Antonio Pirán, former *regidor, conciliar*, and prior of the Buenos Aires *consulado*. The functional relationship between knowledge and class position was instilled in Argentines early in their lives. This lesson was taught to youngsters, for example, by the principal of the elementary school in the town of San Fernando when in 1830 he told them that the best prevention of misfortunes "came by way of study and application in your infancy . . . , guiding yourselves by the irrefutable principle that knowledge enlightens the rich and facilitates the livelihood of the poor."[7] The subject of childhood education will be discussed within the context of the social and political values of the dominant elites; the model of citizenship that these custodians of order tried to implant is the backdrop of the analysis.[8]

Education in this part of the Spanish Empire had not been a privilege limited to the aristocracy. The interest in education was widened considerably in the viceroyalty of the Río de la Plata by the functional aspects of the region's commerce and administration; the services needed by Buenos Aires could be carried out by officials formally trained in the managerial and legal skills adaptable to the most important center of commercial and bureaucratic activity in the south Atlantic. Thus, the number of urban educational establishments tended to increase in the first half of the century. In 1815, the city was served by thirteen elementary schools, five of which were administered directly by the religious orders, but all of which taught the curriculum based on church doctrine. These primary schools were attended by over 1,200 students, estimated to represent barely 5 percent of the city's school-age children.[9] Increases in the school population were registered very slowly; for example, 130 students attended the elementary school in the parish of La Piedad in 1815, while only 126 were enrolled three years later.[10] Similarly small increments in school enrollments were registered in other barrios where the total increase reached barely 5 percent between 1815 and 1817:[11]

School	1815	1817	School	1815	1817
Catedral	150	147	Piedad	130	143
Monserrat	114	144	Hospicio	59	62
Concepción	59	69	TOTAL	642	674
San Nicolás	130	113			

TABLE II

Changes in Population in Public Primary Schools, 1815–1831

School	Population				Net percent change		
	1815	1817	1829	1831	1815–17	1815–31	1817–31
Catedral	150	147	90	148	− 2.0	0.0	0.0
Monserrat	114	144	85	123	+ 26.3	+ 7.9	− 14.6
Concepción	59	65	82	89	+ 7.4	+ 50.8	+ 36.9
San Nicolás	130	113	73	81	− 13.1	− 37.7	− 28.3
Piedad	130	143	83	111	+ 10.0	− 14.6	− 22.4
Hospicio	59	62	52	55	+ 5.1	− 6.8	− 11.3
San Telmo	—	176	93	119	—	—	− 32.4
Socorro	69	150	0ᵃ	140	+ 117.4	+ 102.9	− 6.7
TOTAL	711	1,000	558	866	+ 40.6	+ 21.8	− 13.4

SOURCES: *El Censor*, Apr. 24, 1817; AGN X-6-1-1, Instrucción Pública, 1812–35; AGN, Sala X. División Gobierno Nacional, Censos, 1813–61.
ᵃThe archival records show that this school was closed down for lack of an available building (*vacante por falta de casa*).

Moreover, the number of registered students in any given parish fluctuated significantly from one year to another; Table 11 shows the percent changes in the number of pupils who attended the city's public elementary schools in various neighborhoods between 1815 and 1831. This was indeed a checkered record for a generation of revolutionary leaders whose educational ideology had committed them to casting off the Spanish system, which, in the words of *alcalde* Prudencio Sagari, had been aimed at "keeping us ignorant in order to perpetuate our slavery and [the Spaniards'] despotism."[12] But by the early 1870's, approximately 107 public schools and 120 private institutions operated within the city.[13] Over 7,700 students, or nearly 22 percent of the school-age population—defined by the government as children between the ages of 6 and 15 and then numbering nearly 36,000 boys and girls—were attending classes.[14]

The eventual proliferation of educational institutions continued, nevertheless, to express certain colonial roots, values that had originated in a Bourbon administrative system in which the locals who had received training in the liberal professions had been rewarded with positions. It was one of the earlier manifestations of formal education as an instrument of social advancement, and, consequently, of social stratification. University formation, for example, "attracts not only the sons of the upper classes," Halperín Donghi observed about late colonial porteño society, "[but] it is also true of the middling groups, who aspire to receiving these degrees, as they were con-

sidered to form a very efficient mechanism of social ascent; in the
Buenos Aires of the latter days of the viceregal era, the possession
of an academic title had been transformed into possibly the clearest
expression of entry into the circles of the elite."[15] Law degrees and
practical bureaucratic experience were especially valued by the royal
administrative apparatus; without these *letrados* and *doctos*, the efficiency sought in governance—a cherished value of the Enlightenment—would have been difficult.

The basic nature of the interplay between education and social
advancement was redefined after independence. The advancement
derived from formal training during the colonial period had been
inherently individualistic; education had been considered a surplus
commodity of a sort, which could be marketed insofar as it had situated the educated individual in competition for place. The returns
on the investment of education had been largely self-centered: the
individual, along with his family, would reap the benefits of salaries
and other emoluments in addition to the contacts that would further
his position in this clientelistic society.

Independence increased the importance given by the state to the
system of education by politicizing it. This process included both
the infusion of ideological content into the curriculum and the belief—derived from the republican ethos among the original revolutionaries—that formal training was a basic element of the new and
liberal communitarianism. Thus, General Manuel Belgrano's motive in founding public schools in Jujuy in 1813 was patently political: he held the ultimate goal of education to be "the formation of
the citizen's conscience." The school regulations drafted by Belgrano
himself called for a teacher who was concerned with instilling in his
students "a love for order, respect for religion, moderation and
sweetness in dealings with fellow men, a deep sense of honor, a feel-
ing of love toward virtue and science, abhorrence toward vices, a
favorable disposition toward work [and] selflessness, contempt for
anything materially extravagant or luxurious in matters of food,
dress, and other necessities of life, a spirit of nationalism that would
guide them to work for the public well-being rather than for private
benefit, and a higher esteem for everything that is American over
and above anything foreign."[16] Belgrano's intent appears to have
taken root with some students, such as the young boy attending an
elementary school outside of Buenos Aires who delivered his completed assignment with a note at the bottom: "This was written by

the Citizen José Ignacio Villarino in San Fernando on May 14 of 1818."[17]

Belgrano's determined nationalism soon became heavy-handed; equations were quickly drawn between political loyalty to the revolution and place of birth, usually to the advantage of well-placed creoles. In Córdoba's Colegio de Monserrat, for example, xenophobic considerations are clearly manifested in the following letter to the political authorities: "The junior positions of Vice-Rector and Teaching Assistant were provided by the Government, and following this same procedure, when the posts become vacant, the Government should decide unilaterally who should fill them, giving preference to committed Patriots in order to benefit our Holy System. . . . And since Dr. Bustamante—excessively European and, consequently, educated and nurtured in [Spanish] fashion . . . is thus presumed suspect, and is perhaps even a spy, he should immediately be fired from his Teaching Assistantship to be replaced by a true Patriot, someone like Dr. Patriño, *Catedrático* in Grammar at the University."[18]

In other attempts at fostering republican consciousness, the revolutionary leadership of Buenos Aires early on ordered the dissemination of Rousseau's *Social Contract* among the schoolchildren in the elementary grades.[19] More than a decade later, the educational authorities required students on vacation to read the daily record of the sessions of the short-lived national congress in 1826 so that they "would learn the rationale on which our nation's constitution is founded."[20] The results of the new curricula were expected to contrast sharply with the particularistic privileges associated with the hierarchical society of castes that had existed under the defunct monarchical regime. The content of the curriculum that pertained to civics and history would, of course, extol the visionaries who held progressive values, but the fundamental responsibility of the hagiological curriculum was to provide the community with young men and women upon whom the nation could rely for spiritual and material progress. Formal training would continue to furnish the means that would advance individuals, and their families would continue to be the beneficiaries of their children's success. Yet the new republican ideology held that benefits from such advancement must be shared beyond the narrow confines of the private individual and familial worlds. Liberal reformers of the revolutionary era were thus adding a novel and divisive ingredient to the realm of education by challenging the traditional dominance of the family and the household over the child, particularly during the formative years. Indeed, educational and social reformers throughout the West shared the hope that progressive schools would drive a salutary wedge into the habits and loyalties that traditionally had been shaped and maintained by home and church.[21] In the view of social conservatives in Buenos Aires, however, the revolutionary principles that affected children created the "Jacobin family," wherein "paternal authority was forced to relax by the intervention of the State in all conflicts."[22]

Insofar as schooling had the potential to disestablish traditional community norms, conservatives in Buenos Aires and other areas where early nineteenth-century reformers held political influence were justified in their fear of a consequent alienation of their children: in the revolutionary ideology, republican virtues were public virtues established by extrafamilial interests, and the achievements of the nation's youth became the foundations of the nation's, not simply the family's, progress. Moreover, if the inspiration for reform was republican, its instruments came from cultural environments that were historically antagonistic to the Iberian traditions: "Instruction should not be limited only to instructing," preached one of the city's liberal weeklies in 1817. "It is necessary to form the heart, to awaken and stimulate its useful, lofty, and patriotic sentiments; in sum, we are obliged to inculcate virtuous habits in our children. . . . They [should be taught] the subjects of justice, truth, well-being, and love for the country. . . . Happy are those nations that know how to form the inheritors of their rights . . . , and the zealous guardians of *order*."[23]

If "nation" was still a distant political construction rather than a reality in a disunited revolutionary Argentina, the ideal was no less powerful a decade later; indeed, the ideal, which combined order with deference to authority, became increasingly urgent after the completion of the revolution and the schisms of the 1820's. The search for stability was expressed in the relationship between political order and education; in the following comment written in 1827, a porteño urges the masses to read a treatise published by London's Society for the Promotion of Useful Knowledge:

A paternal and just government receives the natural support of the people when they become enlightened. The spread of knowledge brings with it this decorous submission, which is supportive equally of both power and public order. Learned men obey better than do ignorant men, because the motivation among the former is based on being convinced, while among the latter it is terror. . . . Let this be known among the bandits who have broken the ties among our deluded provinces. Perverts! They speak about the national will, of balance among the various authorities, of the bases of federalism. What do those unfortunate people know about political theories? What need do they have for further turmoil? What they need is elementary instruction: schools, books, means to cultivate their lands, elements to stimulate their industries. Let them be given teachers . . . and not conspirators.[24]

As occurred with other theoretical formulations of the era, however, educational and cultural ideals, too, conflicted with political, financial, and ideological cycles. In an oblique reference to the military conflicts that ensued from the antagonisms between federalists and unitarians and from the generally acrimonious style of relations, Ramón González Gorostizú, secretary of the Society for the Promotion of Enlightenment in the town of Chascomús, equated education with social and political stability: he hoped that the town's elementary school "would eliminate the animosities engendered by the state of ignorance."[25]

According to some traditional analysts, these conflicts resulted in the dangerous erosion of the foundations of colonial education, one more victim of the destructive forces of the revolutionary storms. The intelligentsia that had emerged from the centers of learning had failed in its attempts at inculcating the masses with its own enlightened and liberal values. The "doctoral class," not having elevated the mass of common men to its own cultural level, was forced, instead, to descend to the behavior and values of the plebeians. Matters would not become progressive again until the second half of the nineteenth century, during the process of national organization. These were judgments passed on the state of educational affairs by intellectuals who adhered to the liberal *sarmientista* view.[26] Indeed, conservative authorities made it their business to restore the sense of deference to established authority among children, perceived to have been lost in the wrongheaded application of unfettered individualism during the liberals' reign. In a note sent to the inspector general of schools in 1831, Tomás Manuel de Anchorena, the minister of government, reasserted the political function of education, but from the antithesis that had been generated by the preceding Rivadavian political generation:

> One of the most efficient means that must be employed for the sake of establishing an orderly society is the provision of a careful education for our youth. If children become accustomed from their early years to observe the laws of the country which saw them come into this world, and to respect the authorities, such impressions will become indelibly engraved. . . . But they must be educated in accordance with the views and political objectives of the State in order to plant the seed of hope that they will, in turn, support it.[27]

Minister Anchorena went on to instruct the inspector of schools in a written directive of March 11, 1831, that not only must school employees wear the red emblems in support of the Federalist Party led by Rosas, but it also became the duty of the students to wear them, while the authorities made clear to them "the origins of such a determination in a manner calculated to instill in them love and respect for the [Federalist] System and for the Laws of their Fatherland."[28]

From the earliest stages of the revolution, the city's meager educational resources were placed at risk. The growth of the militia following the victory over the English invaders in 1806 had made it necessary to convert the old Colegio San Carlos into barracks. The premises would not be returned to educational purposes until 1818, following Pueyrredon's decree reopening the school under the secular—and optimistic—name of Colegio de la Unión del Sud.[29] By September 1810, barely four months after the *cabildo abierto* sessions of May 25, Mariano Moreno was already sounding a warning about how political events could quickly undermine educational achievements. "The blood of the citizens is not the only sacrifice that accompanies triumphs," he wrote. "The Muses, frightened by the horrors of combat, flee to quieter regions, while men insensitive to everything that is not disastrous or thunderous leave unattended all those institutions that in happier days had been founded for the sake of promoting the sciences and the arts." If nothing were done to prevent this state of affairs, warned Moreno, "the gentler customs of a people will be followed by the ferociousness of its barbarous habits. . . . Buenos Ayres finds itself faced with this terrible lot; and four years of glory have silently undermined the very enlightenment and virtues that had made such glory possible."[30]

One generation later, Moreno's warning was reconstituted in the draconianism of Rosas, illustrated by a memorandum the governor circulated among all private and public schools in which he warned teachers that no discussion of politics should be allowed by anyone within school grounds. Furthermore, the government urged teachers to try to prevent any political talk by the children outside of the schools in order to limit any further dissension among Argentine families. Finally, any infraction of this new regulation would result in the immediate closing of the school.[31]

Thus, from the first republican moments, matters related to education did not stand apart from matters political and military. One of the clearest examples of their inseparable relationship comes from a simple but telling event in 1821. A brigantine sent from Buenos Aires to the southern coastal town of Patagones carried cargo that included fresh supplies of "weapons, ammunition, uniforms, tools and some money to repair the forts, and twelve artillery pieces of high caliber and gun carriages." The supervision of this shipment was predictably in the hands of a military officer, Colonel Don Gabriel de la Oyuela, who had been given command of the military detachment of 20 men on board; the colonel had also been provided, however, by the Buenos Aires cabildo with "the most complete training necessary to begin teaching the youth of that important population."[32]

Because of the close relationship between education and the formation of political values, the officials of learning establishments had to deal with the effects of their politically fragile and conflictual society. Under Rosas, the membership of each school board was selected by the juez de paz of every district and barrio. Thus, in 1830, Minister Tomás Guido instructed every juez de paz in the province to prepare reports that would include lists of suitable candidates, the condition of every school, and a list of all students and faculty.[33] A more overtly dangerous feature of the era, whether during the May revolution or during the sporadic rebellions that dotted the first decades of the century, were the military storms that sometimes blew down the structures of learning. For example, during the military and political disturbances of the years 1827–29, which were marked by Lavalle's revolt, the execution of Governor Dorrego, uprisings in the province, and the eventual coming to power of Rosas, schools were forced to shut down for lack of funds or were occupied and ransacked by armed bands.[34] The financial picture of the 1830's was much more conducive to military and police expenditures than to educational or other nonmilitary needs.[35] Teachers went without salaries for months; their schools, reported the authorities in July 1829 following Lavalle's uprising, were "looted horribly by hordes of criminals." A teacher in the outlying town of San José de Flores was forced to flee from his post and take up a new one in Buenos Aires' Monserrat parish.

The city's educational establishments were, therefore, not immune to the violence that accompanied political turbulence: the inspector of schools protested on July 23, 1829, that returning troops had occupied the school in the zone of Recoleta and were in the process of destroying it. The response given by the minister of war tersely instructed the official to relocate the school elsewhere, despite the well-known lack of available properties for such purposes. Three months later, the records indicate that the school in Recoleta, among others, was still closed for lack of space—*vacante por falta de casa.*[36]

These were just a few of the consequences that schools suffered in a troubled political environment. Even private schools for girls were forced to close down so frequently that teachers sometimes found themselves "obligated to start with the first lessons over and over again."[37] Under such circumstances, it is not surprising that porteños began their informal education in political socialization early in their lives. This learning process contained two avenues of contact between children and figures related to politics or the military. On the one hand, the effects of instability touched them in ways over which they had no control; on the other hand, educational leaders and teachers did well to seize their own opportunities for contact that might shield them, along with their schools and their students, from such effects. This was clearly the strategy followed by the authorities in charge of the girls' school of the parish of San Miguel shortly after Rosas was installed in the governor's residence in December 1829. In a scene that had been carefully rehearsed, "one of the girls offered His Excellency her best wishes and a floral arrangement in the name of all her colleagues." The calculations worked, or at least had the potential to work; Rosas pronounced publicly his delight at this show of support by the young generation and promised the children and their school "the most definitive protection" of his government.[38]

Warnings of all these consequences and laments by observers notwithstanding, the pervasiveness of war—or at least of a military stance—was difficult to eradicate. The contradiction between the desire for peace and the militarization of society became evident in the nature of the prizes that were sometimes awarded to primary school children who had received good grades. It became customary during much of the nineteenth century for political and school authorities to hold public exams and contests. The ritual of examining children's learning in public in the manner of a competition, followed by award ceremonies and festivities, was a tradition that contained important functions and derivatives. For example, the works of schoolchildren, which would be put on public display in the barrios' churches and in government buildings, served as moral examples for other children and as stamps of approval for the teachers, who could thereby further their careers and their own search for additional employment as private tutors.[39] More important still, the public ritual of judgment and observation of children's school performance served as an overt expression of the state's nominal concern for education, and it clearly established the connection between the style and content of learning and the political values held by the governing authorities in power at any given time. The rituals of 1816, for example, included the public reading of a congratulatory note that had been sent by the governor to Don Rufino Sánchez, director of one of the city's public elementary schools. In it, the political authorities lauded his pedagogical efforts and the high levels of achievement demonstrated by his students. This time, the coveted prizes consisted of weapons.

It was an honorable exam on general subjects that the 8 students under your direction rendered on the afternoon of the 28th of last month at the Church of San Ignacio. . . . As reward for their brilliant performance, I offer 8 carbines with bayonets which you should present to them in my name to each one of them, along with a copy of this note; let each of these weapons from this day on accompany them as a prize for their studies.

Please also accept a carbine and a pair of pistols for your own individual use as a well-deserved reward for your virtuous earnestness, and assure all the children under your care that the Government will continue to provide them with distinctions in accordance to their advances.[40]

The results of students' examinations were published in the city's newspapers.[41] This type of publicity was a double-edged sword, however: for every student who did well, many others were publicly embarrassed, along with their families, for their lower achievements. In addition, the publication of students' levels of performance could threaten the stability of the educational institutions, as happened occasionally in the University of Buenos Aires' schools of medicine and law.[42] One of the most publicized cases of dissatisfaction with the examination procedures came from a number of law students who in 1830 aired their grievances in the city's press. Students complained of unfairness and favoritism in the grading of their examinations and blamed the capriciousness of some professors, thereby opening a heated debate that eventually involved the direct intervention of government authorities.[43] Professors responded with deep concern over the harm done to the university's "moral position" by such publicity. One member of the faculty accused students of covering up their own inadequacies at the expense of the honor of their professors: "Where will we stop if every person runs to the press? I hold a teaching position at the university and I confess that I now tremble whenever I think of how near the day is when I must sit down to test students."[44] Spokesmen for the students argued in return that education was a matter of public concern and therefore it was perfectly proper to have "aired these questions."[45]

But the conservative press echoed the government's sense that the act of student protest on issues related to the university or any other educational institution was improper: "It is unacceptable to experience organized opposition in the schools of the type that we witness in civil society," wrote an editor.[46] For its part, the government took the opportunity to make clear the intimate relationship that existed between education and politics through its own organ, the *Gaceta de Buenos Aires*: "If today we permit the youth to disrespect their teachers, tomorrow they will treat their parents with disrespect, and the day after they will become rebellious citizens who will disobey their government."[47] Finally, because of the military characteristics that contemporaries correctly associated with politics, a porteño suggested that the government take all the dissatisfied students and "give them more plausible occupations by placing them in charge of guarding the internal stability of the province during the period of their vacations, and to dress them in military fatigues, thereby taking over from the industrious citizens who today live on the basis of the sweat of their brows."[48] These discussions represented the last expressions of a continuous lack of discipline on the part of the university's students: it took the efficiency of Rosas' heavy-handed security forces to eradicate whatever felt indiscipline there was by both the students and, occasionally, members of the faculty.[49]

To a large extent, the combination of military with pedagogical needs resulted from the political elites' insistence on dominating the region's formal institutions and, through them, affecting the collective consciousness. Moreover, the infusion of politics into educational matters was reinforced by long-standing regalist traditions that had assigned both pedagogical and political functions to the men circulating in university affairs. Thus, political elites who had received formal university training could realize the advantages that accrued from the socialization they experienced while in school.[50] It has been recently argued that Brazil's relatively peaceful transition from colony to independent nation resulted largely from the value system shared by the administrative corps, formed almost entirely in the law school of Portugal's University of Coimbra. The process of inculcating the same principles and canalizing them into cogent and uniform action by the administrative and judicial elite served to maintain two important sources of elite domination: class solidarity and political order. By contrast, the argument continues, the Spanish American educational system had produced too many diverse and locally formed educated elites to have cemented among them a sense of unified purpose. The result was the fragmentation of political and regional loyalties, which dismembered the relative cohesion of the colonial viceroyalties, leading to costly convulsions and balkanization on the road to nation building.[51]

Too little scholarly work has been done in the case of Argentina to make a full comparison with the Brazilian evidence, but the general indications suggest that objective conditions related to formal training do not appear to be different from what obtained in Brazil. Although the far-flung Spanish Empire produced most of its civil servants from six major universities in Spain, the Río de la Plata's University of Córdoba held a dominant position in the education of southern South Americans until the opening of the University of Buenos Aires in 1819.[52] Thus, until the 1820's, the University of Córdoba had been to the majority of the educated groups in Argentina what the University of Coimbra had been to their counterparts in Brazil; thereafter, the University of Buenos Aires performed a similar function on behalf of the sons of porteño families. To be sure, there had been a significant corps of public officials composed of *letrados* who had migrated from Spain, but their number and their political function had decreased sharply with the revolution.

The basis for the schisms among Argentine elites was not so much the diversity of their university training, but rather the diversity of their social backgrounds. This diversity is brought sharply into focus by the contrasts in both the educational and noneducational training of three notable Argentine contemporaries: Domingo Sarmiento, who never completed more than a formal primary education, but who was deeply influenced in matters of schooling by the North American experience; Esteban Echeverría, who interrupted his studies at the University of Buenos Aires to become educated, formally and informally, in Parisian intellectual circles; and Juan Alberdi, who was born into a well-to-do and prominent family, whose education was complete and domestic, and who grew up to become a conservative lawyer with a solid economic position in the city's legal establishment.[53] Not surprisingly, such men came to disagree on basic policies, including those related to the educational training of the youth.[54]

The most fundamental differences that divided Argentine thinkers on the subject of education, however, were related to functional aspects, such as what role education might play in molding the human resources that would be responsible for the country's political and economic development. On such issues, the child—as a developmental and dynamic concept—was largely missing from their considerations. To be sure, attitudes about the nature of the child were instrumental in determining the nature of his training in school. Philippe Ariès' thesis of the "invention" of childhood in the early modern age is applicable to the attitudes observed by way of the educational practices experienced in Buenos Aires from the late eighteenth century until the 1840's. The freedom and happiness that the medieval child had enjoyed, according to Ariès' central thesis, was severely undermined by the perceived need to manipulate the child. This management, in turn, deprived him of freedom, and resulted in an authoritarian parent confident of receiving support from a tyrannical state.[55] Yet the case of Buenos Aires suggests that official educational policies could become sources of conflict between the domestic and the public spheres. Before 1830, the growing demand for educational facilities resulted in the increased role of the state in the socialization of the child outside the family's protective circle. For conservative Catholics during the anticlerical Rivadavian

era, progressive and lay education posed a serious danger to traditional values: when, for example, Bernardino Rivadavia decreed the
end of autonomous teaching by Franciscans in their monastery in
February 1824, he gave as his reason the crisis of confidence in the
educational preparedness of the religious orders, and their inability
"to provide the state with the guarantees it expects to receive in such
matters."[56] For their part, liberal parents in the conservative restoration headed by Rosas underwent the difficulties inherent in the
same conflict, albeit obtained from ideological opposites.

Differences of opinion on matters of education among members
of any given community could be found on such subjects as the content of the curriculum, the extent to which religious dogma should
occupy the children's daily classroom experiences, or the extent of
influence parents should have in determining the appointment of
teachers. Such disagreements divided the citizenry furiously: for-
merly sociable neighbors stopped talking to each other, and it was
not unusual for tempers to flare and for insults to be shouted out
during school board meetings. In the words of a contemporary observer commenting on the deliberations of citizens' school committees in the mid-1820's, "the discord among various neighbors has
been uninterrupted, and the consistent state of perpetual clashes prevents them from arriving at amicable resolutions. These differences
are based on the failure to achieve a mutual understanding, and on
erroneous perceptions born from opposition to any given set of [ed-
ucational] principles."[57]

The clergy, too, served as a source of factionalism. In 1819, Don
José García Miranda of San Antonio de Areco wrote to Don Manuel
Luzuriaga, the town's *alcalde*, complaining of the inactivity of the
local priests, especially in the rural regions of Buenos Aires province,
and of their obstructionist stance on matters related to educational
reforms. "I wish that I did not have to say this," he wrote, "[but] in
the towns of the countryside, the priest is everything, and because
of his failure to act, all desirable things related to education are missing, regardless of their usefulness. The priest is required to build a
school, and even though this is the wish commonly held by everyone
in town, [nothing has been done]. . . . I am thus appealing to you
for help."[58] The conservative era of Rosas witnessed the reversal of
such attitudes on the part of officials toward priests who got in the
way of strengthening the presence and role of the public school. In
1831, the board of education of the town of Pilar, the *Junta Inspec-*

tora, complained to the government authorities in Buenos Aires that parents would not send their children to school during periods of mass in the churches, even though they had already been warned that truant children would be expelled from school. The government wasted no time in responding to their complaint by outlining clearly the conservative order's limits on education: "Nothing calls for our attention more," read the official reply, "than the learning by the youth of the principles of healthy morality and religious respect toward the Supreme Being, and it is thus a lesser evil that they not know how to read or write than they turn into bad Catholics."[59]

The composition of the *Juntas Inspectoras* was changed in the alternation between liberal and conservative regimes. Under Rivadavia, each school board was composed of the local justice of the peace and two residents; beginning in 1830, shortly after Rosas' coup, each board was brought under the government's closer scrutiny by replacing one of the residents with the Ministro del Culto, a sort of minister of religion. These changes formed part of a generalized turn away from the secularizing trends of the liberal past and toward the renewed prominence of the clergy in various institutions of learning and high culture. For example, when José Ignacio Grela, the director of the Buenos Aires Public Library, resigned for reasons of health in November 1833, the government appointed a priest, Father José María Terrero, as his replacement.[60]

The tendency toward Catholic control of the city's educational system made it more difficult to open private nonreligious schools. Political administrators came to contradictory decisions in awarding such licenses, and they were uncomfortable with the untenable predicament of either precluding the growth of school establishments or maintaining the church's hegemony of education. By way of illustrating this political waffling, one can take the case of Ana Bebans, a Protestant immigrant who in 1845 applied for a license to open an elementary school. The city's chief prosecutor denied her request tersely "on the basis that Bebans is not Catholic." The government's chief counsel, however, overturned this ruling by means of a carefully constructed artifice: "Bebans," he ruled, "with the exception of not being of the Catholic Faith, has demonstrated all other requirements for public teaching. Such an exception does serve to prevent her from reaching her objective, but [the dilemma] can be overcome by keeping Doña Ynés Amaya as the school's principal, since she could be in charge of teaching our religion to our country's daughters and Bebans could teach her religion to the daughters of her country."[61]

Financial considerations added to the conflicts between the public sphere and the domestic domain, conflicts that developed as a result of the enlarged role played by the state's authorities in the evolving educational establishment. The expansion of primary schools threatened to weaken the economic links that tied parents to their children's labor among families of humble means. As early as 1819, the teachers of the primary schools located in the poorer barrios, such as the one in the Hospicio and those in the parishes of Piedad and San Nicolás, reported that it "was a constant struggle" to teach basic skills to their students because of "the general lack of resources and because of an ineffective attendance record that results from the jobs the children have at home." By contrast, they attributed the superior level of performance of the students at the school in the parish of Catedral to "the efficient [cooperation] of the good parents who are economically well off."[62]

The children's attendance and the quality of training they received in public schools were positively correlated; in turn, both depended equally on the socioeconomic positions of their families. "As soon as parents believe that their children have managed the barest understanding of the first lessons in reading and writing," reported several teachers in 1819, "they resolutely try to remove them from school, and they thus deprive them of the greater enlightenment that could make them more developed and that could raise their general standing in the community. The sad situation in which those fathers and mothers find themselves provides a powerful explanation for the general dislocations preventing a complete education." In a similar vein, Juan Alexo Guaux, the teacher of the primary school of the humble barrio of San Telmo, informed his superiors that because of "the poverty of so many parents, they cannot provide their children with the required educational materials." Guaux was asking approval from the director of schools, Don Manuel Bustamante, for a plan to provide the paper, ink, and quills to needy students out of his own pocket, to be repaid by the parents some time later. But such parents often failed to see any economic value whatsoever in educating their children; "I cannot bring [the children] by force," wrote José María Conde, a teacher in the county of Concepción, "and their parents either do not want to send them, or if they do send them they remain uninterested in their advancement."[63] Similarly, José

Rodríguez, the teacher in the town of Morón, was convinced in 1825 that the cause for the "very small" number of students attending school was the placement of the children by their parents at the service of the town's bakers to sell sweet cakes on the streets.[64]

Parental resistance to reformist education and disregard of educational ordinances were not peculiar to the Argentines, who were merely demonstrating attitudes found in contemporary Europe and the United States. Parents, particularly those toward the bottom of the economic scale, forced compromises and succeeded in evading goals established by middle-class reformers.[65] In the end, the financial dependence in Buenos Aires of lower-class parents on their children and the state's insistence on childhood education created tensions that were never fully eliminated. It remained for a more efficient system of monitoring school attendance at the start of the twentieth century to make compulsory education a reality.[66] In the meantime, even children from humble positions who were determined to complete their education ran into disappointing realities. This was the case of young Lucas Barrenechea, a student in the city's Academy of Arithmetic, who was unable to take his midterm examinations in May 1816 because he lacked "a decent suit" to wear during the public testing.[67]

Thus, in Buenos Aires, as elsewhere in Latin America, childhood was variously defined; that is, the moment at which this period within one's life span was terminated depended on the socioeconomic conditions of the parental home. Childhood, a construct that took on operational meaning with its accompanied dedication to learning in school, came to a premature end with the youngsters' entry into the realm of adulthood, expressed in their full occupation with gainful labor. This transition was determined for the child by the impersonal forces surrounding his parents' station in life. Although the most conspicuous differences in the consideration given to childhood appeared in the contrast between urban and rural environments, intraurban differences were also very noticeable. Thus, the public authorities' insistence that their own bourgeois modes of behavior be internalized by the entire citizenry was fundamentally contradicted by the very conditions that differentiated the socioeconomic strata. For children, these differences meant that the parameters of youth, for example, were not universally agreed on; rather, youth was dynamic, insofar as it responded in great part to the objective material conditions surrounding each youngster. Moreover, youth itself would not become a societal construct uniformly held by the elites until the end of the century.[68]

School Regimen and Parental Resistance

Parental reluctance to cooperate with officials on matters of educational policies was not simply the result of rural backwardness nor of their own illiteracy. Among the city's *gente decente*, too, school authorities and teachers found many recalcitrant fathers and mothers who objected to specific educational reforms, such as the monitorial system, which had been ardently welcomed by progressive liberals in the late 1810's. The monitorial system was predicated on enlisting proficient students as aides in the instructional regimen—thereby maximizing the number of students while minimizing educational expenditures—and on completely subordinating every child in the classroom to the teacher's demands. In this context, the drill became one of the monitorial system's all-important features, and—by means of the insistence on instantaneous responses to questions and to unspoken signals—the students' attention was supposed to be assured.

The monitorial system of simultaneous instruction was originated in England by Andrew Bell and Joseph Lancaster in the late 1790's. Their contribution to the field of education rested on a "scientific" approach to the curriculum, meant to convert it into a systematic, consistent, and economical mechanism of instruction. The procedures represented the pedagogical version of the rationalism that pervaded the Industrial Revolution. The educational regimen also reflected the industrial entrepreneurs' deep concern for workers' efficiency and absenteeism by including detailed plans for the classroom in order for the teacher to monitor the students' behavior and attendance. In fact, Lancaster emphasized greatly the need to stimulate students' attention and to set clear limits to unacceptable performance. The result formed an odd combination of progressive didactics, authoritarian rule, and impersonal attention.

The actual teaching of the basics of reading, writing, and arithmetic was founded on a breakdown of the components of acquired knowledge in each subject and on a clear progression of specific goals. Attendance was to be taken by number instead of the students' names, a natural consequence of the increased ratio of students to teacher that the new system permitted. There was also a marked turn toward strict regimentation, specified in the instructors' manual: "The classes are numbered—each beginning at number 1, and ending its series of numbers at 30, 70, 130, or any other number of which the class may consist. . . . The monitor calls his boys to muster—the class go out in due order—go round the school-room; and, in going, each boy stops, and ranges himself against the wall, under that number which belongs to his name in the class list. By this means, the absentees are pointed out at once—every boy who is absent will leave a number vacant. The monitor of the class then passes silently round the school-room, and writes on the slate the numbers which are vacant."[69]

The system's economy was based on the use of children who, on mastering the material, would then teach other children. These monitors were responsible not only for the execution of the concept of peer education, but also for monitoring behavior and enlisting fellow students in guarding the orderliness of the classroom. Social control was thus applied to the children by other children, albeit under the adult supervision of the school's inspector, all within an authoritarian structure that frequently used public embarrassment to correct the behavior of students who broke the rules. For example, Lancaster's guidelines for treating truants invoked the principles of peer pressure and public shame: "In the case of truants being reported, when they are brought to school, either by their friends, or by a number of boys sent on purpose to bring them, the monitor of absentees ties a large card round his neck, lettered in capital letters, TRUANT; and he is then tied to a post in the school-room. When a boy repeats the fault many times or is incorrigible, he is *sometimes* tied up in a blanket, and left to sleep at night on the floor in the school-house. When boys are frequently in the habit of playing truant, we may conclude that they have formed some bad connections; and, that nothing but keeping them apart can effect a reform."[70] Indeed, Lancaster outlined in great detail the various "Instruments and Modes of Punishments," which included the use of shackles and yokes, suspending incorrigibles from the roof, the proclamation of students' faults before the whole school, and other forms of humiliation.[71] The appeal to improved behavior was made on the basis of public shame, that is, by pointing out to the the entire classroom community the student's unwillingness to submit to the ideals imposed from above (by way of the school authorities). Scholars have speculated that such forms of noncorporal punishment must have hardened the "coarser children and wounded to the quick many others whose sensibilities were more refined."[72]

This authoritarian style of treatment, coupled with its publicly punitive rituals, was in the end especially suitable to the porteño political elites of virtually all ideological preferences, as eager to establish orderliness among the youth as to restore order in the nation. Ironically, such treatment had been specifically forbidden by the first wing of radical revolutionaries. Manuel Belgrano's educational regulations, prepared for his Schools of the North during his revolutionary campaign in the northern regions of the old viceroyalty, did not rule out corporal punishment, but they did forbid psychological torture: "Under no circumstances will [youngsters] be exposed to public shame, such as making them walk on hands and knees, or any other improper form of embarrassing punishment." Furthermore, if it became necessary to dismiss a student from school, the procedure would be carried out quietly and privately.[73] Ultimately, however, the bitterness that resulted from the revolutionary and civil wars hardened attitudes and diminished tolerance for any relaxation of acceptable standards of behavior. "In all the years of Revolution, we have not done one good thing," wrote Father Francisco Castañeda, echoing the sentiments of embittered revolutionaries and subsequent generations. "The republic will never achieve institutional stability, unless everyone is taught, from infancy, to observe faithfully every single act that is useful and beneficial to the State."[74]

Not surprisingly, the Lancasterian model of instruction—which was first imported to Buenos Aires in 1818 by James Thomson, an emissary of the British and Foreign School Society of England, and fully applied in the 1820's—was hailed by influential porteños as the greatest and most efficient innovation in the field of pedagogy.[75] To the enlightened, it carried the legitimacy born of its English origins; to the rational, it offered scientific design; to the liberal and the anticlerical, it became positively associated with secularism; and to the authorities, always short of capital, it promised economy.[76] And yet it met parental resistance, forcing the authorities to spend some efforts instructing teachers in how to soothe public concerns in order to convince fathers of the value of sending their children to the reformed schools. Still, parents were "not taking this well," reported Florentino Zamorano, a school principal, in 1819. According to his testimony, families generally resisted the implementation of the

Lancaster method of teaching, and continued to ignore pleas by officials to give the new system a chance.[77]

Evidently, educational reform had become an element of community division, albeit less salient than others generated by the political ferment of the May revolution.[78] Policies and programs that threatened to undermine patriarchal authority were opposed by the older generations. Their education had served them well, and they defined the subordination of the child—and his mind—to the household as essential for the maintenance of the societal order. For their part, educational reformers insisted on the close interplay among their stated goals of intellectual development, political independence, and the general progress of a people. In some ways, the division of opinions reflected a generational split.

Perhaps the earliest illustration of this generational schism on the subjects of pedagogical styles and educational curricula comes from a case lasting from 1811 until 1812 that pitted reformers against traditionalists in the region of Paraguay, then freshly occupied by revolutionary forces. Don Luis de Zavala had been charged by the Asunción junta with reforming the educational structures, but in February 1812 he abruptly submitted his letter of resignation. He felt that it had become impossible for him to effect meaningful changes in the face of resistance from the obdurate elders of the educational establishment. Impatience showed through his language:

> My judgments against the obstinate habits of that already decrepit, cold and fruitless literary education, which Your Excellency so appropriately hopes to banish, have scandalized the most Elderly Individuals of the Patriotic Society during its first two meetings. This is the reason for finding myself in the compromising situation of either agreeing to a shameful condescension to them in the hopes of avoiding greater problems, or by continuing my legitimate functions, of maintaining endlessly a set of deeply rooted differences. I beg Your Excellency to accept the resignation of my honorific appointment.[79]

However, the political authorities could not yield so easily—the reformation of children's minds and the implantation of a new civic spirit were goals too important for the revolutionaries to surrender easily. Thus, Zavala's resignation was not accepted, and he was instructed, instead, to follow the same diplomatic and labyrinthine course of action that became a feature of the more successful political antagonists in other places in the Río de la Plata during the decade of revolution that followed the *cabildo abierto* of May 25, 1810. He was to convince his adversaries without cajoling them and to promote the idea of progress in education without impugning the learning of the patriarchs.

You have not sworn an oath of allegiance to the vestiges of the antiquarian notions of our elders, but rather to the adoption of the scientific rules that are observed in cultured schools. Our elders taught us all that they knew, but they never achieved what we know. Never, said Seneca, will ingenious novelties be created if we remain satisfied with what others have found and if we merely follow their lead without searching further. If we want to avoid making mistakes, it is essential not to subscribe to what is taught to us by those who, by virtue of their prestige, profession, or office, have been in the position of holding our knowledge captive.[80]

In addition to difficulties brought about by the financial hardships of parents and by generational differences, well-to-do families were reluctant to send their children to schools where they might mix with the less fortunate members of porteño society. The city's authorities had established a few scholarships designed to educate children orphaned by the loss of their fathers in the service of the revolution. Some school principals and teachers, however, were pressured by the barrios' parents not to accept these children into the schools; indeed, school officials themselves were reluctant to comply with the scholarship regulations. The sharp-edged terseness that Antonio Segurola, the director of the city's school system in 1817, used in his message of September 30 to teachers and principals suggests how severely the new and progressive ideals related to public education had irritated the relations between the state and the gente decente.

By order of its Excellency, the Municipality, you will receive in the schools under your charge every orphan who, upon receiving prior approval by the Office of the Director, Don Saturnino Segurola, should present himself before you. There will not be permitted the slightest excuse nor pretext for not complying; on the contrary, you are to take great pains in providing for the education and learning of these poor unfortunates who, by their very nature, demonstrate their worthiness. All this should be carried out, be it understood, with the certainty that the slightest complaint will bring about the most serious penalties.[81]

These warnings against discriminatory practices did not signify, however, that authorities considered the plight of "these poor unfortunates" from any other perspective than their own. Consequently, a good deal of attention was given to the instruction of social relations deemed proper—that is, as expressions of the custodial elites' value system. For example, the porteño child in the early nineteenth-century school received his training in sociability within a framework designed to instill in him an acceptably inferior position in domestic society and an unquestioningly deferential attitude toward authority. Reading and writing exercises, reinforced by constant drill, formed the typical mechanisms used for instilling these patterns of sociability or *urbanidad*, as the subject was formally known. Teachers graded the children's handwriting and spelling as they copied down value-laden maxims on their *planas*, or slates, after reading them and discussing them with the teacher. The following handwriting assignment from the public elementary school of the parish of San Telmo in 1817 illustrates the behavior expected from children in relation to their superiors:

A person must be very conscious of himself at the dinner table, since it is there that he must observe an infinite number of rules in order to avoid all forms of rudeness and ill-breeding. Parting from the notion that cleanliness is never more necessary than at the table, the Child will wash his hands after all other persons superior to him have done so, taking care not to wash at the same time as these others, unless he is expressly not forbidden to do so, in which case the man-servant should be nearby to provide a towel.

In the same school, students copied the following maxim:

The fourth [*sic*] Commandment of the Decalogue indicates to us in the strongest fashion the reverence and respect that must be shown toward our parents. It is the first precept imposed on us by the second tablet of the Law of Grace, and which must be obeyed in the strictest fashion after the first three precepts of the first tablet which refer to God. The Child will look with horror upon all deeds or words that may be interpreted as disobedience, contempt, mockery, or inattention toward his Parents. He will kiss their hands upon entering the house or wherever He encounters them.[82]

Mariano Rivero never completed one of his handwriting assignments, but the lesson in male civility remains clear: "A hurried walking cadence is seen poorly, as is the heavy step, while the artificial

and effeminate form of walking suggests arrogance or shallowness.
Shaking the body, or walking in a slanted fashion, or too straight,
is . . ."[83]

The drive to inculcate a deep sense of subordination among children was shared equally by liberals and conservatives. "We have just
happily seen in practice the Lancaster system, by which not only do
the children learn to read and write, but they also become accus-
tomed to order," reported the utopian liberals of 1821.[84] During Rosas' government students and faculty alike were required to wear the
red pins that signified loyalty to the federalist party. The wording of
the decree of May 1835 contained a logic easily found in the earlier
liberal and republican rhetoric: "The government is convinced that
when children are made to observe the laws of the country from the
time of their infancy, and thereby they are taught the respect owed
to the authorities, such impressions become permanently en-
graved."[85] For their part, hardened and more realistic liberal voices
expressed themselves even more fully: "From subordination emanates good order," wrote Sarmiento in the 1830's, "and it is therefore
of the utmost importance that the students respect and obey their
superiors without any contradiction or opposition to their orders;
failure to do so should be considered one of the greatest personal
flaws, and by the same token, the most severe penalties available to
the School should be applied in such cases."[86] Indeed, Sarmiento's
ideological liberalism in political matters generally, although it did
not extend much to children, displayed the contradictory mixture of
respect for the need of children to be educated and the application
of measures that severely restricted their behaviors.[87]

The hardening of attitudes by the Generation of '37, so succinctly
expressed by Sarmiento, its most famous pedagogue, contrasts
sharply with the tenets held by the previous generation of liberals
of the period shortly following the May revolution. In a handwriting
assignment of that earlier and more optimistic era, Juan Farias carefully wrote out on his *plana* the words as they were dictated by his
teacher: "Both the good and the bad crop of virtuous and literate
men are attributable to the Teachers rather than to the nature of
children, because it is the good Professor who plants—by his own
actions—the selected seed of good doctrine, industriousness, and labor."[88] In time, however, the Rousseauist requirement that education
contribute to the flowering of childhood and to the evolution of so-

ciety was forcefully complemented by the coercive elements of the Kantian call for constraint and for the inculcation of habit in the youngsters' preparation that would facilitate the faithful following of the rules of conduct imposed from above. The adherence to a strict disciplinary order among youths was shared by political thinkers of both the liberal and conservative wings. This was one of the very few subjects on which the two sides arrived at consensus: any relaxation in vigilance or in the school regimen would detract from the much-sought-after order in general society. Thus, the tumultuousness of the independence era gave way to a curious consensus: Argentine reformists and traditionalists came to agree that the supreme guide to life was the law of duty, which was always more or less in opposition to the promptings of inclination.

Not surprisingly, Sarmiento devoted a significant number of regulations to monitoring the behavior of students and to the punishments appropriate to every type of infraction. For example, in the charter he prepared in 1836 for a girls' school in the Province of San Juan, he wrote: "If the nonapplication, disobedience, and transgression of constitutions should go unpunished, such misbehaviors would become so frequent that the hard work and vigilance of the Headmistress and others in charge of education would be in vain."[89] Important differences did remain, however, between conservatives and progressives on the subject of dealing with misconduct. The liberal contribution here was the elimination of corporal punishment in school. Thus, Sarmiento's charter allowed for six degrees of severity in punishments, including "sweet and loving warnings," denials of privileges, religious penance, and, finally, expulsion "in cases of absolute impertinence," but no mention is made of paddling.

Access by children to the world beyond the school was severely limited in private institutions. This rigid circumscription of social contacts was achieved by two methods: by actual prohibitions placed on certain activities, and by a very regimented schedule that did not allow much free time. For example, the young women in Sarmiento's school in San Juan were forbidden to read any book without the prior consent of the headmistress or the director; they were not even permitted to receive letters from home without receiving prior permission. No visits were allowed from one dormitory room to another during the hours reserved for studying. Children were never permitted to use the familiar pronouns or verb forms of the language, not even with each other, and nicknames were expressly forbidden;

no games or pastimes involving physical contact were allowed; no one was permitted near the kitchen or areas where servants were likely to be working. Finally, a general prohibition forbade any "indecorous acts or expressions." The world of the school and the world of the home could meet only by way of contact among adults. Students were forbidden to recount at home any punishments meted out by the school authorities, or any other event that might have given cause to people in the community to speak ill of the school or of any person involved with it: "Parents would be acting criminally if, in satisfying their childish curiosity, they were to foment the dishonorable habit of gossip that is found among their children." By design, an uncritical solidarity with the community in which the youngster lived was fostered early. Here, as in the political realm, the commonweal and the peaceful order were held to depend on blind deference to established authority.

The schedule that these students followed provided them with a very long day during which free time was kept to a minimum. Normally, students began their days at 5:00 A.M. and went to sleep at 11:00 P.M. Their responsibilities included regular studies, musical training, cleaning chores, and lectures on diverse topics generally associated with cosmopolitanism. First came the morning prayers until 5:30 A.M., followed by a study period in the students' rooms until 7 A.M. The first class was then given for one hour. Only then were they fed their first meal. Study sessions and classes continued until noon. During lunch, a student who was the recipient of a financial scholarship was responsible for reading out loud "something moral and entertaining." The rest period lasted until 3:00 P.M., followed by more study and class sessions until 6:30 in the evening. Later, after one hour of free time, the students listened to presentations on various topics that were considered essential for well-bred and worldly ladies. These lectures lasted until 9 P.M., when everyone gathered for prayers, followed by dinner. Finally, lights were put out at 11 P.M.[90]

Until midcentury, educational thinkers and essayists writing on the subject of childhood generally did not consider young children to be naturally endowed with critical thinking abilities. Indeed, the attitude suggested by a number of schoolteachers resembled the theories of Locke on the youthful acquisition of knowledge. Along with some of his seventeenth-century contemporaries, Locke believed that at birth children's brains were devoid of content; knowledge and aptitude were nothing more than the child's capacity to fill his head with the facts provided him by others and by experience. Neither the innate ability of children to learn nor the cognitive prowess of the human mind were recognized; thus, it was not until after the 1850's that any attention was paid to devising teaching techniques that capitalized on the child's own cognitive abilities. Until then, most educators felt the need to shape children's minds in a clearly hierarchical, unilateral, and adult-centered manner, allowing virtually no latitude for youngsters to develop and employ their own analytical skills. Indeed, this attitude toward children, far from being unique to porteños, was widespread enough to have become a leitmotiv in modern Spanish American fiction: for example, José Arcadio Buendía, the patriarch in Gabriel García Márquez's *One Hundred Years of Solitude*, shared in the belief that children's minds were essentially empty vessels: "He was always alien to the existence of his sons, partly because he considered childhood as a period of mental insufficiency."[91] This line of thought, which unites some of the sentiments regarding youth from the Buenos Aires of the late eighteenth and early nineteenth centuries, was noted in the chronicler Azara's comment that a child who asked questions would not have his curiosity taken seriously by adults; instead, he would be treated in all likelihood with disdain and be brushed off with a deceitful answer.[92]

The Structures of Education

The effectiveness of the educational system of Buenos Aires was highly dependent on the quality of its teachers and the quantity of its funds. Advocates of public education and many officials consistently bemoaned the severe shortage of money, a limited infrastructure, and, in the countryside, a limited supply of teachers.[93] In addition, the school system suffered from considerable changes in teaching personnel, teachers who long remained dilettantes, and the absence of a state licensing system. Until the 1850's, the basic requirements for teaching appointments included the applicants' moral standing in the community and the patrimonial leverage they could muster on their behalf. Neither the pay nor the working conditions were sufficiently attractive to dissuade teachers from applying for more remunerative positions; not surprisingly, the high turnover among teachers remained a problem. For example, in February 1818, the *Junta Protectora de Escuelas*, the local school board of San

José de Flores, received a heart-wrenching request for a teaching position from Fr. José Vicente Ortíz. Ortíz wrote from the province of
Santa Fe, where he was mired without any money and caring for his
ailing mother, already in her seventies, and her "four unmarried
daughters." In response, the school board provided him with a teaching post, only to find that several months later, in September, Father
Ortíz returned to Santa Fe on business after having tendered his
resignation.[94]

Teachers had much to complain about. Several of their appeals,
written in the early 1820's, suggest that the educational reforms instituted by the humanistic liberals of the Rivadavian era worsened
teachers' working conditions. This was true, for example, of the implementation in Buenos Aires of the monitorial system. The Lancaster method was embraced in Buenos Aires in the 1820's by virtually the entire liberal leadership of the gente decente as being of
"unquestionable public utility."[95] The system was likewise being introduced in other regions of South America where secular liberals
held sway, including Chile and Uruguay.[96] But despite the liberals'
ideological attachment to the Lancaster method of schooling, it appeared to provide teachers with further administrative and pedagogical problems. Teachers complained that the authorities had mis-
interpreted the reputed economy of the system by grossly increasing
the number of students assigned to each classroom and thereby undermining pedagogical integrity.[97] Moreover, the monitorial system
depended for its success on a reliable supply of young students who,
in their mastery of the subjects, could act as drill instructors themselves; yet these youngsters were not always available, especially in
schools located in barrios with significant proportions of low-
achieving students, victims of the poor school attendance and little
available study time that resulted from their families' strained economic situations.

Before the reforms in higher education were instituted by Domingo Sarmiento in the later 1850's, teachers in Buenos Aires received
no professional training in either carrying out their pedagogical duties or in dealing with problems peculiar to young school-age children. Indeed, any literate person with good handwriting possessed
all the objective requirements to teach in the elementary grades. Insofar as the members of the gente decente—in particular the
males—had received formal schooling and religious training them-

selves, they fulfilled the basic criteria for employment. Teachers' salaries reflected the reluctance of authorities to reward their services as full professionals. In 1828, the inspector of elementary schools of Buenos Aires reported that the city's schools would not prosper until they were staffed by teachers of high quality and training. This could never become reality, he argued, because of low salaries; indeed, teachers were being forced to take on additional jobs to meet their regular expenses.[98] At the time, teachers in Buenos Aires received 41 pesos monthly plus lodging at or near the school where they taught.[99]

Beyond the objective requirements for a teaching post, however, teachers needed also to possess moral authority, which they derived from the perception held of them by their neighbors. The need for teachers to be vested with a close working relationship with the barrio residents is illustrated by an event that occurred in 1819. When the teacher of the parish of Socorro died and the process of finding his replacement was begun, a letter requesting a new teacher was sent to the *cabildo* authorities, signed by the parish priest, the cuartel's *alcalde*, and several vecinos. Its contents outline the barrio residents' expectations:

We believe that it is our obligation to express to Your Excellencies our concern that the naming of the elementary school teacher take into consideration the requirement that the appointee must reside in the center of the Parish, and if at all possible, in the immediate vicinity of the Parish Church, all of this with a view toward benefiting all the children of this neighborhood so that they can attend in comfort the daily mass, and be observed closely in order to insure that the children benefit from a high level of morality, from healthy religious principles, and from the many other advantages accruing from the proximity of the parish priest and from the care provided by the parents who zealously oversee their children's improvement, all of which is made easier by observing and monitoring their learning from up close.[100]

The emphasis on the schoolteacher's direct accessibility to the barrio's parents remained a feature of the popular construction of educational accountability. In the late 1850's, the authorities were still insisting on locating public schools in the very center of a parish, if at all possible.[101]

In this face-to-face society, the public standing of the pedagogue was an essential component of his teaching abilities. The difficulties encountered in satisfying parental concerns regarding public education, however limitedly public that education may have been, were thus based in part on the requirement that teachers command respect inside and outside the classroom; the orderly regimen of schooling demanded it. When, in the view of barrio residents, teachers failed to carry out their duties, it became a matter of public debate. In the parish of La Piedad, Thomás Rebollo, the juez de paz, had had enough of the barrio's elementary school teachers:

The low attendance by youngsters in the State's School has no other basis than the failure of the teacher to discharge his duties. It is notorious that one block away from the public school there is a private one, and yet, despite the costs that parents have to bear in order to send them [to this private institution], they feel they have no alternative but to undergo the necessary sacrifices so that their children do not spend the major part of the day on the streets acquiring the most pernicious form of education, as is the case of [the students] of the State School. And this entire neighborhood is witness to the lack of concern that these teachers have toward the education of the youth. It is nothing but a scandal among the neighbors who have observed that the school has not been opened at the scheduled hour, thereby permitting that the children gather in the streets sometimes for hours, even until noon. It follows that parents have taken their children out of the school, having become convinced of the need to remove them from a school in disarray and place them in another which at least does not permit such scandalous procedures.

Because virtually the same conduct has been observed in general among the teachers of this State School, we find that today there are hardly three or four children enrolled there, while the opposite is true of the private school . . . with an attendance of no fewer than sixty children; indeed, this is the case even though the behavior of the teacher of the private school is not the most conducive for the education of the youngsters, since it is well known that he is usually inebriated in the hours when school is not in session.[102]

The inspector went on to fire the teachers of the public school who allegedly had failed to carry out their duties responsibly. Furthermore, he forced a Portuguese man named Barboza to close down his private school on the grounds of his drunkenness. The minister of government, however, rescinded the order, reminding the inspector that the state had no right to meddle in the conduct of private entrepreneurs; the business of education, wrote the minister, was a business.[103]

As a consequence of the political turbulence of the first half of the nineteenth century, the moral standing of teachers also rested on their political legitimacy. In fact, one of the important considerations for all professionals who depended on the public authorities for their employment and well-being was their proven deference to authority during their own days as students. The obedience that Adolfo Peralta had demonstrated in the course of his studies in the medical college of the University of Buenos Aires served him well when he petitioned to become a licensed physician. One of the advisors to the minister of government summarized the young Dr. Peralta's personal talents in a note dated August 27, 1847: "He has demonstrated in a substantial fashion that he is a loyal follower of the National Cause of Federation, no less than he was submissive and obedient in his dealings with his superiors during the course of his studies." The same characterization was given to José María Real and Claudio Megía, also medical doctors, and to Francisco Villar, freshly graduated as a doctor in canon law.[104] Deference by students in the era of political tensions was defined politically. Thus, *sumisión y obediencia* was equated with adherence to the federalist party during Rosas' rule; in fact, university students regularly petitioned to be exempted from the requirement of documenting their good and submissive conduct in school on the basis of their federalist loyalties.[105]

The daily activities of children in school allowed little free interplay between teacher and student. There was no such thing as discussion of the educational subjects to any meaningful degree. Teaching was unidirectional and hierarchical, always stemming from the teacher and not subject to debate among students; indeed, successful education was deemed to rest more on the teacher's total domination of the class than on his own mastery of the material. Thus, the two basic instruments of instruction for each subject included the monologue and the attendant practice-and-drill session. A typical schedule for the elementary public schools of Buenos Aires included a six- or seven-hour day, depending on the school, always divided into two sessions. The school of the parish of Socorro, for example, held classes from 6:30 to 10:30 A.M. and from 2:30 to 5:30 P.M. Every morning session followed the same strict regimen: the first 30 minutes were spent in sharpening the writing quills; the following hour was devoted to handwriting drills; the next 45 minutes were spent attending mass; then came 30 minutes of drill in arithmetic, followed by 15 minutes of correcting the arithmetic problems; the next hour was spent in oral examinations in front of the class; and for the rest of the morning period, the children enjoyed recess. The afternoon session also began with 30 minutes of sharpening quills; one hour of writing assignments followed, these offering the opportunity to teach Christian and civic norms to students through the dictation of appropriate maxims containing social and religious themes; the next 30 minutes were devoted to examining students; then came an hour of actual teaching in the form of lecturing; finally, grammar and spelling were taught during the last hour of the afternoon session, just before afternoon prayers. This was the daily reality for Baltasar Sebastiani and his 69 students of various ages in the Socorro parish in the late 1810's.[106] This pedagogical system required a great deal of passivity on the part of the youngster and thereby conspired against students with short attention spans.

The attrition rate among elementary school children was significant. No systematic breakdown of ages among schoolchildren is available for the years preceding the 1870's, but the indications of sharp attrition are clear from the significant decrease in the number of students at each of the six levels of handwriting skill. The rudiments of handwriting were established with *cartilla y catón*; at this stage the child wrote on a large sheet of paper with a thick and blunt quill. The student then progressed to *libro y proceso*, which in actual practice meant using a slightly sharper quill and a scrapbook. The next several levels signified a progressive shrinking of the written letters and the quills, and a concomitant increase in the number of lines per sheet.

The number of students at each of the six levels of handwriting ability in the school of the parish of La Piedad demonstrated the continuous erosion in enrollments as the students' ages increased. Of the total school population of 130 children, the numbers of students at each level, beginning with the lowest, were 45, 17, 21, 22, 14, and 11. For his part, Juan Alexo Guaux, the teacher responsible for 183 students registered at the start of the academic year in 1816 in the school of the barrio of San Telmo, witnessed similar declines: 41 children were beginning their training in *cartilla*, and only 22 were at the highest level. Evidently, most parents were interested in having their children acquire merely the rudiments of reading and writing.[107] The period's only available statistics on the ages of elementary

school children come from the school in San Fernando, outside Buenos Aires. In 1818, this school had an enrollment of 41 students ranging in age from 4 to 12:

Age	Number	Age	Number
4	1	9	4
6	2	10	5
7	13	11	2
8	7	12	6

The authority of teachers depended not only on their moral superiority by virtue of their pedagogical status, but also on their
assertedly indisputable knowledge of the subject; teachers thus
brooked no question or doubt from any student on the execution of
the curriculum. Students who questioned the established procedures
ran the risk of public humiliation and ostracism. For example, in
July 1816 José Gabriel Colina wrote a note to the headmaster of the
Academy of Arithmetic in which he announced his intention to quit
the school after having been enrolled for only two months. José had
taken his examinations, even though he admitted that he had not
studied very much; furthermore, he had been at the school only a
brief time and could not have prepared adequately for the examinations. When he received the high grade of "Very Good," he began
to question the grading and promotion procedures, and even the
amount of learning he had been given. "The way things work here,"
he wrote tersely in a message to the headmaster, "is that today one
copies down the lesson, and if tomorrow he knows it, he then passes,
and if he does not know it, he is passed just the same. In the end, I
learn nothing. Thus, instead of merely taking up space here, it would
be best for me to retire. [In addition], my withdrawal should be interpreted as an expression of solidarity with [Faustino] Lezica [and]
Avelino Díaz." Lezica and Díaz had apparently studied much more
and, at least in Colina's view, they had mastered the material better
than he had himself; still, Lezica and Díaz had received the lowest
passing grade, "Satisfactory."[108]

The city's educational administrators reacted to Colina's "insulting and indecorous" letter by permitting him to leave the school, but
only after he was made to "understand the respectful method and
form that he should have used to make his request." Colina's lesson
would take place during the three days that he was sentenced to
spend in jail. Furthermore, the penalties were to be announced pub-

licly so that all the other students of the Academy would learn from Colina's mistake. Not satisfied with handing down the jail term, however, the authorities began a slander campaign against the young student by methodically attacking his moral and civic character. Felipe Senillosa, the Academy's director, turned over to the authorities documents designed to prove Colina's poor attendance record. Apparently, he had been penalized on three occasions, although no one reconciled the apparent inconsistency between his good grades and his poor attendance. Ironically, Faustino Lezica, who had barely passed his midterm exams in May, received the highest grade of "Excellent" during the subsequent examination period on September 7, 1816. Avelino Díaz received a "Satisfactory" grade once again. By then Colina no longer figured in the class roster. Colina was not the only student to suffer stiff penalties and incarceration. These were often applied to students with military affiliation, as the school inspector of Buenos Aires showed whenever he requested help from the army's commanders to carry out the arrests of cadets who were also troublesome students with "such perfection that it should serve as a corrective to their flaws."[109]

Colina's statements had not only raised doubts about the proper means by which to examine and evaluate students' efforts, but—perhaps unknown to their author—they had also threatened to jeopardize one of the basic mechanisms by which educators improved their professional and financial positions. Teachers and educational administrators used the improved grades of their students to legitimate requests for higher positions and salaries. Thus, while grades were quite good on the average, it is difficult to gauge the educational efficacy of teachers, since the system of advancement encouraged grade inflation. Felipe Senillosa wasted no time in making his own bid for advancement. The day following the first set of public exams taken by his students, he wrote a letter to a highly placed government aide asking him to forward his subtle request for an increase in salary to the highest authorities:

When I took charge of the Academy, I was given a provisional salary of 800 pesos until the time that the first examinations could provide some tentative results from this enterprise. . . . The results are now clear; and these are perhaps the first examinations that have ever been given anywhere in which the entirety of pure arithmetic has been taught in the short amount of time of barely two-and-a-half months. Indeed, many of the students had even less time. Moreover, I had offered my services for the education of only twelve students, as I am certain Your Excellency knows, but for the sake of the general welfare, I have received up to forty with the greatest pleasure. . . . I have the honor or providing Your Excellency with all this information for any results which may be deemed appropriate.[110]

The characteristics of the educational system of Buenos Aires remained basically unaltered until the 1850's. Then the school regimen, the formative experiences of teachers, and the definitions of childhood with their attendant epistemological concerns constituted the line of considerations that distinguished the old from the new approaches to the education of youth. As precedent to action, however, the very purpose of childhood learning had to undergo a fundamental redefinition, while the role of the state in the field of education had to be expanded considerably. The fall of Rosas signified that the extremely hierarchical structure of learning within the classroom and the ad hoc nature of the personnel and the curriculum were subject to review and amendment.

Reform and Professionalization

The ascent of liberal reformers to political power in the 1850's bore significant consequences for the educational system. Not since the Revolution of 1810 had men come to political leadership with a renewed sense of the value of education; they demonstrated a heightened awareness of the pedagogue's power to shape the political consciousness of the citizenry. In addition, they now brought into play a greater sensitivity to the innate learning processes of children. If the reforms did not bring significant increases in the percentage of literate porteños, at least the needed infrastructure was put in place for the quantitative increases in school attendance that would be registered at the turn of the century.[111]

At the root of the changes lay a functional definition of the masses that distinguishes clearly the conservatism of the Rosas era from the liberalism of the Generation of '37. Rosas' political elites considered the illiteracy of the gente de pueblo to be the natural condition of a prepolitical folk. In other words, ignorance of matters of the mind—as distinguished from matters associated with the practical end of artisanship and rural functions—was inherent to a people who not only lacked political influence but had been destined never to have it. As such, the gente de pueblo represented the large majority of Argentines who posed a political threat only insofar as they could be led into battle by a politically calculating individual. Without such a leader, however, the gente de pueblo merely served the ends of the governing elite. Malleable and unable to apprehend either the subtleties of the art of politics or the machinations of their patrons, plebeians were in no need—indeed, they were not capable—of being redeemed. Instead, they merely served as clients and servants of their custodial elites.

At the heart of Argentine conservative thinking on learning, we find the construct of an educational system that would insidiously worsen social and political conditions. In a letter written by Rosas from his English exile in 1872, the former caudillo warned against enlarging the system of public education: "Thanks to free public education, the most noble of professions is converted into the art of exploitation, favoring the charlatans who profess ideas that are false, and that subvert morality and the public order. Free education introduces anarchy into the ideas of men, who are then formed under principles that are self-contradictory and infinitely variable. In this way, the love of the fatherland will become extinguished, [and] constitutional government will become impossible because, in the midst of a confused public opinion, much as the languages in the tower of Babel, there will never be formed a solid enough base of a sufficiently large majority to follow one system."[112] Rosas was obviously not an advocate of universal education, nor did he consider the state to have any educational responsibilities. By contrast, his contemporary, Mitre, considered education to be an indispensable instrument of material progress; the state was therefore required to promote it in order to increase the returns on this social investment.[113]

Allowing for the considerable differences found among the liberals of the Generation of '37, their school of thought presented a significantly different definition of the purpose of the masses. Post-Rosas liberals certainly viewed the illiterate and rustic peoples with disdain, much as did their conservative counterparts, but they distinguished themselves from both their liberal and conservative predecessors on the basis of two facts. The first was simply generational: they had breathed the stimulating and rarefied atmosphere of the Parisian salons alongside Romantic socialists who believed in the perfectibility of all segments of mankind. They thus stood in sharp contrast to the traditional elites, who accepted the immutability of the ignorant state commonly found among the lower classes. The second distinction was derived from their formal study of the Spanish American experience; the Generation of '37 viewed the nature of Argentine and Spanish American politics as historically conflictual, and it was from the acceptance of this reality that they defined the value of a literate public.

These two constructions synthesize the explanation for the actions of the Generation of '37 in matters of education: the redeemability of the ignorant masses was possible not only as a universal proposition of unavoidable progress, but also as an urgently needed prescription for the elimination of armed struggle to resolve conflicts. These calculations were clearly aimed at the realignment of the mental states related to identifications, for the average individual in Argentina identified his political self with one leader or another and his retinue. The Generation of '37, by contrast, aimed at inculcating in the masses the popular identification with the abstract, specifically with the state, thereby eliminating two historical tendencies: the centrifugal dispersal of political authority among the surfeit of actors in the constellation of power, and the centripetal tendency of hegemonic caudillismo.

The second half of the nineteenth century was the ripe time for these ideas to be tested in Argentina; they circulated in the realm of values attendant on a capitalism that, already mature in parts of Western Europe, was now advancing with greater strength than ever across the Atlantic. The growing presence of market forces was altering radically the nature of contractual obligations, including the rights and obligations among citizens and between citizen and state. In the material realm, the oral promise proved inadequate to the exigencies of financial transactions. Along with more stringent requirements of accountability for human will, the market was inculcating the needed lesson of attending to the remote consequences of human action.[114] What was true of the world of industry, commerce, and finance had become obvious also to the political inheritors of the more than forty years of tensions encompassed by the revolutionary and Rosas eras: that private promises of friendship and political loyalties among caudillos served poorly as mechanisms for the maintenance of stability, and that alternative means had to be found to attain a firmer basis for action and accountability.[115]

At the legal end of things, codified and constitutional principles would be established that would, in due course, at least provide relatively clear standards of appropriate political behavior. But at the much more complex level of establishing normative action, education was considered to be the principal mechanism that over the long run would alter the popular character and the gente de pueblo's disposition toward authority. They would no longer be easily available for use by political adventurers and caudillos; they would instead make their own political calculations on the basis of reasoned will. The age of caudillos would come to an end, not so much because such men would cease to arise from the ranks of the politicized gentry, but because they would be uncertain of commanding a mass following. Public action, which before depended on the ability to muster men of arms, would come to depend on garnering affinities to political ideas. Freedom could not be guaranteed except by an educational system made to fit a generation's new necessities and break its old habits, wrote Esteban Echeverría in a guide for teachers while living in exile in Montevideo.[116] Echeverría's goal was to establish a society that, in the course of history, would be able to exercise sovereignty through the use of reasoned thought rather than through traditionally visceral motivations. The link he traced between education and political action was more discrete than the one traced earlier by the first generation of revolutionary liberals: "Only the prudent and rational part of the social community," he wrote, "is called to exercise that sovereignty."[117]

Thus, these liberals considered that prudence, rationality, and conscientious political action depended on the ability of the majority of the Argentine public to internalize the values generally associated with contemporary Western Europeans: delay of gratification, attention to remote consequences, and conceptualization of the self as a functioning member of the social and political community. The basis for success would rest on the ability, not the willingness, of the public to learn and act out these new behaviors. Willingness, or rather the will to have these values and behaviors adopted by porteños, rested with the state, which enlarged its responsibilities to include education and the regularization of the educational system. Education was thus a metaphor for civic apprenticeship to a new generation of leaders who endowed themselves with the mantle of political power on the basis of their self-asserted intellectual superiority. In a way, this represented an updated liberal variant of the political schema of the traditional Thomist perspective on authority:

the purpose of the supreme political organization known as the state was to rise above the fallibility of the popular constituency in order to consummate public action in accordance with a higher morality and for the benefit of the common good in opposition to private consideration.[118]

The political hegemony of the generation of men who followed Rosas' fall was justified by their insistence on turning the problematical masses into passive elements of society.[119] The *hommes de lettres* then simply had to fulfill their duty of molding the masses in accordance with the contemporary sense of a civic society. Men of ideas ruled, therefore, by virtue of their tutorial talents, the political novelty of which was based on the addition of education to the realm of public action. Furthermore, the new liberals' concepts related to the masses and their education represented a significant departure from the revolutionary liberal ideology of the 1810 generation. To the revolutionaries, education was the means to the liberation of each and every individual of the community in the common pursuit of republicanism; it had been an ideal with direct lines of argument from the Enlightenment's optimism about mankind's political future. The course of the revolution and the subsequent erosion of the constitutional ideal had dramatically demonstrated to the young liberals who grew up under the caudillo political order the need to eliminate the individual from active participation in exchange for his passivity, in effect his depoliticization. If for Belgrano the classroom had been the cauldron in which the ingredient of fervent republicanism would stir up Americans seeking liberty, for Sarmiento it represented the containment of passion and the instrument for inculcating subservience to the abstraction of the state.

In sum, the ultimate goal of the education process did not and could not stand apart from matters more overtly political. It represented the planned elimination of the atomization of popular loyalties and the depersonalization of authority. The end of an Argentina defined as a political construction of hostile regions would come from the efforts exerted by two forces pushing from opposite ends of the societal structure toward the center. From the top, that is, from the structures of government and its executive officials, would come the pressures to conform via the organized political parties—associations, really—and the accumulation of military prowess capable of eliminating regional dissidence with updated war-making technology. From the bottom came the pressures for union exerted by generation after generation of youngsters who, through a peaceful and longitudinal program of education, had come to understand political authority in terms of the moral superiority of the nation as the fundamental abstraction, in which all were joined in the common goal of peace and deferred to men of letters—not warlords—in the interest of stability.

Nineteenth-century Argentine political elites could not accept the existence of personalities that would not defer to their construct of the social order; they were much more willing to analyze the unacceptable behavior of the uneducated masses from the perspective of centuries of Spanish colonial cultural training than from that of the social environment that affected them. In sum, they did not codify such behavior and such a personality within a theory of the unity of the individual—a personage indivisible, free, goal-directed, and whole.[120] What the porteño elites did not understand, however, is that the structure of personality is determined and conditioned by the individual's relations to all of his environment, including the intrinsic factors related to physical stimuli or handicaps. To understand the composition of the "plebeian personality," one had to explore the meaning and the understanding that the plebeian individual gave to his relations. This the elites were not ready to do. Indeed, as the century wore on, political leaders became more intolerant of the lower classes and began to define illegal and immoral action more broadly, thereby circumscribing acceptable behavior more narrowly for the poor.

Social psychologists of the turn of the century, like José María Ramos Mejía, began to understand the relationship between the youth's environment and his social and moral formation.[121] But even these more perceptive students of Argentine society were limited by their own judgmental biases against the lower classes, and they did not share fully the views of Alfred Adler, one of the most prominent social psychologists of the time. In the Adlerian view, individuals were healthy to the extent that they internalized their participation in the integral whole we call society. Normal behavior is thus based on social acceptance of rules and conventions, and it is controlled by an implicit understanding of Kant's moral law, which asserts that an individual must act so that the principles of his activities can be made the fundamentals of a general code of law. Men and women who fail to understand this principle, Adler felt, become excessive individualists, circumventing convention and acting with their own "private logics." Unfortunately for the concept and execution of individualism in Argentina, as the nineteenth century wore on, and as its tortuous routes wore down the early manifestations of liberalism, the boundaries of accepted behavior were narrowed. The room allowed to achieve individual fulfillment was restricted more and more by a state increasingly intolerant of untoward and unwholesome behavior. This was unthinkable: that plebeians' behavior could not help being what it was, owing to the nature of their participation in the economy and the untoward distribution of privileges accorded to them and their young.

An example of the degree to which the new educational curriculum tried to depersonify political authority comes from the most widely used book of Argentine history in elementary and secondary schools in Buenos Aires during the 1860's and 1870's, Luis L. Domínguez's *Historia argentina*.[122] The book contained nearly 400 pages on the history of Latin America, beginning with Columbus' voyages and, in a significant avoidance of political polemics, ending with the defeat of the British invaders in 1807. In sum, despite its title, the formal initiation of youngsters into their nation's past was carried out with a literature that culminated before the actual formation of the independent country, leaving much of the republican history's facts and interpretation up to individual teachers. Domínguez's history reflected the linear version, popular at the time, of the development of peoples: "Everything is logical in the life of every nation . . . the invisible chain links one cause with another culminating with the final consequences."[123]

In the prologue to the first edition, published in 1861, Domínguez summarized the perspective held by generations of regional and national leaders on the fundamental nature of the Argentine problem: "[With the Reconquest] begins the era of the Revolution. The Argentine Nation thrusts itself in uncharted directions . . . but always firm in the task of resolving the great problem of creating *order within freedom*."[124] Independence was itself the result of the discord generated at the time of the reconquest, which tended to dissolve the bonds that had previously existed among the governing elites.[125]

Furthermore, as an element of instruction, Domínguez's work retained the traditional characteristics of the period's hagiologies and school texts: great attention to minute details, many dates, birthplaces and life experiences of the principals of history, and general tediousness. The text was thus perfectly suited to the evaluation of students on the prevailing index of excellence, which was memorization. It was not until the 1880's that Argentine history would be rewritten with an overtly liberal and anti-Rosas content; the first educational reformers led by Sarmiento avoided any quick revisionism by avoiding the national period altogether, thereby bringing to the students' consciousness only the abstractions associated with the nation, not its leading personalities.

Along with new curricular texts, the Generation of '37 also brought philosophical and attitudinal changes on the subjects of childhood and the cognitive capabilities of children. Marcos Sastre was one of the early reformers of nineteenth-century thinking on childhood. Born in Uruguay, he served as educational administrator under Justo José de Urquiza in the province of Entre Ríos in 1850. His reforms were applauded by exiled opponents of Rosas, including Sarmiento, who, with characteristic directness, characterized Entre Ríos' schools as second to none in South America.[126] Sastre proposed that, in order to mold the future adult citizen, teachers must work with—and not against—the natural inclinations of children, their sense of fair play, justice, and morality. Flaws in children's characters might exist, but they must be corrected with great prudence and patience. Thus, Sastre would not tolerate corporal punishment, which had continued despite its legal prohibition. In the regulations he drafted governing the schools of Entre Ríos, he also abolished practices that tended to create a misplaced sense of pride among students, such as public awards of frivolous prizes, including medals and honorific titles. Instead, the new regulations called for awards of books, stamps, and other objects appropriate for the instruction of children, rather than the previous awards, which "fomented presumptuousness and pride."[127]

Sastre also expressed the beginnings of the concept of teachers as professionals. His regulations called for teaching appointments to be awarded on the basis of examinations and competition; furthermore, teaching was to be a full-time occupation, and any activity that was not related to the education of the children was to remain outside the school.[128] Finally, Sastre admitted the notion of a flexible curriculum to accommodate the social and environmental realities of the different communities of children; thus, the curricula of schools in the countryside would contain less emphasis of arithmetic beyond the basics and would devote more time to matters of practical value in the rural setting.

Marcos Sastre figured among the precursors of educational reform; these men, who also included Esteban Echeverría, analyzed the political flaws of the Argentine nation as the result of educational weaknesses.[129] Substantive changes began with Sarmiento's appointment as chief of the department of schools of the State of Buenos Aires in 1856. Sarmiento began the practice of instituting textbooks suitable for children in the educational processes involving reading and writing. Sarmiento's contributions to Argentine education earned him a prominent place in the histories of the reforms undertaken by the Generation of '37. In fact, however, his main contribution consisted of his willingness to bring specialists and new personnel to the task of curricular design and pedagogical execution. The most important of these reformists was Juana Paula Manso, who returned from exile in 1853 to become the most influential pedagogue among Sarmiento's collaborators.

Manso's efforts raised considerable resistance, and she was ultimately forced to resign her position as headmistress of an experimental school in 1865. Among her most progressive—and, to conservatives, more alienating—reforms were coeducational instruction and teaching on the basis of following young children's natural instincts. This philosophy of education expressed the return of Rousseauist principles that accompanied the fall of Rosas' Catholic conservatism. Manso, a devoted follower of the educational ideas of Johann Pestalozzi and Friedrich Froebel, followed their belief that children learn best when motivated by impulse and emotion in an environment conducive to learning and "self-activity." The affront to traditional thinking on childhood, to the accepted process of learning, and to political subservience was very clear to conservatives: since children were now recognized to have minds and cognitive abilities at virtually all stages of their development, teaching was transformed from breaking infantile habits and will to working in concert with the child's mind.

Free will, however childishly expressed, subverted the centralizing and authoritarian traditions of the past. Manso's opponents sensed that whatever else could be said on behalf of the progressive educationists, they were planting the seeds of a potentially dangerous revolution with social and political consequences that could jeopardize the political solidity of the old custodial elites; would the generations that would grow to adulthood under such a subversive system continue to defer to traditional lines of authority? Manso's advocacy of Froebelian ideas thus represented a particular danger to established values on the subject of children. Froebel, who had died only the year before Manso's return to Buenos Aires, considered play to be a fundamental employment for children, from which he derived the concept of kindergarten. The kindergarten's major role was to allow the young child to learn his place in a wider world of social relationships and related duties. In this small society where social skills were to be learned, instinct could be gratified, but in equilibrium with self-preservation. The goal of socialization had two parts: "On the one side," wrote Marvin Lazerson, "stood the emancipation of the child from traditional and insensitive restrictions, the enhancement of spontaneity and creativity. On the other, emphasis was given to uniformity and control."[130]

Clearly, Manso represented a generalized movement of educational reform that was reflected in other areas of the West. For example, the most respected promoter of ideas related to early childhood education in late nineteenth-century Massachusetts was Elizabeth Palmer Peabody, who also followed Froebelian principles. Peabody and her reformist colleagues introduced play objects and frolic to the learning environment: "Of the two evils," she wrote, "extreme indulgence is not so deadly a mistake as extreme severity."[131] Manso shared these beliefs and introduced the methods of play, in accordance with Froebelian prescriptions. But to sectors of a porteño culture that had long considered children for their practical value both politically and economically, the idea of apparent pedagogical "uselessness" or experimentation was difficult to accept. By contrast, the general tendency of the era among both the wealthy and the poor families was to define early on the occupation that their young boys would pursue. Children of both the rich and the poor tended to follow their fathers' occupation, whether a profession or menial labor. This pattern of settling early into an occupational pattern, argued Joseph Kett, was in part responsible for a lower toleration of flexibility and experimentation in the early years in nineteenth-century America in general. Adolescence, however, was prolonged under circumstances that postponed choice and allowed a certain amount of stumbling and false starts.[132] In the end, Manso's prescriptions did not take hold after the years of her activity. What remained of the Sarmiento and Manso era were superstructural and organizational reforms, but substantive matters—always the thorniest for politics to incorporate—were much slower to sink roots.

By the end of the 1860's, the city of Buenos Aires contained nearly 230 public and private schools, many more than ever before, although they still served less than one quarter of the school-age population. The educational system was composed of schools with five different administrative structures: there were municipal schools, provincial schools, educational institutions supported entirely with public funds but administered autonomously by the Sociedad de Beneficencia, private schools that received government subsidies, and private schools with only tuition-paying students and no public support.[133]

Despite the significant increase in the number of schools, the internal weaknesses of the public educational system still showed; indeed, they would not be eradicated until many years after the enactment of the compulsory education law in 1884. Public schools continued to be deficient in instructional tools, books, and appropriate surroundings; moreover, the racial and socioeconomic position of the vecinos continued to determine the quality of teachers, school libraries, and the physical environment of the barrios' schools. Although the absolute numbers of students had increased, serious deficiencies in attendance remained, a problematic legacy of previous decades. The reluctance of middle- and lower-class parents to send their children to school after the youngsters had reached a certain age suggests a continued competition between the schools and the families of modest and low means in determining the proper activities of children.

To judge by the attendance figures, there continued to exist a natural antagonism between the economic function of the child as part of the household economy and the state's definitions of childhood within general society. Here the evidence comes from the age and sexual characteristics of the enrollment and attendance data. Public coeducational schools almost always had much lower enrollments of boys. Furthermore, the attrition rate was dramatic among boys 10 years of age and older; indeed, it was not unusual for public schools to have only girls between the ages of 10 and 15. To be sure, by 1872 the city provided 15 public schools for boys only, which enrolled a total of 1,676 youngsters, but even these schools saw a significant decline in enrollments after the age of 9. In only four of the 15 all-boys public schools did the number of 10- to 15-year-olds equal or surpass the number of 5- to 9-year-olds. The attrition rate among boys above the age of 10 averaged over 50 percent in both the 11 remaining all-boys schools and in all of the 35 coeducational public institutions. Clearly, the humble porteño family that had internalized the value of education for its children had, on the average, done so on the basis of minimum functionality: once the boy had learned basic reading and writing, plus the rudiments of arithmetic, he was removed from school and made to help in providing for the family's sustenance.

But poor families were not alone in associating schooling for children of the poor with its practical functions. In its own way, the educational authorities also shared this philosophy, to judge by the gross disparity in the educational curricula and environments for black children and their white counterparts. Among the 12 all-girls schools operated by the Sociedad de Beneficencia was the Escuela del Rosario, located on Venezuela Street in the parish of Monserrat, part of cuartel 19, and classified at the time as a school of *clase de color*. Only four subjects were taught at the Escuela del Rosario: reading, writing, arithmetic, and domestic skills (*labores de mano*). The school was totally lacking in maps, illustrations of plant and animal life, three-dimensional geometric figures, blackboards, and books. The two teachers planned their lessons without the aid of any textbooks, which meant that students received the lessons and attendant drill only to the extent that the teachers were willing to create them.

The contrast with another of the schools run by the Sociedad de Beneficencia, also located in the parish of Monserrat but attended by white girls, was dramatic. This was the Escuela de la Parroquia de Monserrat, located on Lorea 149, where the girls learned—in addition to reading, writing, arithmetic, and the predictable *labores de mano*—geography, history, Spanish literature, French, singing, and the playing of musical instruments. The school also had several flat maps and globes, three-dimensional shapes for learning geometry, two blackboards along the walls, and a library containing 150 volumes. The dual philosophies of the educational authorities, each applicable to either the rich or the poor, had not changed much in the course of the nineteenth century. The words of educators to students 40 years earlier had retained their essential truth: for the rich, knowledge was meant to enlighten, while for the poor, it would facilitate livelihood. Another case of privileged education beyond the reach of the poor and the nonwhite was Juana Manso's Escuela Graduada No. 1, a public girls' school with a pupil-to-teacher ratio of 12 to 1 at a time when ratios of 60 to 1 were not unusual. In addition, the school also served as a training ground for young women studying to become teachers. Manso's students received the latest style of education, complemented by a full range of didactic tools and illustrative materials, including a library of nearly 200 books.

Despite the shortcomings of Buenos Aires' educational system after more than 50 years of republican rule, however, certain constructive changes had in fact taken place, and the basis for others was being laid. A professional approach to teaching had been established, complete with a training facility, the Normal School, which was the precursor of the higher-level training institution, the Profesorado de Buenos Aires. If some schools lacked textbooks or other instruments and educational materials, at least the principle that they were necessary was accepted and would eventually achieve fuller implementation during subsequent decades. And, in the end, the state won over the recalcitrant parents by establishing the principle of compulsory education, although here again, its full execution lagged for some years.

At the same time, certain characteristics of the society of old were retained, including its clientelist and patrimonial aspects. The schedule of the school day still required much of the students' time: for example, youngsters of the 1860's were attending classes Monday through Saturday, from early in the morning to shortly before sunset, with a noontime break. The growing bureaucratization of the educational system did not eliminate the continued reliance on structures that were established at the barrio level and that were designed for the promotion and execution of municipal policy. Thus, peer pressure among vecinos served its traditional purposes in matters of public education in the late 1850's much as before: "By way of the Parish Educational Commissions, [the Municipality] expresses its greatest desires for parents to send their children to school, thereby conquering the indolence which unfortunately still exists," reported the city's educational administrators in 1857.[134] In fact, the barrios' authorities retained the right to nominate local students to be examined publicly on festive days commemorating important events in the nation's history, typically May 25 and July 9, when the city celebrated the *fiestas patrias*.[135] Additional continuities can be seen in the clientelist style of elite members whose positions in political society made it possible for them to profit from renting their urban properties to the Department of Education, which seldom if ever owned any real estate. The list of owners of the properties that schools rented included some of the more prominent figures of the city's gente decente.

In the end, the elites who would steer the educational system through the course of the economic boom and mass immigration that began after 1870 would accumulate and centralize authority more efficiently than ever before. They would eliminate the considerable latitude that the barrios had retained through the revolution, the early liberal period of the 1820's, the Rosas years, and the tutelage of the Generation of '37. Writing in 1891 to the minister of education, Ernesto Quesada proudly asserted that "secondary education among us is meant fundamentally to prepare youngsters for the liberal professions, and to form the general culture of the minority of people who take advantage of it."[136] Juan P. Ramos, the federal government's inspector general of schools in 1910, gave the reasons for the concentration of educational administration in the state's hands. In his view of the educational regimen that had existed until 1870, the old political elites had been mistaken in their belief that schools could be managed by an administrative system that combined official and popular representation:

In theory, the people longed for education. But, in practice, did they truly want it? The two highest groups, the politicians and the enlightened classes, acted on the theory's universal truth, when, in fact, they were simply acting on the basis of their own values, all the time believing that they were accurately observing the people. They therefore believed in the existence of a sufficiently high level of *social capability* throughout the land. All that they theorized, however, failed completely to materialize. And this could not have been otherwise. At the risk of uttering banalities, it is important to repeat it: culture is not spread except as a function of a long and progressive process of adaptation.[137]

Thus, an even more fundamental level of patrimonialism not only survived, but also went on to become codified in governmental practice: the educational principles that would eventually become acceptable in Buenos Aires and the rest of Argentina continued to be driven by cultural and socioeconomic prejudices. Universal education would thus mirror society: the quality of educational opportunity would reflect the socioeconomic position of the student. Therefore, as late as 1914, the graduates of elementary and secondary schools who became the typical students at the University of Buenos Aires represented virtually the same social and economic strata as had their predecessors from the Generation of '37, all the way back to the youngsters who had felt the spark of Belgrano's popular but all-too-optimistic republicanism.[138]

6

The Political Dimensions
of Household Changes

This chapter analyzes the fluctuations in the structure and composition of households in the city of Buenos Aires. The analysis concentrates on the changing relationships among family members and on the role played by the state in creating those changes. The materials related to household size and structure are based on detailed analyses of the homes in which approximately 36,000 porteños lived, and on the archival documentation that detailed their personal situations insofar as they had a bearing on their domestic constitution.

The principal sources for the quantitative data are the three pre-national manuscript census returns from the years 1810, 1827, and 1855. These census tracts represent an ample and detailed cross-section of urban Buenos Aires society. The fluctuations in household structures over the course of time provides evidence to support a theory that includes a demographic dimension to explain caudillo rule in Argentina. The research paradigm employed in this chapter is based on the propositions that Argentine political instability was reflected in the home; that thousands of families were sucked into a maelstrom not of their own making; and that public purpose also had its expression among the anonymous plebeians. Beyond this, the proposed thesis on the relationship between strongman leadership and popular following is based on interpretations that employ classic sociological theory. Finally, the conclusions address the nature of early nineteenth-century political culture and should afford opportunities for fresh explanations of the period's *caudillismo*. The data are thus presented with the hope of broadening the plane of discussion about political leadership during the early stages of nation building in Spanish America.[1]

The Political Context

The period of Argentine history that underlies this analysis was punctuated by dramatic political cycles. The Revolution of 1810 heralded a decade of war waged against both external enemies and internal oppositionists: in the Platine area, the war for independence from Spanish domination and the struggles for political hegemony among Argentines blended into massive, enervating movements. The republican porteños' formula for political leadership met at the earliest stages with strong resistance from various sectors in the important regions of Córdoba, Santa Fe, and elsewhere. In the ensuing military confrontations, men were uprooted from their native environments to fight for causes they only vaguely understood; of his own men, Rosas commented in 1820 that "the majority . . . are not so immediately conscious of the imminence of the risks or of the need for sacrifices."[2] The enlightened formulations of Locke and Rousseau, espoused by liberals like Manuel Belgrano and Mariano Moreno, sharply conflicted with the patrimonial traditionalists who did not equate the political independence of the state with the diffusion of power among its citizens.[3] At the outset, the utopian liberalism shared by Bernardino Rivadavia, Bernardo Monteagudo, and the youthful Moreno was at odds with what José Ingenieros called the "inherited forces [*fuerzas de herencia*] which constituted the traditions that consolidated the past."[4]

Differences in political philosophies were compounded by conflicts of material interest. Animosities spread among regions and, consequently, among the participants who derived their incomes from the activities afforded them by the regional economies. Thus, elites who depended on the silver output of Alto Perú, with its wide network of affiliated production, service, and plebeian—mostly Indian—servitude, reasonably feared the expansion of a coastal economy founded on pastoral goods, owned by pampean interests, and manipulated by Anglophile creole merchants of Buenos Aires.[5] In their apprehension over their economic future, elites from the interior had calculated the historically disproportionate allocations of silver revenues to the Buenos Aires bureaucracies. Within the viceroyalty of the Río de la Plata, the intendancy of Buenos Aires had been consuming almost 90 percent of the revenues from Potosí's silver mines in order to support its political, military, and ecclesiastical administrations.[6] In the meantime, the fundamental issue to be settled by any emerging nation-state—the formulation of processes of governance and mechanisms for the allocation of power and resources—would not be resolved until the second half of the nineteenth century. Thus, in the absence of consensus on matters related to the political order, the decade of 1810–20 was characterized by war. Offensives, counteroffensives, mobilizations—sometimes of entire populations—blockades, desertions, and all the other consequences of war took their toll on the lives and finances of the people of Buenos Aires.[7] By mid-decade, the aspirations of the first utopian liberals had foundered on the reality of discord and bloodshed and were replaced by a hard-bitten, virtually aristocratic conservatism intent on retaining power over the recalcitrant peoples of the interior.[8]

In the end, however, porteño elites, forced to accept the dissolution of the former viceroyalty of the Río de la Plata and the end of their pretensions to national leadership, resigned themselves to ruling over the reduced space of the city and province of Buenos Aires. Through most of the 1820's, the city was governed by economic liberals, anticlericals, and socially conservative men who had experienced the costs of a generalized war. They were intent on maintaining order, even though they were themselves in part responsible for making order precarious by failing to establish formal and lasting bonds among the various rulers of the different Argentine regions. Stability was also challenged from without Buenos Aires province by the Brazilian threat in neighboring Uruguay, which resulted in yet more war between 1825 and 1828, and from within by the federalists, who opposed the centralist bent of the porteño elites.

Toward the end of the 1820's, centralist liberalism had become enervated and fallen at the hands of conservative federalism. The federalist domination that began at the start of 1829 ushered in an era of tenuous political continuity, characterized by the caudillo Juan Manuel de Rosas, who insisted on stability at the cost of the nominal liberties promised by the revolutionaries of 1810 and restricted by the liberals of the 1820's.[9] The process of redemption of conservative Iberian and Catholic values during the Rosas era, although tailored

to the contemporary needs of the conservative order, would spend
itself by midcentury. The military defeat of Rosas in 1852 signaled
the entrance of a new generation of liberals. Their unwholesome
experiences in Argentina and their European intellectual foundations moved these liberals, known collectively as the "Generation of
'37," to a cosmopolitanism in the art of government, and to exper-
ientially motivated political formulations not seen earlier. Beyond
this, they also put into political practice their inherent distrust of the
masses, on whom they placed responsibility for Rosas' success and
durability. By 1860, leading members of the Generation of '37, positioned in key political offices, had begun to give legal form and
substance to the organization of government in its various functions.
That this process of codification and institutionalization of governmental procedures entailed neither democratization of political
power-holding nor popular electoral politics indicated the continued
concern elites had for the maintenance of order: their collective
memory of seemingly immanent war was a motivating feature of
their governments. But in this they were reconstituting previous generations of politicians all the way back to those men in the early
1810's who had also sensed the illogic of their expectations for early
consensus and social peace. Against this backdrop of turmoil, the
population of the city of Buenos Aires underwent significant
changes. In the process, the porteño family was made to face powerful forces and adopt strategies for survival in order to maintain its
cohesion.

General Characteristics of the Population

The dramatic growth of late eighteenth-century Buenos Aires
was one of the major consequences of the Bourbon reforms applied
to the region of the Río de la Plata. With the legalization of trade
at the port and with the designation of the city as viceregal capital
in 1776, Buenos Aires became the recipient of a considerable number
of migrants from both Europe and the interior. They swelled the
ranks of the population, which increased by almost 70 percent between 1778 and 1810; from little more than a village of 25,000 souls
in 1778, the city had grown by 1810 to a humble but respectable lo-
cality that was home to over 40,000 people. Yet seventeen years later
the population had increased by only 5 percent more, to fewer than

TABLE 12

Population of Selected Wards, Selective Universe, 1810–1860

(N = 28,579)

	1810		1827		1855	
Cuartel	No.	Pct.	No.	Pct.	No.	Pct.
3	838	14.8%	2,779	27.4%	3,373	26.4%
4	1,709	30.2	1,602	15.8	2,283	17.9
12	1,508	26.6	3,471	34.2	3,485	27.3
19	1,609	28.4	2,291	22.6	3,631	28.4
TOTAL	5,664	100.0%	10,143	100.0%	12,772	100.0%

43,000. Almost one generation had passed with no appreciable growth. By about midcentury, the population had expanded again, by 112 percent, to comprise over 90,000 people. This growth preceded the mass immigration from Europe, which did not begin until the 1870's. The fundamental difference between the two periods was that the era of demographic stagnation was characterized by enervating war; the later spurt in the population, by contrast, took place in an environment of relatively few and only sporadic military confrontations.

Porteños of the period tended to consider their domestic groups to be located in a neighborly space, the barrio and the cuartel, as the sample data show. The composition of these neighborhoods was not static, as considerable changes occurred in the proportions of the populations of certain of the cuarteles, especially cuarteles 12 and 19, between 1827 and 1855. The virtually complete data set of cuarteles 4 and 19 between 1810 and 1827 can be seen in Table 12.

One general conclusion is that by midcentury the mostly black and mulatto cuartel 19 had become home to a larger proportion of porteños than before. At the same time, cuartel 12 lost its leading position of 1827 to become the second most populous cuartel in 1855. The city appears to have grown overall, but the increases varied considerably among barrios. Migrants from Europe and the interior swelled the population and increased the pressure on the already relatively crowded zones in the city's southern half and close to the coast. Immigration from Europe ebbed and flowed in response to political and economic cycles. Internal migration, however, appears to have been continuous and, especially in the late 1840's, on the rise.[10]

Heads of Households

Important determinants of a population's demographic growth lie in the characteristics of its married cohort. In the group that constitutes the selective universe, the negative effects of the campaigns of the revolutionary era (1810–20) and, soon afterward, of the war with Brazil over Uruguay (1825–28) are best illustrated by the observed significant increase in the percentages of widowed women, from 10.4 percent in 1810 to 14.8 percent in 1827. In fact, the mortality rate for men—evident in the declining ratios of males to females—is one of the most salient features of the evolution of early nineteenth-century porteño society. There are no documentation flaws that might have skewed the data enough to cause this sexual imbalance. The best estimates for mortality indices during this era come from 1822; they are 30.18 for whites and 59.96 for freedmen.[11] One can only speculate about what share of these figures represents the consequences of war, but the indications from the sex ratio data point strongly in the direction of the military events that took place during the most unstable and militarized period of 1810 to 1830. This is suggested by the following sex ratios:[12]

Year	City	Selective universe	City sample
1810	1.08	1.18	0.95
1827	0.76	0.92	0.82
1855	0.95	0.88	0.85

From all three sources, we find the same general tendency, a precipitous decline in male-female ratios between 1810 and 1827. By contrast, the sex ratios in 1855 point in the direction of either recovery or attenuation of the previous decline, depending on the social group. Thus, each of the population's subgroups registered a very different rate of decline, particularly during the first intercensal period: the city as a whole witnessed a drop of 30 percent in its masculinity index, compared to a 22 percent drop for the selected cuarteles, and only a 14 percent decline for those who belonged to family groupings. What accounts for the differences?

Socioeconomic position and race were the primary variables that determined the extent of damage to the coherence of the porteño household, as well as—by way of military conscription and service in troubled times—the life expectancy of men. An indication of this selective mortality process is the fact that both cuartel 12, which contained a large number of lower-class laborers and agriculturalists, and cuartel 19, the most African and Afro-Argentine of all, reported the lowest sex ratios:

Year	Cuartel (N = 28,579 population)			
	3	4	12	19
1810	1.39	1.50	1.10	0.89
1827	0.98	1.80	0.79	0.69
1855	1.07	1.09	0.78	0.73

The smallest drop in sex ratios was reported among members of complete family units; the largest change was registered by single men, servants, live-in apprentices, and other young men not married or not residing with their spouses and children. Many, and probably most, of the latter were men of the lower classes, including the nonwhites. It is an indication that race was an important causal variable in delimiting the life chances of porteño men. The overwhelming majority of the whites in the city sample belonged to family units; by contrast, greater numbers of people of color were listed as solitaries or as lodgers. These findings are borne out by the results of a sample of 1810 and 1827 populations drawn by Reid Andrews. In 1810, almost 83 percent of the sampled black population lived in households headed by whites; the figure dropped to approximately 74 percent by 1827.[13] Thus, whether freedmen or slaves, family units of nonwhites were usually situated in a white household. They were not related to the heads of the households but figured as appendages, dependent to some extent on a white man or woman who was the head. The relatively small decline of 14 percent in masculinity levels for members of families—as distinguished from households—reflected the historical realities that generally sheltered whites from the most extreme ravages of poor sanitary conditions and from military conscription. The policy of military conscription, as it related to marital status, was applied in the city with the same criteria as in the countryside, where single men outnumbered married men in military roles that involved dangerous service. For their part, married men tended to serve, if at all, in inactive regiments.[14] The statistical evidence points to artificial, rather than natural, sources of mortality for young men, such as military service fighting political enemies and Indians; no natural phenomena of the period can account for the consistently lowest rate of masculinity in the age groups 15–19 and 20–24 in the population shown in Table 13.

The brutalization of political relations and the militarization of male society must be taken into account to help explain the slowly draining pool of young men in Buenos Aires; within this generalized demographic disaster, the lower-status groups—the gente de pueblo and the *gente de color*—bore the brunt of the losses. The nonwhite population was drafted into military service in numbers far above its proportion in the city's general population: "Given the province's never-ending quest for men to fuel its war machine," summarizes Andrews, "military service was an experience that virtually every black man who reached adulthood in nineteenth-century Buenos Aires could count on having."[15] Forced military service threatened much of the province of Buenos Aires; to the north in Pergamino, the scarcity of laborers in 1827 resulted from the *leva*. The following year, Manuel Dorrego, the governor, condemned the military draft as a humiliating device of government.[16] This human tragedy, in turn, bore consequences for family and household structures that affected the majority of porteños.

The degree to which concern for the plight of families who lost members in battle became generalized in the consciousness of contemporaries can be inferred from the periodic auctions and raffles held in the city's plazas and other public meeting places for the specific purpose of relieving the burdens of widows and orphans.[17] The practice of making public awards to widows began as early as 1807 in response to the loss of life during the English invasions in the Río de la Plata. The *cabildo* authorities began this practice, but in their allotment of funds they displayed an unfortunate racial bias by donating to white widows and orphans twice the sums given to free families of color.[18] Slaves whose wounds left them invalids were awarded a small monthly pension and their freedom. The names of slave men who had participated in repelling the English and who had not been wounded were entered in a pool along with those of slave women who could prove that their husbands had lost their lives in those engagements. The names of 30 individuals would be drawn and given their freedom. Private donations increased the final number of awards of freedom. In the end, of the 686 slaves who entered this raffle, only 70 were manumitted.[19] During similar procedures a generation later, Rosas' officials turned national celebrations into oc-

TABLE 13
Age Distribution of Selective Universe, by Sex, 1810, 1827, and 1855

(N = 28,579)

Age group	1810		1827		1855	
	No.	Pct.	No.	Pct.	No.	Pct.
0–4						
Male	322	51.9%	419	46.1%	669	49.4%
Female	299	48.1	489	53.9	686	50.6
5–9						
Male	255	51.6	519	49.2	602	48.4
Female	239	48.4	535	50.8	641	51.6
10–14						
Male	367	55.9	596	52.4	579	46.7
Female	289	44.1	542	47.6	661	53.3
15–19						
Male	296	45.5	391	37.5	495	35.9
Female	355	54.5	653	62.5	884	64.1
20–24						
Male	383	53.8	415	39.4	579	41.5
Female	328	46.2	637	60.6	815	58.5
25–29						
Male	351	54.3	448	42.4	631	46.9
Female	295	45.7	609	57.6	714	53.1
30–34						
Male	313	58.5	524	48.7	618	49.7
Female	222	41.5	552	51.3	625	50.3
35–39						
Male	171	64.0	305	54.1	516	54.6
Female	96	36.0	259	45.9	429	45.6
40–44						
Male	180	51.7	400	52.2	396	50.4
Female	168	48.3	367	47.8	390	49.6
45–49						
Male	94	58.0	212	60.9	245	49.6
Female	68	42.0	136	39.1	249	50.4
50–54						
Male	140	53.8	258	54.3	232	50.3
Female	120	46.2	217	45.7	229	49.7
55–59						
Male	54	71.1	78	56.1	137	50.2
Female	22	28.9	61	43.9	136	49.8
60–64						
Male	74	54.0	177	58.4	123	44.6
Female	63	46.0	126	41.4	153	55.4
65–69						
Male	8	61.5	44	73.3	54	46.2
Female	5	38.5	16	26.7	63	53.8
70 +						
Male	54	61.4	87	55.1	109	49.3
Female	34	38.6	71	44.9	112	50.7
TOTAL						
Male	3,061	54.0%	4,873	48.0%	5,985	46.9%
Female	2,603	46.0	5,270	52.0	6,787	53.1

casions for providing charity in order to "alleviate part of the misery and destitution of the families who have lost their fathers in war." At the Plaza de Mayo in 1830, awards totaling 500 pesos were raffled off to twelve widows in a public ceremony "with all the formalities" to celebrate Argentine Independence Day.[20] These official awards, which were eventually phased out by Rosas, were usually meager compared to needs. Neither official proceeds from the government's pension funds for widows nor the ad hoc affairs of charity sufficed: "The only thing my husband left was his military pension," pleaded a needy porteña in 1823. "What will I do under these circumstances . . . hand over my children's hopes to a usurer?"[21]

That fundamental event in the life-cycle, marriage, took place among porteños at considerably different ages. The principal objective factors that conditioned age at marriage included race, socioeconomic position, and ethnicity. Of course, subjective elements also governed the timing of marriage, functions of the emotions of family politics and the resolution of conflicts generated over the choices of partners and even among partners; this was especially true of the gente decente, the social layer composed of those who had the most at stake in their children's choice of marriage partners, including their status among peers in what was still a face-to-face society.

Census data do not provide the ages of spouses at the time of their marriages; we have instead the ages and the familial relationships among the members of households at the moment when each census was taken. From these and other data further information can be gleaned about spouses and their domestic environments. The first trend shown by the data yielded by both the selective universe and the city sample is that age differences between spouses tended to narrow over time. As the nineteenth century progressed, the women of Buenos Aires married men much closer to their own ages. The following figures reflect this decrease in the age difference between marriage partners (partners aged 15 and older; N = number of heads of household):

Year	Selective universe (N = 2,523)	City sample (N = 674)
1810	11.4	9.1
1827	9.6	10.6
1855	7.5	7.6

The data indicate a decline in the incidence of unions contracted by men older than their brides by ten years or more over the period of 1810–55, and in turn reflect the significant decline in the average age at which men married. The proportion of men within the selective universe who were married to women of the same age or younger by less than nine years increased from 38.4 percent in 1810 to 51.4 percent in 1855. In the city sample, this proportion increased from 39.9 percent in 1810 to 47.4 percent in 1855. Yet within these averages, remarkably great differences appeared between creoles and peninsulars. The latter tended to be older than their wives by up to 29 years in 1810 and in 1827, while creole men tended to marry women much closer to their own age. This considerable difference between the two ethnic groups reflected the economic situation that characterized so many of the Spanish men who took up residence in Buenos Aires. Usually, they had come as mercantile agents on behalf of family and kin who owned important commercial houses in Spain. Despite their connections to financially powerful men across the Atlantic, however, these young peninsulars at first experienced the very frugal life that their meager advances determined.

Don Lorenzo de Arco's finances typified the initial constraints that these young Spaniards in Buenos Aires had to overcome. He had been sent by his father in 1777 carrying the following letter of introduction:

My son, a Regimental Captain. . . , is the last of three left to me by his deceased mother. This Captain, as is the case with almost all military men, wastes his savings on vices, women, etc. He has a childless wife, whose retinue I help to maintain. I have already spent much money on him for clothes, etc., for his trip; these should suffice him for another half-dozen years. He can keep all the salary he earns, and I want no one to lend him a thing. I purposely have not given him a letter of introduction [to seek favors]. I am alerting you to these matters lest you mistakenly think that the money on him is mine; should he ask you for a loan, you should refuse him. He has a penchant for borrowing and never paying back, . . . and I will not honor his debts.[22]

On the average, Spaniards like Lorenzo de Arco who came to the viceroyalty of the Río de la Plata would not become financially secure enough to establish their own households until after spending at least ten years in Buenos Aires.[23]

This is not to suggest that creole merchants necessarily had an easier time than Spaniards in starting out in business: transatlantic mercantile activities were a precarious experiment in making a living for anyone. Still, the amount of support given to Lorenzo de Arco by his Spanish father contrasts sharply with the aid given by Don Fernando Maseyra by his porteño father-in-law. Maseyra had accumulated several unpaid debts, as had his contemporary de Arco; in fact, Maseyra had been placed in Buenos Aires' debtors' prison in 1754. The letter of appeal sent by his father-in-law to the authorities was a model of familial solidarity not likely to have occurred in de Arco's family, given his father's observed stringency. Maseyra, according to the letter, had been the victim of greedy speculators, "who insist that [Fernando] has assets hidden away only on the basis of their own malicious assertions, and yet they have failed to prove this Godless and slanderous accusation over the course of the nine months he has spent in prison."[24] Unlike his peninsular counterparts, Fernando Maseyra had not deferred marriage; on the contrary, his financial difficulties had not deterred him from marrying and having a child.

By the mid-nineteenth century, however, Spaniards and natives were no longer displaying major differences in the timing of their marriages. Spaniards, however, tended to marry older women much more often than did creoles, a behavior that may be explained in two ways. First, widows in Buenos Aires found the same difficulties as widows in other parts of the world in exercising complete freedom of choice in marriage; thus, the data probably illustrate the cases of widows who had to settle for marrying younger Spanish merchants who, although objectively not of their peer groups, did show promise of climbing the economic ladder.[25] For their part, the Spanish *comerciantes* who entered into these relationships surely considered the strategic advantages to their local trade that could result from settling into family life in Buenos Aires' small, tightly knit merchant community.

The second explanation is related to the concept of continually reinforcing solidarities, an idea most clearly expressed by Latin America's upper sectors. Diana Balmori and Robert Oppenheimer have demonstrated the vitality of marriage as one of the fundamental techniques of bonding members of upper society in South America. Among nineteenth-century Chilean and Argentine elites, second-generation marriages tended to fuse different wings of the families' networks. If one of the spouses died, "the survivor usually married a brother or sister of the deceased."[26] The unions between younger Spaniards and older creole widows manifested such elite calculations in that they were examples of remarried members of the deceased husbands' families.

Such strategies underscore the value of considering the Buenos Aires experience within the general patterns found elsewhere in Latin America, and indeed in the West: local and regional variations represented differences in the historical timing of Western phenomena, and not oddities of a non-Western culture. Behavioral similarities to other Western regions are especially evident in cross-cultural comparisons of elites. For example, the patterns of marriage selection and fertility among Argentine and Chilean aristocracies of the 1800's were similar to those of their English counterparts during the late sixteenth and seventeenth centuries.[27] Such similarities in familial organization indicate that urban littoral society, far from reflecting a static cultural heritage, responded dynamically to objective and conjunctional forces. Indeed, attitudinal changes toward family formation and the composition of households took root in Buenos Aires early in the nineteenth century, as they would elsewhere in Latin America during the twentieth.[28]

Household Size: The Composition of Heads of Households

Family size and composition figure among the many considerations forming the tenets that modernization theory applies to family strategies. According to the modernization-theory perspective, married couples in traditional families do not observe the rule of joint decision making on the subject of procreation, nor is that subject treated in "rational" fashion; moreover, traditional families retain complex, nonnuclear structures, and their members are heavily influenced by the presence and authority of resident kin.[29] The process of modernization also includes the demographic transition, the sharp reductions in both death rates and birth rates from the levels registered prior to modern behaviors.[30] The following passage, written about Buenos Aires by an observer in the 1830's, summarizes much of modernization theory's sense of traditional family size and structure.

Do you see that uninterrupted line composed of 20 women, slowly walking and lazily swaying to the rhythm of their fans? . . . Well, it is just one family, and you are seeing only its feminine portion, because if the men were not to have opted for strolling on the opposite side of the street, it would be impossible to get around them. Let us count: twelve marriageable and charming daughters; the mother—still young and *good-looking*; three aunts, a bit jealous of their own nieces . . . ; one grandmother, still fresh and *high-spirited*; and, finally, three *maids*.[31]

How "traditional" or "archaic" were family size and structure in Buenos Aires? How young were its married women? What were some of the factors that affected the composition of porteño families in the first half-century of independence? Were families only reactive elements in the political struggles of the period, or did they also have their own adaptive strategies with which to confront the dangers that the era's political instability posed to their coherence?

The available data for late colonial Argentina point to historically small families and households. Here, for example, are the figures for several provinces in the rural interior:[32]

Year	Province	Extended family	Nuclear family
1786	Catamarca	4.2	3.0
1786	Córdoba	5.4	3.8
1778	Jujuy	3.9	3.6
1791	Catamarca	3.1	2.5
1792	Córdoba	6.2	3.6
1807	Catamarca	3.4	2.6

Moreover, although the extended family was indeed a feature of the region's home life, it was not usually much larger than the average nuclear family. Córdoba, the wealthiest region of the group of provinces that also included Catamarca and Jujuy, consistently registered the largest extended family size. It suggests that wealth and family size are positively correlated in the Argentine interior, a relationship that was borne out in the earlier discussion of much higher marital fertility rates among the well-to-do in the city of Buenos Aires.

Demographic changes within the families of porteños can be observed in the trends related to the ages of married women. In 1810 the group of 30- to 34-year-olds represented the single largest age group of married women, comprising 45 percent of all married women between the ages of 15 and 34. Over time, however, younger women came to represent a larger share of married females; the proportion of married 30- to 34-year-olds fell to 40 percent in 1827 and to 35 percent in 1855. This decline corresponded to slight increases in the proportions of married women in two other groups, those aged 15 to 19 and 20 to 24; of greater significance, however, was a considerable rise in the percentages of married women aged 25 to 29. In 1810, this age cohort had comprised only 25 percent of all married women, rising afterward to 30 percent in 1827, and then to 33 percent in 1855, according to the sample data. Thus, the secular tendency was for the women of Buenos Aires to marry at earlier ages over the course of the nineteenth century. The statistic that most succinctly summarizes the tendency of declining bridal age is the women's singulate mean age at first marriage: between 1810 and 1827, it decreased from 17.4 years to 17.1 years; by 1855, it had decreased to 16.9 years (figures from selective universe, N=8,854).[33]

These are very young ages at first marriage by the contemporary standards of Western Europe, where the average age at first marriage was between 23 and 25.[34] This youthfulness strongly suggests the prevalence of consensual relationships, especially among lower-class households, which comprised the majority of the population. Insofar as their financial situations often precluded the expenditure incurred in the sacrament of church marriage, these heads of households bypassed it. Moreover, had these all been church-sanctioned marriages, they would have signified an unusual difference in ecclesiastical norms between two Roman Catholic regions—Argentina and much of Western Europe—that otherwise contained many similar traditions. It is thus much more plausible to assume that wherever women appeared to marry in their mid- to late teens, there were significant numbers of consensual unions.

The extent to which the composition of each age cohort of married women was influenced by socioeconomic considerations is illustrated in Table 14. It demonstrates the proportions of married women aged 15–34 in the city sample gathered into two broad socioeconomic groups aggregated on the basis of the occupational category held by the head of the household.

The manual category consists of workers in unskilled, semi-skilled, and subsistence agricultural tasks; the nonmanual category includes occupations related to commerce, the liberal professions,

TABLE 14
Age Distribution of Married Women and Socioeconomic Status of
Household Head, City Sample, 1810, 1827, and 1855
(N = 330)

Age group	Occupation of household head			
	Manual		Nonmanual	
	No.	Pct.	No.	Pct.
1810 (N = 117)				
15–19	1	1.5%	5	9.6%
20–24	17	26.2	11	21.2
25–29	17	26.2	13	25.0
30–34	30	46.2	23	44.2
TOTAL	65	100.0%	52	100.0%
1827 (N = 99)				
15–19	6	10.9%	0	0.0%
20–24	11	20.0	12	27.3
25–29	15	27.3	15	34.1
30–34	23	41.8	17	38.6
TOTAL	55	100.0%	44	100.0%
1855 (N = 114)				
15–19	4	6.3%	4	8.0%
20–24	12	18.8	16	32.0
25–29	28	43.8	10	20.0
30–34	20	31.3	20	40.0
TOTAL	64	100.0%	50	100.0%

and proprietary landed activities.[35] Women who considered marrying men of low socioeconomic position tended to form unions at
increasingly younger ages over the course of time; much larger proportions of cohorts aged 15–19 and 25–29 were married by 1855 than
had been the case in 1810. Thus, lower socioeconomic groups were
most responsible for the decrease in the mean age at first marriage.
At the same time, the proportions of married females of lower status
aged 20–24, and especially those aged 30–34, declined. Among
women married to men holding nonmanual positions, the picture
provided by the sample data shifted less radically. By 1855, important gains were reported in the representation of the age cohort 20–
24, and small declines were evident in the proportions of the rest. In
sum, women who belonged to the city's upper social levels did not
generally participate in the tendency toward marriage at very young
ages.

Residential location was closely related to the proportions of households headed by married couples. As can be seen in Table 15, significant differences appear between the selective universe and the city sample in terms of their respective married populations. The relative share of the married heads of households in the selective universe increased from 41.5 percent in 1810 to 56.1 percent in 1855, while the proportion of single or widowed male heads of households decreased dramatically from 43.3 percent in 1810 to 27.3 percent in 1855. Considerably different results appear when the same comparison is applied to the city sample of households. Here the proportion of households headed by married men decreased from approximately 72 percent in 1810 to 63 percent at midcentury, while the share of female-headed households rose from 19 percent to more than 24 percent. The differences between the figures in the two sets of data are explained largely by the effects that the mercantile sector had on the city's commercial hub. The sharp distinctions in the early part of the century between porteños and Spaniards in terms of the age differences between them and their wives have already been noted. Because the ages of females who married merchants did not fluctuate much over the course of nearly 50 years following 1810, we may conclude that Spaniards, who formed the city's largest single group of merchants, had deferred marriage. For much the same reason, an abnormally high proportion of single males lived in the city's commercial hub, including cuarteles 3, 4, and the southeastern quadrant of 12—men who were apparently still too immersed in the formative stages of their commercial careers to enter married life.

Although the citywide figures provided by Table 14 are more representative of Buenos Aires at large, they mask the relatively greater protection from violence that the merchants enjoyed during the years of greatest political and military turmoil. The data show that in 1810 the proportions of widows in cuarteles 3 and 4 were virtually equal to the proportions of widows in cuarteles 12 and 19. Yet by 1827 the largest proportions of widows were to be found in the poorer, less commercial, and more racially heterogeneous neighborhoods of cuarteles 12 and 19. In 1810 only half of the widows in the selective universe were residing in barrios encompassed by cuarteles 12 and 19; the figure rose to 70 percent in 1827, and then fell to 60 percent in 1855. The disproportionate rise in the mortality rate among married men in cuarteles 12 and 19 in 1827, which had been equal to that of men in other cuarteles in 1810, indicates how severely

TABLE 15

Types of Household Head, Selective Universe and City Sample, 1810, 1827, and 1855

Household head	1810		1827		1855	
	No.	Pct.	No.	Pct.	No.	Pct.
	Selective Universe (N = 6,310)					
Married couple[a]	460	41.5%	954	40.6%	1,601	56.1%
Male, single or widowed	480	43.3	992	42.2	778	27.3
Female, single or widowed	169	15.2	403	17.2	473	16.6
TOTAL	1,109	100.0%	2,349	100.0%	2,852	100.0%
	City Sample (N = 1,149)					
Married couple[a]	276	72.1%	238	62.1%	241	62.9%
Male, single or widowed	34	8.9	56	14.6	48	12.5
Female, single or widowed	73	19.1	89	23.2	94	24.5
TOTAL	383	100.0%	383	100.0%	383	100.0%

[a]Slight discrepancies arose between the numbers of married men and of married women. They resulted from the incidence of husbands away from the city at the time of the enumerator's arrival and from husbands who were censused at their places of work. The differences were very small, in any event (0.4%). In this table, the number of households headed by a married female is a more faithful representation of homes headed by married couples, since married women were usually censused at home along with their resident family members.

the weight of war had fallen on the shoulders of the families of *peones*, *agricultores*, *jornaleros*, and the other members of the *gente de pueblo* that constituted the city's low-status, casual labor force.

These data combine to distinguish between two types of households, the result of the era's political context, which form a dimension we may refer to as "family coherence"—a term meant to evoke the dangers faced by porteño families, but especially the gente de pueblo, in maintaining their integrity. The two types are plotted in Fig. 1, which shows the distribution of households in both the selective universe and the city sample headed by two types of cohorts: adults without partners and married couples.

Among the households located within the areas covered in the selective universe, the strong representation of unmarried Spanish merchants served to keep the proportion of single heads of households relatively constant until 1827; thereafter, households headed by couples gained dramatically, representing almost 60 percent of all households by 1855. By contrast, the figures in the city sample demonstrate a very different distribution. Because it contains a much

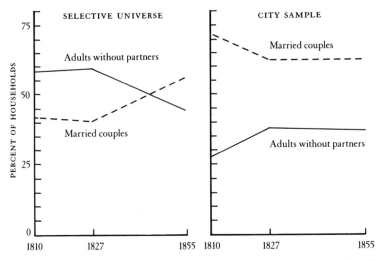

Fig. 1. Distribution of household heads, selective universe (N = 6,310) and city sample (N = 1,149), 1810, 1827, and 1855.

higher contingent of poor and lower-class individuals who could not afford to marry formally in church, whose women were involved in consensual unions, and whose men were the likeliest victims of the *leva*, the city sample's distribution of heads of households is the inverse of the one found within the selective universe: the population of low-status porteños registered a sharp drop in the representation of households headed by couples between 1810 and 1827, with a concomitant rise in households led by widows, a situation that was still evident at midcentury.

Household Size: Children

The average porteño home was strikingly lacking in coresident children. This was especially true for the first intercensal period, as shown by Fig. 2. The number of households without any children, represented by the plotted line, rose dramatically between 1810 and 1827, and then declined slightly by 1855. The number of households that in 1810 had contained 1, 2, 3, or more than 4 children declined thereafter and had failed to recover by 1855. The relatively small number of children at home was not necessarily the result of low fertility rates, since small families and high fertility rates can coexist.

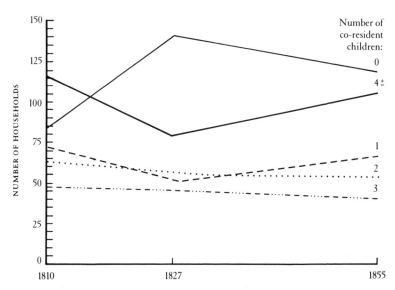

Fig. 2. Number of children living in household with household head, 1810, 1827, and 1855 (N = 1,149 households).

Indeed, the image of the preindustrial household swarming with children close in age is an idealized version of history that has not stood up well to empirical investigation. Among the laboring classes, high infant mortality rates, deferring procreation by suckling infants, and removing children from home in various ways combined to prevent overcrowded conditions.[36] However, this is not the place to discuss vital statistics, since the central subject is household structures: moreover, no systematic evidence of general fertility rates is yet available for all the racial and socioeconomic components of the female population of Buenos Aires.

The porteño household without many children requires precise explanations that are not yet possible with the data at hand. However, two sets of possible explanations—one demographic and the other political—are suggested here for subsequent study and refinement. One set of explanations lies within the realm of vital statistics, which signal that nineteenth-century infant mortality rates in Buenos Aires were too high to permit housefuls of children. Infant mortality indices, available for the period 1827–31, are described as "very high" for both white and nonwhite populations; among infants of color, death tended to occur during the first three months of life.[37] In 1828, infant mortality among families of color was 409.1 per 1,000, 65 percent higher than the incidence of 248.4 per 1,000 among whites. But infant mortality indices are limited in explaining household size and composition. Even high infant mortality rates, especially if they occur within the first few months of life, provide plenty of opportunities for new conceptions to occur, until a house with some minimum of children becomes a constant feature. In the case of Buenos Aires, there is empirical evidence that the lower classes did indeed increase their marital fertility rates over the course of the nineteenth century. This is shown in Table 8 (p. 83), which showed the different marital fertility rates linked with low- and high-status occupations of heads of households in the selective universe. The data in that table indicated that the secular trend for the families of the gente de pueblo was to increase marital fertility rates, while the gente decente lowered theirs.

In the context of household size, one should expect to see some increase in the incidence of coresident children in keeping with the average increase in marital fertility of over 6 percent. Their absence is, therefore, all the more puzzling; it invites a political explanation, fully argued later in this chapter, one that historians might well consider in their own examinations of nineteenth-century Platine society.

Household Size: Coresidential Kinship

The manner in which many families responded to the troubles visited upon them by the period's political and military disturbances suggests that their reactive strategies were designed to ameliorate their personal situations. One of the most frequently adopted strategies was expressed by the existence of extended families, the consequence of an instrumentally motivated reaction that calls into question the applicability of traditional, culture-based variables to explain the structure of Spanish American households.

Affective kinship has long been a fundamental characteristic of Spanish American society: patriarchy was, from the time of the conquerors, an organizing principle of the social order of the Indies. By extending beyond the normal protection and care of subordinate intimates and loved ones to include the forging of networks to carry out transatlantic commerce, landholding patterns, and political power, kinship in Spanish America signified both affective and strategic relationships.[38] The household in Spanish America is thus assumed to incorporate features of this important phenomenon of kinship by housing extended families, often encompassing three or more generations. According to the data presented below, however, Buenos Aires does not neatly fit this model. To judge from the data yielded by both the selective universe and the city sample, coresidential extended families were relatively rare:

| | In selective universe: | | In city sample: | |
Year	No.	As percent of year's total	No.	As percent of year's total
1810	286	5.1%	236	9.5%
1827	618	6.1	202	11.8
1855	1,407	11.0	349	18.9
TOTAL	2,311	8.1%	787	13.1%

Beyond this, however, the historical trend indicated an incipience of complex households; in other words, as porteños edged closer to the modernizing era of the export boom economy of the century's second half, they began to display an increase in the incidence of coresidential kinship.

Within the population of the selective universe, the percentage of the heads of households who shared their homes with their kinfolk doubled from 5.1 percent in 1810 to 11 percent in 1827. The same doubling of percentages was evident in the city at large, from 9.5 percent of the sampled population in 1810 to 18.9 percent in 1855. The great majority of extended families involved the coresidence of only one kinsman: 8.6 percent of the city sample in 1810, 12 percent in 1827, and 18 percent in 1855, according to the data shown in Table 16. Moreover, the data indicate that coresidential kinship was a dynamic and strategic phenomenon tied to the well-being of husbands among the kinfolk who shared homes. The data presented below support this hypothesis. Thus, the extended family, when it developed in Buenos Aires, did not take on large dimensions: on the average, two-thirds of the extended families included no more than five members, or approximately one more individual than in the normal porteño nuclear family.

Who were the likeliest candidates for taking up residence with kin? Table 17 shows that, of all extended families, adult siblings were

TABLE 16

City Sample Households by Number of Kin Living at Home, 1810, 1827, and 1855

(N = 1,149)

Number of kin at home	1810		1827		1855	
	No.	Pct.	No.	Pct.	No.	Pct.
0	295	77.1%	293	76.5%	241	63.0%
1	33	8.6	46	12.0	69	18.0
2	25	6.5	18	4.7	22	5.7
3	13	3.4	13	3.4	21	5.5
4	2	0.5	2	0.5	10	2.6
5+	15	4.0	11	2.8	20	5.3
TOTAL	383	100.0%	383	100.0%	383	100.0%

TABLE 17

Type and Frequency of Resident Kin, City Sample, 1810, 1827, and 1855

(N = 320)

Relationship to household head	1810		1827		1855	
	No.	Pct.	No.	Pct.	No.	Pct.
Adopted minors	4	4.4%	7	7.7%	4	2.9%
Sons-in-law	26	28.6	5	5.5	14	10.1
Daughters-in-law	7	7.7	5	5.5	7	5.1
Grandchildren	1	1.1	11	12.8	14	10.1
Sisters/brothers	19	20.9	38	41.8	43	31.2
Sisters-/brothers-in-law	16	17.6	11	12.1	23	16.7
Mothers-/fathers-in-law	8	8.8	4	4.4	10	7.2
Nieces/nephews	1	1.1	0	0.0	10	7.2
Mothers/fathers	1	1.1	4	4.4	8	5.8
Unknown	8	8.8	6	6.6	5	3.6
TOTAL	91	100.0%	91	100.0%	138	100.0%

the principal type of relative to share a home in 1827 (41.8 percent) and in 1855 (31.2 percent); in 1810, by contrast, they represented 20.9 percent of all coresidential kin citywide. Coresident sons-in-law dropped dramatically in their representation from a high of 28.6 percent in 1810 to 5.5 percent of all coresidential kin in 1827. Closely related to this decline in the representation of sons-in-law was the increased representation of coresident grandchildren, which rose from 1.1 percent in 1810 to 12.8 percent in 1827, and then fell somewhat to 10.1 percent in 1855. The congruence between the sharp drop in the presence of sons-in-law and the dramatic rise in the presence of grandchildren reflected the misfortunes of war, as fathers commended their wives and children to the care of their own parents or parents-in-law. Women left alone tended to invite their parents to share their homes, rather than move in with their in-laws; this was illustrated by the rise in the proportionate representations of mothers and fathers of the heads of households from 1.1 percent in 1810 to 4.4 percent in 1827 and 5.8 percent in 1855. The share of the category of mothers- and fathers-in-law, however, diminished.

A note of some interest is raised by the data in Table 17, which show the rise and subsequent decline in the adoptions of young children with no apparent relationship to the head of the household. These wards fulfilled household needs which, although usually domestic in nature, did not imply positions of permanent servitude. Sometimes called *entenados* in the census tracts, these boys and girls tended to appear in homes headed by elderly persons, where they found temporary shelter. It was a tradition of the domestic family that was somewhat helpful in housing some of the city's many abandoned children, as noted previously. In light of the high rates of abandonment, it is not surprising to find the slight rise in the absolute number of *entenados* between 1810 and 1827. By 1855, the percentage of complex households that contained unrelated minors dropped to 2.9 percent, and this informal variety of charity fell victim to the rise in the privatization of the family, an ideal that grew in importance in the course of the nineteenth century, especially among young married couples.

Coresidential kinship often resulted from offering the use of a home to people related to the head of the household by marriage. The citywide incidence of households made complex as a direct result of marriage declined from nearly 63 percent of all complex households in 1810 to slightly over 39 percent in 1855; these figures represent the proportion of households that included in-laws. At the same time, the incidence of consanguineous relations (including sisters, brothers, nieces, nephews, mothers, and fathers) of the head of the household increased from 23 percent of all complex households in 1810 to over 44 percent in 1855. In Table 18, which shows data from marriage-related complex households for the selective universe and the city sample respectively, two important characteristics appear. The first reflects cultural norms, which included the prolonged

TABLE 18

*Complex Households Resulting from Marriages, Buenos Aires Households,
1810, 1827, and 1855*

In-laws present in household	1810		1827		1855	
	No.	Pct.	No.	Pct.	No.	Pct.
Selective Universe (N = 573)						
Sons-in-law	39	38.2%	29	17.0%	50	16.7%
Daughters-in-law	8	7.8	16	9.4	33	11.0
Sisters-in-law	24	23.5	70	40.9	100	33.3
Brothers-in-law	16	15.7	24	14.0	44	14.7
Mothers-in-law	15	14.7	27	15.8	59	19.7
Fathers-in-law	0	0.0	5	2.9	14	4.7
TOTAL	102	100.0%	171	100.0%	300	100.0%
Pct. of households	—	9.1%	—	7.2%	—	10.5%
City Sample (N = 136)						
Sons-in-law	26	45.6%	5	20.0%	14	25.9%
Daughters-in-law	7	12.3	5	20.0	7	13.0
Sisters-in-law	10	17.5	7	28.0	16	29.6
Brothers-in-law	6	10.5	4	16.0	7	13.0
Mothers-in-law	5	8.8	2	8.0	9	16.7
Fathers-in-law	3	5.3	2	8.0	1	1.8
TOTAL	57	100.0%	25	100.0%	54	100.0%
Pct. of households	—	14.9%	—	6.5%	—	14.1%

protection of females in general and daughters in particular. In Table 18, the component of coresident sons-in-law is much greater than that of daughters-in-law, which indicates that, considering the relative infrequency of young married couples living with one set of parents, daughters were more likely than sons to remain in their parental homes after marriage.

The second characteristic brought up in the data is congruent with the cycles in household structures noted earlier. In 1827, households experienced a general decline in the proportions of coresident sons-in-law and a rise in coresidence among adult females, that is, daughters-in-law and especially sisters-in-law. The sharp increase noted in the presence of sisters-in-law in porteños' households is directly related to the need of married women, left alone by their husbands (away at war, perhaps forcibly recruited to defend the frontier against Indians, perhaps warring against Brazilians, or very possibly

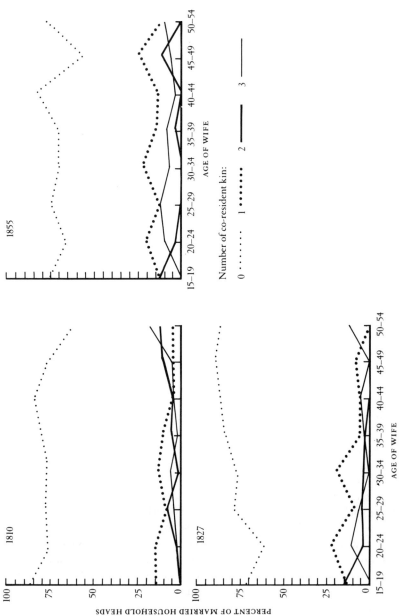

Fig. 3. Distribution of married household heads by number of kin in household and age of wife, 1810

killed during the revolutionary era of the 1810's), to move in with family and kin until the time when they could again set up their own homes.

The lower classes in 1810 were much likelier than the upper classes to form complex households by incorporating kinfolk into their homes; this was found to be as true of the population in the city sample as it was in the selective universe. Coresidential kinship for the well-to-do was in 1810 relatively rare, although a sizeable minority (approximately one-fourth) of the complex households were composed of well-to-do extended families. By 1855, however, coresidential kinship was as common among the poor as among the wealthy. The evolved congruence between rich and poor in their tendencies to form extended families is not easily explained by standard models of modernization theory. These models posit that, over time, the poor tend to retain the traditional characteristic of forming extended families and complex households. Over time, however, material conditions improve, educational levels increase, traditional values are left behind, and the household tends toward nucleation.[39] Apparently, the Buenos Aires situation was the reverse of this model: well-to-do families increasingly imitated their poorer counterparts. It should be noted, however, that the porteños' tendency toward extended households over the course of time was not exceptional. For example, for reasons derived from their own historical experiences, Florentine households were much more laterally extended in the sixteenth century than they had been in the early fifteenth.[40]

Extended families represented the numerical exception in Buenos Aires, where family nucleation was the norm for married couples. Beyond this generality, however, lies the question of how dynamic or static the nuclear model was within the lifespan of the heads of the households. Fig. 3 summarizes the information presented below.

In 1810, coresidential kinship tended to increase at about the time when a mother was likely to have fewer coresident children of her own, which was at the age of 40, on the average. This was also the time when both husband and wife began to prepare the composition of the household to fit the needs that would be occasioned by the eventual death of one of the marriage partners; this pattern was equally true in 1855. In 1827, however, the cycle was very different; the incidence of married households without any kinfolk at home remained uniformly high—on the average, 85 percent—for the 40–

44, 45–49, and 50–54 age cohorts. Instead, the incidence of coresidential kinship in 1827 appears to have been significantly strongest at the time when the wives of the heads of households were aged 20–24 (38 percent); this was the result of the increase noted earlier in the numbers of sisters-in-law, contemporaries of the wives, who moved in with them. Thus, the married couple tended to retain its private, nucleated quality under normal circumstances; if any extended family was to be formed in Buenos Aires, however, its existence reflected less the Iberian or Mediterranean peculiarities of porteños than their fundamental affect, together with the practical function of providing needed care and lodging to the aging patriarchs and to the desolate young.[41] Their practices manifested the principle that there has been everywhere and at every point in time a social norm that has placed on grown children the requirement of caring for their elderly parents.[42]

Political Crisis and Familial Integrity

The part that the militarization of political dissent in the Río de la Plata played in undermining the completeness of the family is seldom noted; the usual references skim along at the macroscopic level to highlight gross tendencies related to total populations. We know, for example, that Artigas' movement served to deplete a great percentage of the rural population of the Banda Oriental. Likewise, the male labor force of the rural littoral was seriously undermined in the course of the civil wars in the 1810's.[43] But we know virtually nothing about the effect of war on the coherence of the urban household. How successful were porteño families in escaping the worst effects of the warmaking that plagued the Buenos Aires environment? It would be helpful for students of this era of political and military turbulence to see the political state as a fundamental agency of familial destruction or, conversely, as an agency of melioration and familial coherence. This is the context in which we place the changing household structures of the residents of Buenos Aires. To be sure, the contemporary literature contains little directly related to the subject. But this does not mean that we are completely lacking in indications, that there are no pointers suggesting that the wars that ensued between 1810 and 1852, especially during the years before the implantation of Rosas' regime, were disastrous for the porteño household. The issue of childless homes provides the opportunity to explore the relationship that existed between two factors: militarization that ensued from political dissension, and familial cohesion.

It took a relatively short time at the start of the nineteenth century for porteños to integrate the concepts of militarism and militant politics into their collective conscience. These new considerations naturally created important roles for young men and even children. Ironically, the presence of youngsters as military fighters had not been a historical feature of the region, but the heightened value of the urban militia ended that tradition. The militia had only recently taken on a more practical meaning as the Bourbons sought to minimize expenditures and maximize the defensive readiness of their possessions in the Indies.[44] In the region of the Río de la Plata, the Crown's greatest concern was the military presence of the Portuguese in the Banda Oriental, the motivating factor for elevating the Buenos Aires militia after the creation of the viceroyalty in 1776 to something more than an instrument for bestowing status on its members.[45] Ultimately, the militia served as the most effective instrument of war against the English, who were defeated after their invasion of the city in 1806. Soon after this *reconquista*, the notion of military service took on a connotation of honor and glory never before experienced among porteños. New units were formed, identifying characteristics and titles were awarded to these regiments by the authorities, and a newly heightened urban military consciousness appeared in the city.

The manpower that was used in war tended, naturally, to be young. But how young were these men? In the case of Buenos Aires, there are indications that boys as young as 12 were being recruited into military service; in this euphoric and generalized sense of prideful obligation, children—heretofore absent from such affairs other than as spectators—now took their active place alongside young men in the military formations. As the fortunes of war determined the need for men, the *leva*, the legal device of forced recruitment, became the single most dangerous instrument of destruction of the porteño family's coherence. The regulations regarding the *leva* contained some relief for sectors of the male population considered to be economically vital, with the consequently disproportionate recruitment of the unskilled and the unemployed.[46] The inequalities in the system of military exemptions had become notorious enough that Rosas' spokesmen were forced to announce their restrictions of "this scandalous abuse" early in 1830, even if in practice the system continued.[47] Despite the existence of laws regulating military con-scription, it was not unusual for authorities to exceed them on their own initiative. Men who had broken no laws and who were fully employed were nevertheless recruited, often in raids on cafés and pulperías.[48] "This form of ill-treatment occurs repeatedly," com-plained an observer in 1827. "These procedures, whereby *under the name of the 'leva' and the necessities of war* citizens are forcibly taken away, must be eliminated."[49]

The political state's contribution to the perpetuation of military confrontation came by way of its close monitoring of the city's pop-ulation, and its increasing demand for young men to serve in the military, a policy that did not spare male youngsters.[50] During the first decade of war, beginning in 1810, and even until the mid-1820's, the political and military authorities "had been mostly successful in limiting their military recruitment to the socially marginal sectors."[51] The strains on the affected families had begun to show.

But recruitment needs deepened and conscription policies hard-ened as the authorities implemented the military campaign against the Brazilians over the contested Banda Oriental with two consid-erations that were very reminiscent of the earlier revolutionary era. Both of them can be discerned in the dialogue that took place on October 8, 1812, between the leaders of the coup that was about to depose the revolutionary junta and the junta members themselves.[52] First, it became clear that the prosecution of war—at that time, against royalists and internal dissidents—could not be carried out except with a full-scale commitment on the part of the political au-thorities. This meant a radical increase in the resources, including manpower recruits, to be devoted to the military efforts—an in-crease that would quickly result in the forced conscription of the lower classes and the almost universal conscription of the city's slave force.[53]

The second consideration of the revolutionary era, which was re-constituted in the politico-military generation of the 1820's, can be gleaned from the euphemistically contradictory language that José de San Martín employed to address the besieged junta: whatever the decisions of the political authorities, they would, of course, be obeyed by the military officers, as was proper, yet politicians would be unwise to take the military for granted.[54] A generation later, sim-ilar types of pressures and dangers loomed over Rivadavia's govern-ment in its approach toward the Brazilian enemy. The results were reminiscent of those observed during the previous military era: massive conscription, especially of the lower classes, and the eventual fall of the government. In June 1827, with the failure of the other provinces (except Tucumán) to adopt the centralist constitution drafted the previous year, "it only took the imprudent preliminary peace agreement . . . , signed in Rio de Janeiro, to hasten the fall."[55]

Thus, the sensed failure to prosecute war vigorously had its antecedents in the 1810's. Manuel Dorrego, the governor of the province of Buenos Aires and Rivadavia's political enemy, summarized the militants' analysis of the failed prosecution of war: "Blood still pours from the wounds inflicted on us, and much time will have to pass before they become healed. Whenever one would look over the brave and virtuous army in the field of battle along the borders with Brazil, one would gaze upon the naked soldier, without any pay; the number of troops quite low, and everything in danger of complete dissolution."[56] Even normally calm observers not given to bleak prophecies reported that any sort of peace with the Brazilians would ignite a lengthy civil war throughout the country.[57] From all perspectives, social, political, and economic, it appeared to "be a return to the past thought to have been forgotten and gone forever in 1820, [and yet] it would soon be seen as a process much worse than the previous one."[58] The financial tailspin of the porteño economy, caused by the port's blockade by the Brazilians, affected virtually all porteños, but especially the lower classes, petty traders, and artisans.[59] Other studies have detailed the political and economic effects of the period, but the data on households presented here indicate the effects visited on the quotidian lives of porteño families by political and military instability.

Were matters so different after the fall of the unitarians and the advent of the Rosas regime? *Rosista* conscription policies were moved by philosophical tenets quite similar to his predecessors'; indeed, the efficiency of his machine in supplying his needs was far superior and meant that, if anything, more recruits were gathered. The military regulations, drafted in 1823 to incorporate the unemployed and the troublemakers (*vagos y malentretenidos*) into the ranks of the provincial army, were vigorously followed. This policy resulted in the growth of the military apparatus and the increased dependence on the army as the single largest purchaser of goods from important segments of the urban productive and commercial sectors and the rural foodstuff providers.[60] Furthermore, the French blockade of 1837 was certainly instrumental in promoting some home manufacturing. Whatever the principal stimulus was, the provincial economy expanded considerably in the period of Rosas' rule.[61] There were other indications of relative stability and growth by the 1840's: for the first time in a long period, a modest number of immigrants arrived, and political émigrés returned to reclaim confiscated properties.

Political Patriarchy and Political Reciprocity

Are these indications of an idyllic existence? Of course not. They do suggest, however, that we should distinguish the consequences of the growth of the military establishment per se from those of its actual use in bloody and protracted wars. The differences were considerable. The Rosas era was marked by two characteristics that required large numbers of men under arms: actual military conflicts and political security needs. The military conflicts were, however, qualitatively different from the military encounters of the previous eras. They were sporadic, and although Rosas consciously engaged in the rhetoric of war, each conflict was terminal and self-contained. This was the nature of his Indian campaign in 1833, of his war against Bolivia in 1837, of his nationalist crusade against the Anglo-French forces in 1845, and of his reactions to the periodic challenges to his domination from unitarians like Paz and Lavalle. Even though deserters from the army were a constant feature of both federalist and unitarian forces, the danger of military service was considered to have diminished enough to encourage volunteers from the lower classes to join during the economically restrictive period of the 1840's, much as their predecessors almost two generations earlier had joined the evolving urban army in 1810.[62] Halperín Donghi speculates similarly for both periods: of the formative era of independence, while lower-class enrollments prevented the need for forced conscription, he asks, "Why were the plebeian classes in the city so deaf to the appeal to their own interests in orderly government and diminished military expenditure? It may have been the case that militarization in fact proved to be more of a boon than a burden to them . . . transferring wealth from the higher to the lower social groups [in the form of soldiers' pay]."[63] Furthermore, he notes elsewhere that in the era of the late 1830's and early 1840's, the economic conditions found in the city encouraged similar military voluntarism from the lower classes. Despite the absence of any "direct testimony to this effect," enrolling in the army must have offered the "guarantee of subsistence (and not much more than subsistence) to individuals located within the city's least prosperous groups."[64]

That the lower classes sensed the differences between "peacetime" military service and protracted campaigns of war, and, furthermore, that they retained their collective memories of the destructive effects of previous wars, are suggested by the lackluster performance of the troops during Rosas' last battle at Caseros in February 1852. Even before Caseros, the observations made by contemporary British diplomatic agents in Buenos Aires to their superiors in London urged that they not become too concerned about a protracted war in Argentina. They noted that, despite the militant articulations of porteño demonstrators, popular sentiments could not hide the clear differences between voluntary enrollments, with their attendant military drills, and actual warfare. In October 1850, wild mobs paraded through the streets of Buenos Aires calling for war with Brazil. Yet Henry Southern noted that this was so much rhetorical emotionalism, that behind the apparent enthusiasm there was much real hostility to war. This was particularly true of the Buenos Aires region, where "the evils of war are nowhere felt more cruelly . . . [and where] war strikes at the very root of the well-being of nearly every person in the country, whether native or foreign."[65]

Similarly, Robert Gore, writing at the beginning of 1852, observed that people were not interested in war, preferring, instead, a swift and painless victory by Urquiza, because although "there is no sympathy for Urquiza in Buenos Aires, . . . there is a very general desire for peace, to permit people to attend to their private affairs."[66] In the end, Rosas' army dissolved before the enemy on the outskirts of Buenos Aires: the apparent enthusiasm with which the lower classes had recently enlisted in the army yielded to the ennui they demonstrated at the time of actual battle.[67]

If it is accurate to say that "Rosas preserved the inherited social order, reinforced it, and handed it on intact," he succeeded in part because his political supremacy resulted in the attenuation of the actual loss of life on the field of battle.[68] This was something that neither the authorities of the independence era nor the revanchist leaders on the subject of Uruguay in the 1820's had understood as clearly as Rosas. The differences between Rosas and his predecessors did not rest on kindness or human concern—Rosas was no more respectful of the rights of the masses than were the more overtly aristocratic unitarians who ruled before him—but on understanding the limits that defined plebeian loyalties. The patrimonial aspects of the *rosista* formula were moved by fundamentally political considerations, based on his assessment of his predecessors' failed policies toward the lower classes. By contrast, noted the caudillo, "I thought it important to gain an influence over the people of this class in order to restrain them and lead them. . . . I found it necessary to . . . protect them and to look after their welfare."⁶⁹ Before Rosas' formal arrival on the Buenos Aires political scene at the end of 1829, his supporters had paved his way by publicizing within the city the peace that reigned over the countryside commanded by Rosas: "While elements of discord are being manifested in the city [even] among people loyal to the same cause, nothing but the most complete harmony reigns in the countryside, where only one sentiment prevails—that of *living in peace*."⁷⁰

Conclusions: Toward a Classical Theory of Caudillo Rule

The analysis presented here of census data spanning half a century of life in Buenos Aires underscores the complex changes experienced by the families who lived in a region in search of political stability. The dislocations created by the struggles for independence, the violence attendant on the absence of political and organizational consensus, and the campaigns against Brazil all took their heaviest toll on the gente de pueblo. The militarization of much of the male population and the brutalization of political relations had an especially severe impact on the families of porteños insofar as their mean family size was relatively small to start (4.7 persons in 1810). The data show that by 1855 the losses of the 1810's and 1820's had been recuperated, and the total growth of the city's population since 1827 represented an increase of over 100 percent. This cycle is consistent with the European pattern of rapid rise in population following a period of high mortality rates. Historically, years of crisis have been followed by years of much lower mortality. If marriages—whether consensual or sacramental—had been postponed or interrupted because of externally imposed hardships, a rush of new or resumed marriages would follow the end of the crisis "and a spurt of births would coincide with the reduction in the numbers of deaths to give a few years in which population could rise rapidly."[71] The rise in the number of births would result in a sudden jump, approximately 20 years after the crisis, in the number of young adults. If these young men and women started families, it would result in a wavelike surge in numbers with a periodicity of about a generation. Each baby boom produces a demographic echo about 25 years later as those former babies themselves begin to form families. This is precisely what occurred in Buenos Aires, as can be seen by applying a cross-sequential design to the census data. This design offers the advantage of simultaneous cross-sectional (in this case, age cohort) and longitudinal (that is, age-time frame) analyses.[72] In 1810, the population of boys under the age of 10 represented nearly 19 percent of the city's males. The toll exacted by nearly two decades of political and military turbulence, however, showed in the attrition of this group; in 1827, this population of young boys, now between the ages of 15 and 24, was merely 16.5 percent. For their part, girls under the age of 10, who in 1810 had accounted for 20.7 percent of all females, had grown by 1827 to represent 24.5 percent. By contrast, the second intercensal period, spanning the years 1827 to 1855, showed no drop in male population. On the contrary, the rate of growth for the group of youngsters under the age of 10 was virtually the same for both boys and girls. During this period, this subpopulation showed an increase of 0.6 percent for males and 0.4 percent for females. In sum, young males after the 1820's had a better chance than their predecessors of surviving to adulthood even after experiencing military service; indeed, they stood the same chances as their female counterparts.

In the light of the evidence presented here, can we go beyond the demographic data to broaden the explanatory perspective from which we may see more clearly and understand better the behavioral aspects behind the durability of the caudillo political order, so well expressed by Rosas? Support for Rosas among porteños reflected both their fear of his repression and—from a constructive perspective—the most fundamental personal benefits they derived from his imposed domestic peace: much-improved chances of life. This benefit was particularly true for the lower classes and the city's black population: Reid Andrews has demonstrated that as late as 1840, the blacks' representation in the city's population, which in 1838 stood at approximately 26 percent, was the highest since 1810, when blacks constituted 29.5 percent of porteños. The figures for the 1830's represented significant increases from the declines shown by city's censuses following 1810, despite the very high infant mortality and the sexual imbalance registered among blacks. While Andrews asserts that official statistical data hid the real extent of the black population, it appears that the rise in their population resulted in large measure from the reintegration of lower-class men of all colors with their families following their prolonged military involvements.[73]

Porteños of the period did not know, of course, the detailed demographic implications behind their political struggles. But they did experience the general implications of those struggles enough so that, even among men who would in the long run oppose Rosas, an appreciative realization of his regime's stability was noted. Marcos Sastre, in whose home the *Salón Literario* first met on June 23, 1837 (giving rise to the term "Generation of '37" to identify the group of anti-Rosas liberals), noted his appreciation of the stability of his times and of Rosas' government "because [it] is the only suitable one, the only one powerful enough to pave the way toward national prosperity."[74] Even Domingo Sarmiento, who of all the members of the Generation of '37 unswervingly expressed the harshest condemnations of Rosas, saw the caudillo as a man who comprehended the whole Platine sociopolitical framework, rather than as simply a mindless barbarian. According to Sarmiento, writing in 1844, no one knew Argentine society better or felt the need to control the masses more than Rosas: "He is the owner of the [masses], and is very much aware of their power and of their instincts . . . ; he has come to have such total understanding of the state of South American society that he can, at any time and by his highly unusual cunning, pluck just the right social chords to produce the sounds he desires."[75]

As a political exile in Chile, Juan Bautista Alberdi admitted in 1847 that "the unitarians have lost, but unity has triumphed."[76] Moreover, Alberdi had the acumen with which to analyze the passivity of the masses in the face of authoritarian leadership as a behavior that did not derive so much from popular inertia and ignorance as from salutary political deference. In a sharp criticism of romantically Europeanized liberalism, Alberdi accused Sarmiento of not understanding the needs and motivations of the peoples of South America. Responding to Sarmiento's call for the masses to rebel against those who would keep them under the federalist yoke, Alberdi wrote from the Chilean city of Quillota in 1853:

It is not "resistance," Mr. Sarmiento, that good writers must teach our Spanish America, so vitiated already by rebellions; rather, it is "obedience." "Resistance" will not provide "freedom"; it will only serve to make impossible the establishment of "authority," something that South America has been searching for since the beginnings of its revolution and that forms the starting point and the cornerstone of its political existence. . . . The current symbol of civilization in South America is the principle of authority; anything that prevents its establishment is merely barbarousness and savagery with gilded exteriors. "Authority" is not established by discussion, nor by "resistance." Instead, it rests fundamentally upon "obedience."[77]

Most of the members of the Generation of '37 were fundamentally correct in assigning the "rabble" its role as the most numerous and basic source of Rosas' support, but it was in their assignment of the masses' motivations that they erred. These were not simpletons, unaware of reality and blindly following any demagogue who came along to stir their passions. Calculations were made on both sides, by the methodical, literate ruler and by the amorphous, inarticulate masses. To a large extent, what has been said of a typical nineteenth-century Spanish American liberal intellectual may similarly be said of many an individual among the porteño masses: "Forced to choose between liberty and order, he chose order."[78]

A transactional exchange of sorts was taking place in nineteenth-century Argentina, which did not always require exact and material reciprocity, but which was conditioned by cultural elements, including patriarchal traditions. Such traditions, in turn, were further reinforced by the behavioral traits of politico-military leaders that were recognized and valued by Platine workers, including good horsemanship, military abilities, and the most subjectively valued expressions of charisma. These were the elements of a system of political patriarchy that permitted the existence of war and its dysfunctions but brought the recognition of war's practical limits, and thereby a popular and conservative version of an appreciation for the positive functions of relative stability; this recognition carried with it the political support of warriors and their kin for the leader who, in turn, succeeded in eliminating his enemies as far as necessary to impose that stability.[79]

These propositions and conclusions involve us in the mental states of people who, in the vast majority, could not reify their thoughts in the form of written testaments. This leaves us today with the thorny problem of incomplete empirical evidence, something obviously not peculiar to Argentina or the rest of Latin America. Indeed, family history draws its empirical base everywhere from the top 5 or 10 percent of the population, the share of historical actors who have left disproportionately large amounts of documentation. This discrepancy between the overwhelming evidence of a small minority and the meager literary evidence of the vast majority remains "one of the major unsolved weaknesses of family history."[80]

Can we show conclusively, then, that the masses of Buenos Aires indeed calculated their life chances with the authoritarian caudillo to have been higher than with anyone else? Of course not; the history of mental states, particularly among the inarticulate, does not turn on the issue of conclusiveness.[81] Nor should the employment of cliometric techniques be expected to resolve such matters, since the weight of proof in history, as in a number of other disciplines, is related less to technique than to the inescapable limitations of incomplete evidence, which force us to conceive of the human experience in terms of probabilities only. In other words, the explanations that we articulate in terms of "proof" are really no more than solidly grounded expectations of plausibility; and it is a good thing, for if historical plausibility were equivalent to historical proof, explanatory propositions would have to be so self-evident as to turn into exercises in trivialities and constructions of truisms.[82]

Moses Finley was perspicacious in noting that improvement in historical techniques is a side issue within the larger and more meaningful framework of historiographical progress. "All the possible statistics about age at marriage, size of family, rate of illegitimacy," he wrote, "will not add up to a history of the family."[83] This issue is hardly relevant to the worn-out debate over the relative worth of cliometrics, but rather to the absolute worth of such techniques. It would be myopic to consider that, in the absence (or impossibility) of cliometric resolution, nondemonstrable causal relations should be avoided in the name of explicit data support. As numerically based as the historical demographers' evidence is, the richest answers to their questions come from the wider world that combines the actual evidence and the plausible conclusion, among which, notes John Noonan, figure the "fragile, intangible, and nonquantifiable human ideas themselves."[84] This is because historical demography, as practiced by historians, aims ultimately not at demography, but at history: it deals with human behavior, which is necessarily moved both by objective factors and by thought. Put another way, behavior points to thought in apodictic fashion insofar as that behavior is plausible—that is, logically, not statistically, certain—from the available evidence, including the quantitative variety. By contrast, the field of demography has its roots among the political economists of the era of industrialization, and it remains oriented primarily to the study of the numerical relationships between the forces of production and the cycles in populations. Finally, historians of the family have become increasingly aware that economic variables have their proper role in making us understand certain types of family changes, but only among other factors, such as social structures, political cycles, and psychological attitudes.

There has been a growing awareness of the complexities behind the constellation of causal variables that can account for family and household changes over time. This awareness has been enhanced by noticing two historical tendencies: first, attitudinal changes take place before alterations in the economic forms of production, and second, changes in attitudes occur in classes largely unaffected by production changes when they finally take place. These observations point to the existence of attitudinal malleability among the inarticulate in a manner relatively independent of economic determinants.[85] Thus, the outlook and behavior of individuals within the domestic group are modulated even in the preindustrial, so-called face-to-face societies.[86] This, I suggest, is what we find in Buenos Aires and probably in the rest of preconsolidation Argentina.

Of all the complex relationships formed among political, economic, and demographic factors, the *rosista* formula for authority signaled a respite from the massive loss of life with the consequent recuperation of the porteño household's cohesion. The destructive challenges to the integrity of the family in the first two decades after 1810, and the subsequent relief from the virtually continuous loss of young men's lives after Rosas' advent, formed the poles between which historians of authoritarianism can analyze a caudillo's support and his consequent durability. Rosas' populist touches, his close relationships with the Afro-Argentines, his support among *estancieros* in the countryside and among gauchos in and around the cities were rhetorical and stylistic forms not without substance.[87]

The enmities of the first half-century of Argentine nation building illustrate the classical propositions submitted by Georg Simmel and elaborated and ordered by Lewis Coser, which suggest the positive functions of social conflict. Rosas' imposed stability provided his fundamental legitimacy: the maintenance of life and production—even if intolerant of certain lives and favoring landed production almost exclusively—was a goal, value, and interest that, far from contradicting the basic assumptions on which the relationship between governor and governed are founded, tended to be positively functional for the membership of the social structure.[88] The concrete result was that between 1830 and the early 1850's, an entire generation had been permitted many more opportunities than before to be born and to mature under the frighteningly efficient authoritarianism of *rosismo*. This meant, among other things, that if the caudillo formula had become an enervated form of political rule in Buenos Aires by the 1850's, its dissolution took place before an adult population that contained a large contingent of men and women inexperienced in the costly and seemingly endless convulsions of 1810–29. It was a population willing to run the risk of yet another political experiment, this time with a new generation of liberals at the helm; this generation, politically less utopian than the early revolutionaries, would reconstitute the power of the urban elites during the century's second half.

7

Conclusions:
Masses and Political Obligation

This book began by posing a series of questions designed to elucidate the connections between family and polity in Argentina's principal city during the first half of the nineteenth century. The intent was to identify the manner in which the family in Buenos Aires was affected by the elites' political and social designs, and the means employed by the masses in adapting to them. The analysis of the contact between state and family was accompanied by the undercurrent of tensions that characterized the era and that, because of political acrimony and militarism, periodically upset the quotidian rhythms of porteños. This was the environment in which heads of households in the region of Buenos Aires made calculations for their own welfare and that of their families. In addition, the analysis of the relations between family and polity focused on the mechanisms and processes by which authority—and deference to any given authority—were established. Along the way, we attempted to discover how the rules of the political and social games—specifically, rights and obligations—applied in a preconstitutional and preconsensual order.

The social categorization employed throughout this book— gente decente and gente de pueblo—was admittedly simple; more- over, it ran the risk of masking economic and occupational distinc- tions that existed within the population of Buenos Aires. Still, these two categories afforded two advantages: first, they were used and recognized by the historical actors for their contemporaneous social meaning; and second, they forced us to focus our attention on be- havioral matters and on the differences in the social and cultural value systems of the two groups. Political beliefs and preferences were consequently subsumed under the two major categories in our contention that, at least in the case of the gente de pueblo and of an indeterminate proportion of the gente decente, we are dealing with members of a society that was largely prepolitical; in other words, public action by the majority of porteños was determined by matters of personal consideration and emotional affinities rather than by calculations based on ideological abstractions regarding the commonweal. However, the construct of a limited range of considerations held by nineteenth-century porteños, although useful for explaining their public action, was not equivalent to irrational or unpredictable behavior. On the contrary, the period's documentation is striking for signaling how closely the gente de pueblo, in pursuing their own survival and advancement, adhered to the vocabulary and to the styles of action normally associated with the gente decente. It suggests the existence of a significant political sagacity among masses of people who, ironically, played no obvious or direct role in affecting governmental policy. Furthermore, it suggests that the absence of formal political legitimacy did not preclude a people's access to political decision makers.

The style used by the state to rule this region of the Río de la Plata evoked the links that had traditionally joined political authority with patriarchal traditions. Such a style on the part of the officials combined their authoritarian traits with their willingness to engage the largely inarticulate masses on a subtle but meaningful level of interplay. Iberian culture, including its traditions of a familial and patriarchal ethos, persisted in various forms well into the nation-building era. This was evident, for example, in the similarity of manner in which both gente de pueblo and gente decente managed to reach the ears of the officials in charge of the region's criminal justice system; indeed, they often succeeded in affecting legal decisions. The basis for the maintenance of social control rested on a variety of factors, among which figured the resolution of acrimony and the adjudication of cases at the level of the barrio. This involved vecinos in all the attendant roles, as parties in the disputes, as officers of the court, and sometimes even as prisoners. Officials were expected to mediate between the demands of the highest authorities of government and the realities of the local vecinos. The extent to which the higher political and judiciary authorities respected local considerations varied over time, insofar as their adherence to local traditions reflected either their conservative or liberal ideology: the more liberal ideologues—especially after midcentury—centralized decision making at the higher administrative levels. Decentralization and respect for local norms, which were associated with conservatives at the state level of federalism, were reconstituted at the local level of the city's barrios.

By contrast, the latter part of the nineteenth century witnessed the upward accumulation of authority attendant on growing bureaucratization. This process, inherent in all modernizing states, was accompanied and reinforced in Argentina by the liberals' distrust of the masses, who, they felt, were devoid of "collective reason," as Echeverría characterized them.[1] Conservatives were no more enamored of the concept of popular rule than were the liberals, but their very conservatism, translated into public action, meant that they naturally favored the leadership styles of the traditional *gran aldea* and rejected political novelties as alien to the region's cultural and social characteristics.[2] Liberals, although similarly distrustful of the masses, charged themselves with the tutelary role of altering such characteristics, which necessitated authoritarian impositions by the bureaucratic elite of an enlightened and more complex state.

The access by vecinos to influential administrative levels of authority was likewise displayed in constructs and actions related to children. The perception that some authorities were ignoring local traditions and considerations led to either conciliatory or rancorous petitions, depending on the issue and the style of the actors, for their removal or for the restoration of deference to local interests. While the supervision of children in public was the responsibility of the state, it was also accompanied by the insistence of vecinos that a barrio retain the right to monitor the behavior of teachers and aides. As had been established by long-standing colonial traditions, the imposition of authority without regard for local sensibilities—in the case of Buenos Aires, this meant the vecinos of different barrios—threatened to interrupt the flow of rights and obligations between elites and masses. Here we can see in operation the interplay between two systems of community, one at the uppermost level of province and nation and the other at the opposite end on the scale of governance, at the barrio.[3] By the same token, sensitivity to local concerns provided greater access by the individual, regardless of social station, directly or by proxy, to official circles. As a general model, federalists tended to reconstitute the principles of national federalism at the level of the urban community of Buenos Aires. Liberal unitarians, by contrast, gravitated at a slow and deliberate pace toward the concentration of authority in administrative elites. As the foundation of the future Argentine society, the youth attracted the considerable attention of the state. The child, representing the parents' most intimate concern and the state's ideological ward, telescoped emotional and political interests into conflicts between family and polity. To conservative political elites, the child represented the continued basis of the traditional order: lower-class children would continue to function in their adult years as their parents had before them, guaranteeing the supply of deferential laborers in an expanding pastoral economy. For their part, elite children would grow up to take their place in the retinue of the commercial and political leaders. Such a construct required a limited role by the state in the training of youth; put more concretely, the state's role rested in the adjudication of limited access to the necessary schooling, pretty much along the traditional socioeconomic and racial lines, always adjusted for the political tenets of republicanism and the elimination of aristocratic privileges.[4]

The conservative constructs of childhood contained their own basis of authoritariansim, to the extent that children were not given credit for their own emotional and cognitive abilities until the liberal regimes of the second half of the nineteenth century. But here, too, one notes the similarities between liberals and conservatives. The educational ideologues of the Generation of '37 differed significantly from their liberal predecessors of the revolutionary era. Latter-day nineteenth-century liberals were no longer imbued with the republican utopianism of the earlier generation. Indeed, latter-day liberals shared the opinion of post-Rivadavian reactionaries that the political aspirations of the revolution had gone too far and, in any event, had been premature. The differences between liberals and conservatives on child-oriented issues rested principally on the extent to which they believed the state should become responsible for reforming the forthcoming generations through the instrument of education. Reform of the educational system meant bringing more children under the aegis of the state; this, in turn, meant continued conflict between families and political authorities, reflected in the disappointing attendance records of children who had learned the rudiments of reading and writing. The parents of these sons and daughters saw the state, with some reason, as an obstruction to their children's economic contribution on behalf of their families.

For its part, the liberal state would not turn away from its intent of reforming what its leaders saw as the unwholesome popular attitudes toward fundamental abstractions: authority, nationhood, rights, and obligations. The new order, if liberals had any influence in shaping it, would eventually eliminate the excesses of Iberian individualism in favor of "modern," consensual, and deferential attitudes. This promised the liberation of the new generations by imbuing them with a larger sense of purpose and belonging than the context afforded them by their families and their barrios. At the same time, however, the consequent greater freedom was not the equivalent of pluralism; on the contrary, the potential for greater freedoms was conditioned by the oligarchical state's needs. And, of course, this task along the road to nation building also required authoritarian modalities, no less effective for the different rhetorical styles employed by later nineteenth-century liberals. Domingo Sarmiento's obsessive concern for the establishment of order and of deference by children, coupled with a very busy school schedule and closely monitored communications with the world outside the school, suggests that the liberals' sharply different rhetorical and curricular contents did not replace the tradition of authoritarianism. Indeed, the differences were of dimensions: later nineteenth-century liberals succeeded in applying their tenets over a wider space than ever before in republican Argentina, and they thus enhanced authoritarian traits while subverting the local tradition of consent.

Finally, the concept of political rights and obligations in a pre-constitutional order can help us to understand the foundations that lay underneath the mass of demographic and quantitative evidence that was presented. The system of political patriarchy had a number of dangerous characteristics. If weak, the political patriarchs could fall, and with them public order. If strong, they eliminated enemies and protest with daunting efficiency. The immediate benefit of this terror was the attenuation of civil war; the long-term results included a salutary demographic reconstruction. The victim was political pluralism. Insofar as pluralism's day was not yet at hand, the gente de pueblo concentrated on the practical results of terror. Players in the political game came almost exclusively from the ranks of the gente decente, and there one could be only a partner of the regime—either as active supporter or passive nonparticipant—or an oppositionist. For the gente de pueblo, playing in the game of politics was reduced to serving as a military recruit of one side or another.

Thus, a protracted period of politico-military turbulence could only have immediate and personal repercussions for those recruits. The elimination of enemies by liquidation and the retention of power by terror tended toward greater peace for as long as enemies could be kept at bay. In practical terms, the gente de pueblo—the large segment of the population that the utopian revolutionaries had expected to embrace enlightened liberalism—appeared to have benefited from such forceful imposition of power. Here we can find the logic of the link between domestic and political patriarchy: the absence of consensus had precipitated events that were unwholesome for the integrity of both the domestic and the political family. The gente de pueblo and the gente decente, in their own ways and motivated by their own self-interest, capitalized on the opportunities that such authoritarianism afforded them: supportive *estancieros* improved their economic standing in this growing pastoral economy, and the lower classes lengthened their life expectancies.

Deposition was the result not of subjugation per se, but of the injustices that developed within a particular manner of subjugation. The prevailing system of subjugation was questioned by some of the liberal elites, but not usually by the masses, whose familial concerns overrode political philosophies. Indeed, masses and elites shared this characteristic, both concerning themselves with particularistic familial interests that overrode most other considerations. Robert Kern borrowed from Edward Banfield when he pointed out that among the obstacles faced by political regimes in Spain and Spanish America was "amoral familialism." Banfield had coined this unfortunate term in his unfortunately titled book, *The Moral Basis of a Backward Society*: amoral familialism was to be found in societies where the state had failed to create meaningful national institutions, and where individuals sought to maximize family, class, or fortunes in the conduct of public life.[5] Undoubtedly, public figures in Argentina acted rapaciously while in office, but the more calculating ones tempered their self-gratification with an instinct for maintaining stability in society and thereby themselves in office. Moreover, morality was very much an issue for them, insofar as they respected the traditional values of property and place in society. Tulio Halperín Donghi has noted the economically conservative nature and the law-and-order orientation of Argentine caudillos by highlighting their emphasis on returning laborers to their prerevolutionary tasks and their insistence on policing everyone's movements.[6] In contrast to the Banfield-

Kern concept, it may be more helpful to consider political relationships in less formalistic ways: whatever was missing in the way of
state-led national institutions, the result was not equivalent to an in-
stitutionless state. "Familialism" was such an institution, and it performed a central function precisely because of the particularistic nature of the sociopolitical system.

Natural law and social contract theories coincided on two levels:
the political state evolved from the family, and the obligation of subjects depended on the ruler's performance in maintaining their lives.
The Argentine political context—in the absence of constitutional
norms and of formal and representative institutions for smooth
administration—required that a time-honored and widely recognized principle of authority be used in lieu of an institutional apparatus. Here lies the component of political authority that patriarchy provided, but not the absolutist version proposed earlier by
advocates of divine authority—absolutism was considered to be
anachronistic even by nineteenth-century Argentine conservatives.
Modified and nonabsolutist political patriarchy was employed instead: consent was furnished by the region's elites, who vested military caudillos with the defense of their vital interests, while the social contract was maintained to the extent that a particular
strongman protected the popular classes and allowed them a certain
amount of latitude within the existing patriarchal system. Advantages thereby accrued to the parties that encompassed the three
points that sustained the political order: elites, popular classes, and
caudillo. This thesis of modified political patriarchy accepts the historical reality of a patrimonial political system, but—insofar as the
system contains consent and contractual elements—the thesis is also
required to account for the durability of individual caudillos. In
sum, the theoretical premises regarding nineteenth-century Spanish
America would do well to focus on the caudillos' performance in
terms of how well they maintained the lives of their people; furthermore, we should account for the turnover among these leaders
from perspectives that include the "obligated" masses.

The notion of accountability as a causal variable that helps to explain the duration of any given ruler in nineteenth-century Argentina implies that the Weberian concept of rationality or competence
can apply as well to preindustrial and traditional societies, but only
if, as Glen Dealy has noted, competence is not equated solely with
technological and formal rationality. "Competence forms the basis

for authority within caudillaje society," wrote Dealy, "and this competence has its grounding in a wholly rational life. Behavior comes tied to a rational calculus of means adapted to ends. Without a high level of individual competence the aggregation of a following would be impossible; and without a following, authority becomes impossible." It is thus particularly important that in *caudillaje* culture rational authority rests on a competence whose acceptance depends fundamentally on its performance.[7] I submit further that competence in patriarchal society was measured by the Argentine plebeians only as much as by the notables, insofar as both groups shared the historical and cultural principles of particularism and familialism. Moreover, familialism as an exclusivist normative behavior was reinforced all the more and over a greater majority as one descended the urban socioeconomic scale. Thus, the concept that moral authority and not constituency satisfaction was the prerequisite for ascent to political leadership fails to consider the concept of durability, which is determined by competence and performance as perceived and evaluated in the familial context.[8]

Consent and obligation could not be formally articulated or practiced in Argentina during the period covered in this book. The Lockean principle of consent and contract rested on foundations of political obligation that did not easily prevail in Spain or Spanish America. However, there was a nonconstitutional consent and a non-articulated contract that operated under patriarchy for the best of reasons: they provided the most easily recognizable form of rule to the greatest number of people, and they generated a *mentalité* toward authority that was very conformable to the Iberian historical context.

Moreover, political patriarchy gained further legitimacy in pre-constitutional Argentina from two objective conditions: first, it was easily and widely—almost instinctively—recognized by a society molded in Iberian traditions that contained fundamental elements of patriarchy in many forms of clientelistic association; and second, the bureaucratic superstructures had only recently been put in place as the Río de la Plata's economy was uplifted from its backwater status in the late eighteenth century. Subsequent republican forms of rule and representation had to confront the legacy that had provided great latitude of action to individuals who often represented merely their own interests. Considerable autonomy and informality had accrued to a wide cross-section of local society, a feature that was shared by the gaucho in the countryside and the contraband merchant in the port.

By contrast, the era of independence reinforced the tendency toward greater authority by the political elite—now equipped with military and administrative accouterments—at the cost of familial autonomy. This process had begun with the establishment of the viceroyalty of the Río de la Plata in 1776 and would proceed in earnest during the course of the nineteenth century. Caught in a turbulent era between the state's need for order and the family's own needs, porteños and their families were being required to become part of the larger community. "The government's vigilant defense of the pursuit of happiness among the people will be in vain," admonished the revolutionary junta member Bernardo Monteagudo in 1811, "if those who could assist in this goal, limit themselves instead to applauding agreeable ideas heard within their domestic circles and to discussing progressive reforms and plans only among their friends without ever sharing them publicly."[9] In his own way, Monteagudo, like others who followed him in power, sought to implant the linkages responsible for stable systems of community. These linkages were particularly important during changeful eras when political, cultural, and social traditions stood to be undermined. These were the times when the elites heightened their conviction that the conduct of the individual could threaten the stability of the known order.

In Argentina, this anti-individualistic trend signified the fundamental transition away from particularism, a goal commonly sought and only imperfectly established by Buenos Aires' elites, regardless of other ideological biases that divided them. In its ideal, the transition is related to the Erasmian notion of the state as a true monastery, meaning that the communal life ought to inspire the entire membership of the civil society, which should not consist of semi-private cliques.[10] This endeavor was generally observable in all emerging political entities, at least in the West, and reflected an inherently conflictual characteristic in the conjunction of state and family. André Burguière notes that in the apparent weakness of the state, expressed variously, including the inability to protect its people, "the family expands, assumes control of every aspect of the individual's life, and becomes a bastion." Conversely, the state gains strength at the cost of previous familial autonomy in determining choices for the individual, "who is then more readily integrated into society as a whole."[11]

But this transition also threatened political leaders in Spanish American cities with an untenable situation in which their traditional roles would become incongruous with the new circumstances, for behind the attempts at establishing systems of community, one may discern the conflict that success in eliminating medieval, particularistic features might have meant for elites who were still dependent on clientelism for the maintenance of their own position. Tribalism and rural kinship circles no longer prevailed in the city, which now—as correctly noted by Richard Morse—"constituted *public* order, but a public order in chronic conflict with the private one of patriarchal familialism."[12] As the more obvious corporate privileges of the colonial era disappeared, Spanish American society needed to establish alternative axes around which to balance rights and obligations. In the process, one of the advantages of the colonial corporatist style was lost: its institutions had been utterly clear, perfectly visible to one and all, and although subject to manipulation, corporate institutions had possessed what may be called representative clarity. In the formative period of the Argentine nation, this clarity was obfuscated by the elimination of some of those corporations (such as the *Audiencia*, the *Consulado*, and the *Cabildo*), by the attacks made on them by republican rhetoric, and by the variously—and conflictingly—defined democratic ideals. The power of the state was in flux, suffering alternate thrusts of crises and renewed strength. As François Furet noted, nothing is more difficult or dangerous for a monarchical political and social system in the throes of revolution "than to alter its essential ways of functioning and, above all, to liberalise itself. But the same holds true for social classes; and not only for the nobility, but also for the popular classes, which are particularly vulnerable to disruption of the traditional equilibrium."[13] This period of searching for the new equilibrium between rights and obligations in an urban public order provided a widening cross-section of families of Buenos Aires with a double-edged sword: an enlarged access to influence in the state's administrative mechanisms, and a much increased danger to familial integrity posed by that state's intent on imposing and cementing its rule.

Of Lorenzo the Magnificent, Machiavelli wrote that "he put a stop to the wars in Italy, and by his wisdom established peace." One cannot reasonably assign such an avuncular image to the more successful caudillos of Argentina's nineteenth century, but the principle of consent is nevertheless implied, and it serves the useful purpose of directing our attention to commonly held values related to the concept that we termed familialism and that in turn served to forge a political contract that drew meaning from an Iberian past not very distant from the actors' own lives. One would, of course, like to write with certainty about these matters, but certainty is reserved for few historical actions and for no historical mentalities. The empirical evidence provided by the statistics on population and changes in household structures, fitted into the expressed model of a modified and nonabsolute political patriarchy, can only speak suggestively of a collective consciousness geared toward the maximization of survival and familial coherence.

By the 1860's, the city of Buenos Aires was poised to embark on the significant changes that would be brought by the *belle époque* of the export boom and mass immigration. Men and women who grew to adulthood in the late 1800's recalled, often with melancholy fondness, how much more sedate and accommodating life had been in the old days of the *gran aldea*, before all the bustle and confusion of tongues that came to characterize the modern port city of immigrants—"before the times of mercantilism in which everything is charged by the hour," as Pastor S. Obligado lamented.[14] The outward signs of change appeared throughout the city, although unevenly, as the population swelled to approximately 180,000 people by 1870, and the buildings reached higher toward the skies.[15] By contrast, others boasted of the major strides in the nation's progress, which Buenos Aires reflected best. Thus, Sarmiento wrote laudatorily about the shifting style in the city's urbanization in the 1860's, when "the architect begins to replace the mason, the flat-roofed, single-story house [*casa de azotea*] definitively loses its predominance, and starts to become the unworthy habitat of a free people. Let us break with our traditions by demonstrating, for the first time, the human ability to diversify the forms of housing, since we have already seen that the Indian hut, the shack, and the *casa de azotea* are the forms which belong to the savage."[16] To be sure, the political house of Argentina would remain in some disorder for another few years as the *cuestión capital* continued to simmer with varying degrees of intensity until the city's federalization in 1880; this was evident in the sporadic outbursts of *montoneras* in the interior during the 1860's.[17] But in the end, Buenos Aires' own intolerance for political and territorial secession eventually succeeded in integrating the Argentine territory under its wing and concentrating effective authority in the uppermost levels of the growing state bureaucracy.

This slowly evolving political transition from confederacy to de facto centralization at the national level was also being expressed, but without weaponry or formal political bands, within the city of Buenos Aires. For what marked the *gran aldea* was not merely its antiquated material culture and urban landscape, as the Sarmientos of the post-Rosas era believed, but rather the long-standing traditions of respect for the communal rights of barrios, vecinos, and *gentes de familia*. Urban growth and cosmopolitanism were the necessary consequences of an aggressive, outward-looking, and mostly xenophilous elite, which culminated in the "Generation of '80." But an equally necessary consequence was the growing distance and the weakening of affinities between state and local society: in the paradigmatic terms employed in this book, growth signified the widening distance between the political estate and the familial estate. In the decades that followed, sectoral organizations would come to replace the old webs of local affinities: trade unions, ethnic voluntary associations, and interest groups with influence at the national level, including the Sociedad Rural, the Unión Industrial Argentina, and the Jockey Club, and finally, political parties in their mature form, which in the twentieth century would try to articulate the heterogeneous concerns of classes and regions into an integral whole, but only with checkered results. The evolving systems of community—those links that bind a public sharing a common space and heritage—were to operate at levels in which barrio, vecino, and gente de familia would lose much of their original meaning, and public action its parochial purpose.

Methodological Appendix

Methodological Appendix

The population considered in this study consists of two data sets, both drawn from each of the city's manuscript census returns for the years 1810, 1827, and 1855. The two data sets culled from each census overlap in some variables, but generally each data set addresses different issues. One set of data includes every person residing in four wards (*cuarteles*) selected for this study on the basis of their representativeness. This "selective universe" corresponds to cuarteles 3, 4, 12, and 19 (see map on p. 240). Two objective criteria had to be met as closely as the archival data permitted in order for a cuartel to be selected for inclusion. The first criterion was that the census returns had to be as complete as possible for each cuartel in each of the three years under consideration. The second was that, in their aggregate, the cuarteles would have to provide a reasonably representative picture of the porteños' socioeconomic and racial composition. The cuarteles, each consisting of a 16-block square, have the same numerical designations and territorial coverage originally established by the census enumerators in both 1827 and 1855. In 1810, the numbering system and the area included in each cuartel (12 blocks) had been quite different. It was decided that, for the sake of historical continuity and geographic standardization, the population that in 1810 resided within the same 16 blocks contained in each of the four cuarteles used in 1827 and 1855 would be selected from the census of 1810. The numerical designations given to the blocks (*manzanas*) were different for every one of the three census dates. Again for the sake of standardization, it was necessary to provide a universal numerical designation that would facilitate locational definitions and boundaries in the process of large-scale statistical computations.

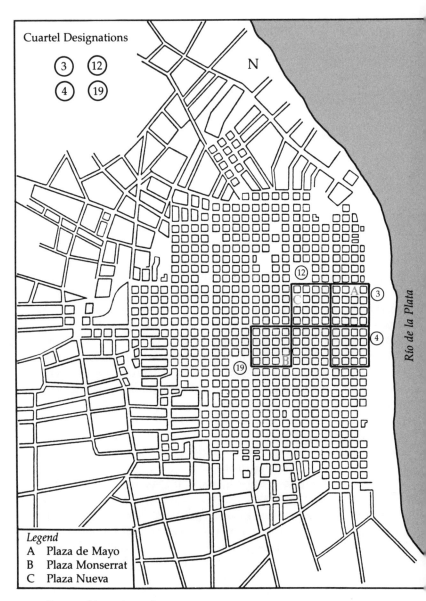

Cuartel Designations

③ ⑫

④ ⑲

N

Río de la Plata

Ⓐ

Ⓑ

Ⓒ

⑫

③

④

⑲

Legend
A   Plaza de Mayo
B   Plaza Monserrat
C   Plaza Nueva

Buenos Aires, circa 1855.

Every manzana number was converted to the designation given in the 1810 census, which had the advantage of having already been sequentially ordered from 1 to 406. The sequentially numbered system employed in 1810 had the added advantage of permitting the assignation of block numbers to manzanas that had not existed in 1810, but that by 1855 had been filled in and occupied; this was particularly appropriate in the case of low-lying areas along the shores of the Río de la Plata that became more populated over time.

In the aggregate, the problem of missing data was kept to a minimum. The 1810 census was missing tracts for nine residential blocks in cuartel 3, none in cuartel 4, nine in cuartel 12, and four in cuartel 19. The 1827 and 1855 censuses contained every block of every cuartel. It is estimated that the data missing from the selective universe amount to 370 households. This means that without any missing blocks the total number of households in the selective universe would have amounted to approximately 6,700 households instead of the 6,310 that were analyzed.[1] Under the conditions of the missing data of 1810, it should be noted that cuarteles 3 and 12 did not contain as much of the city's population as the older and much more densely populated southern cuarteles. Indeed, cuarteles 3 and 12 would not experience much growth or gentrification until after midcentury, eventually becoming the hub of the highly regarded Barrio Norte.[2] We believe that underenumeration is not a problem with the censuses employed. All the folios were first ordered in sequence of pagination and then in the sequence of street names and house numbers that each enumerator followed as he completed his assigned route, manzana by manzana. In this fashion, a number of folios and *libretos* were found to be out of sequence and lumped with inappropriate cuarteles. Comparisons were made of the routes taken and of the populations inscribed; if there was any underenumeration, it appears to have been consistent, thereby making the variations found over time to be reliable indicators of change. In the end, the complete populations of the four wards were gathered, which obviated the concern for statistical significance. These procedures yielded a data base of 6,310 households, the basic unit of analysis, containing 28,579 men, women, and children.

The second criterion for cuartel selection, that of a generally representative profile of the city's social groups, was met with the areas included in the study. Cuarteles 3 and 4, lying immediately north and south of the Plaza de Mayo, contained the strongest concentration of merchants, professionals, and bureaucrats. Within the arc around the plaza lived the scions of governmental and clerical administrations, commerce, and the large retinue of the service sector that encompassed the whole range of status positions, from lawyers and notaries to slaves and freedmen. Immediately northwest of the Plaza de Mayo was cuartel 12, somewhat more recently populated and, even at midcentury, still the site of small farms or *quintas*. Here tradesmen, merchants, teamsters, and agriculturalists gathered as both permanent residents and transients. The wagons and stalls of the marketplace of Plaza Nueva, occupying the site of block number 195, formed the western hub of cuartel 12, while the Plaza de Mayo's larger assortment of goods lay virtually at its southeastern corner. Cuartel 19, situated at the southwest corner of cuartel 12, contained a large concentration of the city's gente de color. This was the neighborhood that was popularly recognized as the *barrio de los tambores*. Within its administrative boundaries, block number 222, occupied by the Plaza Monserrat, served most of the market needs of the population of slaves and freedmen who operated—on their own or for their masters—shops and farms. The socioeconomic position of most of these residents was precarious, and crime was considered a greater problem here than in most other urban wards; its racial composition would change as European immigrants began to settle.[3]

The second data set, the "city sample," was used with two purposes in mind. First, it served as a control device that might provide confidence, in light of missing data, that the tendencies and directions displayed by the computations from the selective universe would be shared by data drawn from the city at large, where missing data are much more likely to be randomized, thereby minimizing error. The second purpose was practical. The caseload of the selective universe was so large that expenditures of time and assets could quickly be depleted. The smaller caseload of the city sample (1,149 households containing 6,020 individuals) provided greater flexibility both in coding intrahousehold relationships and in managing the computerized files. The city sample consists of one random sample of the urban population taken from each of the census years available. The emphasis was on the urban population for two reasons: first, to retain compatibility with the locational characteristics of the four cuarteles of the selective universe; and second, because the incidence of missing data increases radically in the suburban wards, the so-called *suburbios* and *campaña*. The sampling technique employed a table of random numbers; it yielded a total of 1,149 cases, representing 383 households for each census year and comprising the records of 6,020 individuals. While no sample size or sampling design will automatically insure optimal results in demographic research, the sample size of 383 households per census year is appropriate for greater Buenos Aires, where the population by 1855 amounted to approximately 90,000 people, and where a 95 percent confidence level was desired. The statistical results of the tables employing the city sample are significant to the .05 level.[4] The city sample was coded and manipulated in such a way as to provide a precise and representative look into the internal composition of the families and households of Buenos Aires. Unlike the situation provided by the selective universe, the city sample's more manageable caseload permitted a wider variety of frames of reference and comparisons among households. In sum, a total data base of 34,599 men, women, and children was analyzed. These individuals were concentrated in 7,459 households.

This book—focused principally on household structures and not on vital records—used little evidence from ecclesiastical parishes. This means that no verification of census listings on marital status was made. However, because this was an era with significant numbers of consensual unions in Buenos Aires and many other regions of Latin America, the nature of the conjugal union must be considered as part of the methodological framework. It would be counterproductive to suggest that only a strictly religious definition of marital status should be applied. From a purely statistical perspective, it would depress significantly and unreasonably the realistic extent to which consensual unions behaved as legitimate conjugal units. From a behavioral perspective, a sacramentally based definition of marital status would falsely assume that both instrumental and affective considerations of the couple toward each other, and especially toward their offspring, were somehow diminished by the lack of the sacramental ceremony. It is precisely in societies with high incidences of consensual unions that it would be unreasonable to expect diminished affective capacities. This book employed the marital status categories reported in the census tracts by the enumerators, regardless of the investigator's suspicions about the reality of illicit relations. In this book, the judgment of the marital status of persons listed in the census tracts followed the inference rules suggested by the Cambridge Group for the History of Population and Social Structure: "Those may be *presumed married* who are of opposite sex, appear first and second in the household and have the same surname [allowing for the retention of maiden names in the Hispanic tradition]. This presumption is strengthened if those following the first two have the same surname and/or are described as children. Those may also be *presumed married* who appear later in the household, i.e., not first and second, but who have the same surname and are followed in the household by those who have the same surname and/or are described as children. . . . An individual may be *presumed widowed* who is described as either mother or father of the head or other member of the household (a spouse not being present) or . . . the head of a household containing either or both a married couple and children (so described) with the same surname."[5] The censuses that were used facilitated greatly the determination of household relationships. In 1810, respondents and enumerators usually listed relationships. The 1855 census contained the question, "What relationship do you have to the head of the household?" In 1827, the inference rules of the Cambridge Group played a greater role.

Reference Matter

Notes

Complete authors' names, titles, and publication data for works cited in short form are given in the Bibliography, pp. 268–99. The following abbreviation is used in the Notes: AGN, for Archivo General de la Nación.

CHAPTER I

1. Ingenieros, esp. vols. 1 and 4; Belgrano, "Fuentes anglo-sajonas."

2. Taullard; Bejarano; Meister; Besio Moreno; Sarmiento, "Arquitectura"; Scobie, *Buenos Aires*.

3. Yujnovsky; Torres.

4. For a discussion of the relationship between modern behaviors and cultural traditions, see Berkhofer, esp. chs. 5–7; Bell; Freeman; Balán, Browning, and Jelin; Kahl.

5. Neighborhood as a historical and operational concept has been employed by Kent and Kent; Andersen; Romano; Sebreli.

6. See, for example, the complaint lodged on March 13, 1822, by a teacher in the elementary school of the parish of Concepción in AGN X-6-1-1, Instrucción Pública, 1812–35.

7. For a model of the relationship between space and the circulation of information, see Sopher; Pred.

8. For a succinct description of clientele and personnel of pulperías, see Slatta, "Pulperías."

9. For the evolution of material culture and personal possessions of the city's well-to-do from the late eighteenth through the nineteenth centuries, see Socolow, "Marriage"; Hernando; Sarmiento, "Arquitectura."

10. Titles dedicated to the construction styles of the late colonial era and the nineteenth century include Domínguez, "La vivienda colonial"; Martini; Sarmiento, "Arquitectura"; Torre Revello; Buenos Aires, *Arquitectura*; Facultad de Filosofía y Letras, *Documentos* (vol. 9); Guido; Kronfuss; Universidad de Buenos Aires.

11. *El Argos de Buenos Ayres*, Aug. 11, 1821.

12. See Juan P. Ramos' use of the term in Consejo Nacional de Educación, p. 167.

13. Quesada, *La época de Rosas*, p. 200.

14. Belgrano, *Historia*; Gondra, *Las ideas económicas*; Palcos; Binayán; Vedia y Mitre.

15. Morse, "Prolegomenon," pp. 361–62.

16. Fox-Genovese and Genovese, p. 213.

CHAPTER 2

1. Excellent material on revolution and race in Mexico can be found in Hammill; Timmons; Di Tella, "Las clases."

2. Argentina, more than any other Latin American nation, admitted European immigrants and their sons into its social and political circles; the many examples include José A. Wilde, Carlos Pellegrini, José Ingenieros, and Miguel A. Cárcano.

3. Shields and Duncan, pp. 3–4; Zehr, "Patterns," p. 45.

4. Seed, "Social Dimensions," p. 576. For reviews of crime in late colonial Buenos Aires, see Bazán Lezcano; Socolow, "Women and Crime."

5. Facultad de Filosofía y Letras, *Documentos* (vol. 9), pp. lxiii–lxxxiv.

6. Demographic data come from the municipal census tracts of 1810, 1827, and 1855; their data are presented more fully in subsequent chapters.

7. *El Censor*, Jan. 16, 1817.

8. Halperín Donghi, *Revolución y guerra*, pp. 313–14.

9. Crónica Política y Literaria de Buenos Aires, Aug. 22, 1827.

10. *Recopilación*, p. 151.

11. *Recopilación*, pp. 353–54.

12. *El Argos de Buenos-Ayres*, Mar. 13, 1822.

13. *Recopilación*, pp. 361–62.   14. Isabelle, *Viaje*, pp. 157–58.

15. Beruti, p. 3730.   16. O'Brien, pp. 238–39.

17. Beattie, p. 47.   18. *El Censor*, Nov. 13, 1817.

19. Henry Zouch, *Hints Respecting Public Police* (London, 1786), quoted in Beattie, p. 47.

20. *El Lucero*, Oct. 20, 1829.

21. Ted Robert Gurr, "Development and Decay: Their Impact on Public Order in Western History," in Inciardi and Faupel, p. 33.

22. *El Argos de Buenos Ayres*, Sept. 1, 1821.

23. *El Lucero*, Oct. 21, 1829.

24. *Crónica Política y Literaria de Buenos Aires*, Mar. 8, 1827.

25. Ibid., May 10, 1827.

26. Extrapolated from population data in Maeder, p. 34.

27. *El Lucero*, Nov. 4, 1829.

28. Among the best overviews of Argentina's economic evolution dur-

ing the first half of the nineteenth century are Brown; Halperín Donghi, "La expansión"; Gondra, *Historia económica*; Ferns; Ferrer; Cortes Conde, esp. pp. 115–53; Burgin.

29. Nationalistic literature flourished after the turn of the century. A few examples are Mansilla; Mejía; Gálvez; Cordero. Literature extolling the values of the Argentine countryside through the gauchesque themes includes the works of Güiraldes; Hernández.

' 30. Quoted in *Crónica Política y Literaria de Buenos Aires*, Aug. 20, 1827; see also *El Lucero*, Dec. 23, 1830, for similar concerns; Foucault, esp. pt. II, ch. 1.

31. *El Argos de Buenos Ayres*, Feb. 23, 1822.

32. Alberdi, *Cartas sobre la prensa*.   33. Reinhardt, p. 444.

34. Chevalier, pp. 359–408.   35. Elton, pp. 7–8.

36. Baker, pp. 28–29.   37. Hay, pp. 27–28.

38. *Crónica Política y Literaria de Buenos Aires*, May 17, 1827.

39. Flory, pp. 119–23.

40. Beruti, p. 3823.

41. *Recopilación*, p. 112.

42. *Crónica Política y Literaria de Buenos Aires*, May 17, 1827.

43. *El Lucero*, Nov. 10, 1829; see also *El Lucero*, Nov. 13, 1829, for an overview of the intricacies of routing a criminal case through the judicial system, and *El Lucero*, Dec. 24, 1830, for further observations.

44. Karst and Rosenn, p. 14.

45. Zorraquín Becú, 1: 256. For additional overviews of the Spanish and Argentine legal systems, see Levaggi; Jiménez de Azúa; Karst.

46. AGN X-31-9-5, Policía, 1823–50.

47. Ibid.

48. Ibid.

49. Ibid.

50. AGN X-43-7-5, Policía, 1850–59, Serenos.

51. *Crónica Política y Literaria de Buenos Aires*, May 8, 1827.

52. *El Censor*, Mar. 13, 1817.

53. AGN X-43-7-5, Policía, 1830–38.

54. Ibid., 1830–38, 1850–59, Serenos.

55. *Crónica Política y Literaria de Buenos Aires*, Aug. 8, 1827.

56. AGN X-43-7-5, Policía, 1830–38.

57. Ibid.   58. Ibid.

59. Ibid.   60. Ibid., 1850–59, Serenos.

61. Beruti, pp. 3868–69.   62. Beruti, p. 3879.

63. AGN X-43-7-5, Policía, 1830-1838.

64. *Teatro de la Opinión*, June 27, 1823.

65. *El Lucero*, Sept. 15, 1829.

66. Isabelle, pp. 158–59.

67. *Teatro de la Opinión*, Oct. 17, 1823. According to Isabelle, the dangerous characters who often made up the police auxiliaries and their poor performance in the discharge of their peacekeeping duties formed the basic reasons for the creation of the nightwatchmen's corps. Isabelle, p. 159.

68. *El Lucero*, Sept. 15, 1829.   69. Beruti, pp. 3909–10.

70. *El Censor*, Jan. 16, 1817.   71. *El Censor*, Sept. 5, 1816.

72. The regimen governing the maintenance of the street lighting system can be observed in the police department's public calls for bids in *El Lucero*, Oct. 21, 1829.

73. AGN X-36-4-6, Policía, Alumbrado, 1834.

74. AGN X-43-7-5, Policía y Serenos.

75. AGN X-31-9-4, Policía, 1825–31.

76. Fausto, "Controle social"; Holloway; Fausto, *Crime e cotidiano*.

77. Beruti, p. 3910.

78. AGN X-42-8-5, Censos, 1813–61.

79. Beruti, pp. 3804–5.

80. Zehr, "Modernization," pp. 121–22.

81. *The British Packet and Argentine News*, Aug. 8, 1829.

82. For a review of the treatment given to rural lawbreakers, including forced military service, see Slatta, "Rural Criminality."

83. *Recopilación*, "Decreto sobre la seguridad individual," Nov. 23, 1811, p. 3.

84. Quoted in Hay, p. 18.

85. Foucault, p. 75.

86. Zehr, "Patterns," pp. 113–15.

87. R. Levine, pp. 15–16. For a review of means of acquittals in an earlier period of Brazilian history, see Aufderheide, ch. 8; Flory. For a view of leniency in colonial Mexico, see Taylor, pp. 98–106.

88. Echeverría, *La cautiva*.   89. Ibid., p. 74.

90. Ibid., pp. 78–79.   91. Isabelle, p. 184.

92. Mármol, *Amalia*, 1: 37–38.   93. Isabelle, p. 153.

94. Chevalier, p. 409.

95. A good analysis of Argentine positivism can be found in Soler. Notable examples of this literature include Mejía; Ayarragaray; Bunge.

96. Sarmiento, *Facundo*.

97. Echeverría, *La cautiva*, p. 91.

98. AGN X-31-9-5, Policía, 1823–50.

99. AGN X-31-9-4, Policía, 1825–31; Slatta, "Pulperías."

100. See Haigh; Beaumont; MacCann; Caldcleugh; Isabelle, *Voyage*.

101. Rico González, p. 143.

102. *Crónica Política y Literaria de Buenos Aires*, May 17, 1827.

103. *Teatro de la Opinión*, July 11, 1823.

104. Hay, p. 41.

105. AGN X-32-1-1, Policía, Correspondencia particular, 1847–62.
106. Ibid.
107. *Crónica Política y Literaria de Buenos Aires*, Apr. 26, 1827.
108. For an overview of elite attitudes toward folk society, see Burns, *Poverty*.
109. *Teatro de la Opinión*, Sept. 26, 1823.
110. AGN X-32-1-1.
111. The term "inorganic democracy" is employed by J. L. Romero, *History*.
112. AGN X-32-1-1. For reviews and judgments of Rosas' arbitrariness see J. L. Romero, *History*, esp. ch. 4; Ingenieros, vols. 3 and 4; Ayarragaray; Saldías, *Historia*.
113. Estrada, 2: 434.
114. Ingenieros, 3: 319.
115. Andrews, pp. 96–101.
116. AGN X-32-1-1, Policía, Correspondencia.
117. Ibid.   118. Ibid.
119. Ibid.   120. Beruti, pp. 3833–34.
121. O'Brien, p. 236.   122. AGN X-32-1-1.
123. AGN X-33-5-5, Policía, Cuartel General, 1847.
124. AGN X-33-10-1, Policía, Notas de ciudad, 1854.
125. *El Lucero*, Dec. 23, 1829.
126. *Crónica Política y Literaria de Buenos Aires*, May 1, 1827.
127. Ibid., Mar. 6, 1827.
128. Caldcleugh, 1: 160ff.
129. Juan Ignacio Gorriti, *Reflexiones* (Buenos Aires, 1916), quoted in Levaggi, p. 163.
130. Quoted in Levaggi, pp. 174–75.
131. For an early version of nationalist conservative sentiment, see *El Despertador Teofilántrópico, Místico-Político*, Dec. 7, 1820.
132. *Crónica Política y Literaria de Buenos Aires*, Mar. 3, 1827; compare with Mar. 6, 1827.
133. *Teatro de la Opinión*, June 6, 1823.
134. AGN X-33-10-1, Notas de ciudad, 1854, Libros 257–59.
135. In fact, the legal training given at the University of Buenos Aires was based on the concept of utility. See the discussion in *El Lucero*, Oct. 23, 1829, and Oct. 27, 1829; see also Halperín Donghi, *Historia*, pp. 15–62.
136. See *Teatro de la Opinión*, June 20, 1823, and July 11, 1823, for the advocacy of such principles. For an overview of the impact of Utilitarianism on Argentine liberals, see Williford, esp. pp. 126–32.
137. Stone, *Family, Sex and Marriage*, p. 236.
138. Quiroga de la Rosa; Alberdi, *Fragmento*.
139. Alberdi, *Obras completas*, 8: 125–26.

140. *Teatro de la Opinión*, Sept. 26, 1823.
141. O'Brien, pp. 20–21.
142. Halperín Donghi, *Aftermath.*
143. *El Lucero*, Jan. 11, 1830.
144. Lynch; Slatta, "Rural Criminality."
145. Stone, *Family, Sex and Marriage*, p. 660.
146. Geertz.
147. Rodríguez Molas; Slatta, *Gauchos*; Luna, esp. chs. 4–5 on the latter-day caudillos Angel Vicente Peñaloza and Felipe Varela.
148. Scobie, *Revolution*. Figures on exports can be found in Martínez and Lewandowski.
149. Blackwelder and Johnson.

CHAPTER 3

1. Slatta, *Gauchos*, p. 32.
2. Socolow, "Marriage," p. 392; Farber, p. 46.
3. Balmori and Oppenheimer, p. 241.
4. Farber, p. 46.
5. Van de Walle, "Motivations," pp. 135–36; Henry and Blayo.
6. Van de Walle, "Motivations," pp. 135–36, 138.
7. *El Lucero*, Dec. 23, 1829.
8. *El Argos de Buenos Ayres*, Feb. 22, 1823.
9. Ibid., Feb. 6, 1822; also Mar. 8, 1823.
10. Correa Luna, 1: 39.
11. *Telégrafo Mercantil*, Nov. 15, 1801, quoted in Correa Luna, 1: 39–40.
12. L. Johnson, p. 261.
13. For arguments countering the numerical decline of the black population, see Andrews.
14. Examples are found in *El Argos de Buenos Ayres*, July 16, 1823; *Crónica Política y Literaria de Buenos Aires*, Apr. 10, 1827; and elsewhere.
15. *Crónica Política y Literaria de Buenos Aires*, Sept. 18, 1827.
16. Correa Luna, 1: 26.
17. For examples of the putting-out system in England, see Schofield; estimates of child emigration figures for England are given in Wrigley and Schofield, pp. 632–35; the case of child migration from the home in Central Europe is discussed in Braun, "Impact."
18. Honorable Concejo Deliberante, p. 15.
19. *Decreto poniendo al cargo de un ciudadano la Defensuría de Menores,* Buenos Aires, Nov. 14, 1829, ibid., pp. 1021–1022; *El Lucero*, Nov. 16, 1829.
20. In 1829, the responsibilities of the *protector de menores* were expanded to include the protection of Indians. *El Lucero*, Dec. 30, 1829.
21. Buenos Aires, *Memoria*, p. 11.
22. *El Lucero*, Jan. 2, 1830.

23. *El Argos de Buenos Ayres*, Jan. 30, 1822.

24. For comparisons with the contemporary perceptions in the United States, see Demos and Demos, p. 633.

25. *El Censor*, Oct. 12, 1815, pp. 5–6; *Teatro de la Opinión*, July 25, 1823.

26. AGN X-31-9-5, Policía, 1823–50.

27. Ibid.

28. For examples, see AGN X-33-5-5, Policía, Cuartel General, Varios Asuntos, 1847, Libros 151–53, leg. 57.

29. AGN X-33-5-5.

30. Goldberg, p. 86; for a view of the statistical results derived from this sexual relaxation, see Braun, "Early Industrialization," p. 315.

31. The economic situations of single men and women conditioned the timing and even the forms of their unions; thus, Western nuptiality and fertility patterns among low-ranked occupational groups during the nineteenth century indicate deferred, more dependent, and perhaps more fragile marriages than those that took place among members of non-manual social groups. Chudacoff, pp. 184–88; Anderson, *Family Structure*, ch. 3.

32. In mid-nineteenth-century Costa Rica, over 40 percent of urban households were headed by females, many of whom were white. See Gudmundson, "Costa Rica Before Coffee," pp. 131–33.

33. Kuhn, p. 43.

34. Finley, p. 139.

35. Mitterauer and Sieder, pp. 41–43; Stone, "Family History," p. 60; Schofield, pp. 261–74; Braun, "Early Industrialization," pp. 291, 320; Shorter, *Making of the Modern Family*, pp. 26–28.

36. Yasuba.

37. Greven, "Family Structure."

38. Easterlin, "Human Fertility."

39. Habakkuk, p. 1.

40. Habakkuk, p. 6.

41. Szuchman, "Family and Household," pp. 10–13.

42. Stern, "Differential Fertility."

43. Ramos, "City and Country."

44. For example, 28 percent of all births in poor rural areas of Chile between 1885 and 1900 were illegitimate. See McCaa, *Marriage*, p. 79.

45. Shorter, "Illegitimacy, Sexual Revolution," p. 246.

46. Halperín Donghi, *Guerra y finanzas*, p. 236.

47. AGN X-17-3-1, Beneficencia y Biblioteca, 1841.

48. Lynch, p. 192.

49. Emilio Ravignani, *Padrones de la Ciudad y Campaña de Buenos Aires*, in Facultad de Filosofía y Letras, *Documentos* (vol. 8), pp. 356–89; Goldberg, p. 84.

50. Little, pp. 97–98.

51. Goldberg, p. 86.

52. *El Lucero*, Jan. 25, 1830.

53. In fact, the age group of 35- to 44-year-olds among Italian women reduced the mean number of children ever born by nearly 31 percent. Livi-Bacci, *History*, p. 272.

54. Livi-Bacci, "Fertility," p. 526.   55. Ibid., pp. 529–32.
56. Ibid., pp. 532–33.   57. Ibid., p. 533.
58. "Ley aboliendo los mayorazgos," Aug. 13, 1813, in *Recopilación*, p. 31.
59. Goldberg, pp. 86–87.
60. Bilbao, *Buenos Aires*, pp. 62–65.
61. Gillis, *Youth and History*, p. 44.
62. From a private set of letters.
63. For a classic study of the political latitude promoted in the Spanish Indies through the conflicts engendered by a uniform standard of administration, see Phelan.
64. Kuznesof, "Household Composition," pp. 80–81. The literature based on modernization theory is ample. For its application to Latin American value systems, see Germani, *Política y sociedad*; Kahl, *Measurement*; Lipset, Bendix, and Germani; Kahl, *Modernization*; Germani, *Sociology*.
65. Judt, pp. 68–69.
66. Kuznesof, "Household Composition," p. 80. Classic literature on the culture of poverty in Latin America includes the works of Lewis *Children of Sanchez* and *La Vida*.
67. A. Johnson, pp. 633–45.
68. A. Johnson, p. 648. Pressures that affected rural populations in Spanish America in the course of the nineteenth century's modernization and export boom are argued from the perspectives of social control and their political implications by Katz; Bauer.
69. McCaa, *Marriage*, pp. 86–90.
70. Quoted in Livi-Bacci, "Fertility," p. 533.
71. Tutino.
72. Ladd, p. 183. For an analysis of marriage patterns in Mexico City, but without a socioeconomic breakdown, see Arrom, *The Women of Mexico City*, pp. 111–21.
73. Clavero, p. 214.   74. Cooper, pp. 239–40.
75. Cooper, pp. 240–52.   76. Felstiner, pp. 177–78.
77. Harispuru.
78. Balmori and Oppenheimer, pp. 231, 239.
79. M. Cárcano, p. 15.
80. Balmori and Oppenheimer, p. 241.
81. Socolow, "Marriage," p. 392.
82. Socolow, "La burguesía," p. 211.
83. Ibid.
84. Peña illustrates this passage into more equalitarian modes of trans-

mission with the case of José Guadalupe González Toscano, born to a sub-lease tenant in 1821 and married to the daughter of the main tenant in 1846. After working for fifteen years, he had saved enough to buy 350 hectares of ranch land in 1861. At the time of his death, his four sons and three daughters inherited equal shares, something the upper class managed to avoid generally. See Peña, pp. 218–21.

85. In truth, speculation, supported by degrees of theoretical plausibility, is at the heart of much of the recent research in demographic history; note the use of conditional constructions and the subjunctive mood in its language.

86. Burguiére, p. 239.

87. Flandrin, "Contraception," pp. 23–48.

88. Thomas Sánchez, *De sancto matrimonii sacramento*, book 9, dispute 19, q. 7, quoted in Flandrin, "Contraception," p. 44.

89. Flandrin, "Contraception," p. 47.

90. For studies of the Jesuits in this region, see Morner, *Expulsion* and *Political and Economic Activities*; Furlong, *Los jesuitas y la cultura*, *Los jesuitas y la escisión*, and *Los jesuitas, su origen*; Cushner.

91. Noonan, pp. 303–40.

92. Much literature was written by the nineteenth-century Latin American elites bemoaning the racially hybrid character of the majorities and wishing for the superior qualities of Europeans. The Argentine intelligentsia excelled at writing sociology of the future from such perspectives; a fine example of this literature is Sarmiento, *Conflicto*; see also the excellent synthesis by Pérez Amuchástegui. For a review of the ways that nineteenth-century Latin American elites thought of Europeans, see Burns, "Ideology."

CHAPTER 4

1. Río, p. 95; Mármol, *Poesías*, vol. 2, "A Rosas el 25 de Mayo de 1850," p. 162.

2. *El Lucero*, Oct. 29, 1829; Pérez Amuchástegui, p. 232.

3. *El Lucero*, Nov. 19, 1829.

4. "As an Argentine," wrote Alberdi in 1887, "I would have fewer difficulties in accepting the Constitution of the Government of Brazil in my country, than the Constitution of its civil and domestic society, that is, its Civil Code, which organizes the Brazilian family in accordance with the climactic influences of the torrid region, with the principles of empire, and with the enslavement of the Black race." Alberdi, *Obras completas*, 7: 125–26.

5. *El Lucero*, Jan. 2, 1830.

6. *Recopilación*, p. 1020, "*Mandando a cerrar las pulperías en dias festivos*" and its *considerandos*, published in *El Lucero*, Nov. 9, 1829.

7. See, for example, Guido's instructions to the chief of police in *El Lucero*, Jan. 7, 1830.

8. *El Lucero*, Sept. 23, 1829.

9. Slatta, "Pulperías," p. 347.

10. *Teatro de la Opinión*, July 11, 1823.

11. V. Quesada, p. 276.   12. *El Lucero*, Jan. 9, 1830.

13. Bushnell, p. 51.   14. Bushnell, p. 65.

15. *Recopilación*, pp. 420–21.

16. AGN X-42-8-2, Educación, 1826–55.

17. Cf., for example, *Crónica Política y Literaria de Buenos Aires*, Apr. 10, 1827; May 3, 1827; July 12, 1827; and Sept. 4, 1827.

18. *El Censor*, Apr. 4, 1816.   19. V. Quesada, pp. 64–65.

20. Ariès, "The Family," p. 228.   21. Isabelle, p. 148.

22. Ariès, "The Family," p. 231; for perceptions of pulperías by the gente decente, see Slatta, "Pulperías," pp. 349–54.

23. AGN X-32-10-1, *Libro de Policía*, 1, May 20, 1812.

24. Slatta, "Pulperías," p. 349.

25. N. Davis, p. 41.

26. García Belsunce, *Buenos Aires . . . salud y delito*, p. 200.

27. AGN X-32-11-2, *Libro de Policía*, 25, Sept. 21 and 22, 1827.

28. Bilbao, *Tradiciones*, p. 413.

29. Quoted ibid.

30. Scenes of the home as a locus of nineteenth-century political haven and conspiracy are captured in Mármol, *Amalia*.

31. Sebreli.

32. Sosa de Newton, p. 65.

33. This public character would in fact be a growing feature over the course of the nineteenth century as both human and capital migration patterns to Buenos Aires resulted in an increased proportion of the citizenry vitally concerned with public policies. For a discussion of the familial implications of the relationships between space and action, see B. Laslett, pp. 480–92.

34. Bilbao, *Tradiciones*, p. 417.

35. The first Italian opera was shown only in 1810. Beruti, p. 3773.

36. Halperín Donghi, "Revolutionary Militarization," pp. 101–2.

37. Beruti, pp. 3683–84.   38. R. Cárcano, p. 14.

39. Felstiner, p. 170.   40. Obligado, pp. 135–42.

41. Obligado, pp. 140–42.

42. *Gaceta de Buenos Aires*, Sept. 19, 1811, quoted in Binayán, pp. 86–87.

43. *El Despertador Teofilántrópico Místico-Político*, May 7, 1820.

44. Ibid., May 14, 1820.

45. *Decreto inculcando que no se haga uso de azotes en las escuelas,* May 22, 1819, in *Recopilación,* p. 139.

46. *El Lucero,* Dec. 17, 1830.   47. *El Hablador,* Sept. 19, 1855.

48. R. Cárcano, pp. 15–17.   49. Quoted in M. Cárcano, p. 40.

50. Sarmiento, *Life,* p. 234.   51. See Lynch, pp. 222 and 227.

52. Araoz de la Madrid, p. 183. For descriptions of pillaging involving innocents, see Bernárdez, pp. 118–19.

53. Beruti, p. 3990.

54. Beruti, pp. 4088–89.

55. Shorter, "Illegitimacy, Sexual Revolution," "Female Emancipation," and Shorter, *Making of the Modern Family,* pp. 80–89.

56. *El Censor,* May 8, 1817.

57. Szuchman, "Continuity and Conflict in Buenos Aires: Comments on the Historical City," in Ross and McGann, p. 58.

58. AGN X-17-2-7, Registros Parroquiales, 1840; AGN X-16-10-7, Defunciones y Matrimonios en Buenos Aires.

59. Fairchilds, pp. 627–67.   60. Little, pp. 97–98.

61. *El Censor,* June 12, 1817.   62. Ibid., Jan. 8, 1818.

63. Parish, p. 606.   64. Isabelle, *Viaje,* p. 126.

65. Beruti, p. 4116.

66. Shorter, "Illegitimacy, Sexual Revolution," p. 237; Flandrin, "Contraception," p. 45.

67. Shorter, "Illegitimacy, Sexual Revolution," p. 246.

68. Beruti, p. 3840.

69. Beruti, p. 3800.

70. Quoted in V. Quesada, p. 274.

71. For example, in the generalized humility of the Costa Rican economy prior to the coffee-based boom, the incidence of illegitimacy in the urban sectors was high: at least 40 percent of the households in Costa Rican cities in 1840 were headed by women, half of whom declared themselves to be single. Gudmundson, "Household Structures," p. 5.

72. V. Quesada, p. 7.

73. Alberdi, *Cartas sobre la prensa,* pp. 2, 6, 9.

74. *El Censor,* Jan. 15, 1818.   75. *El Hablador,* Sept. 5, 1855.

76. *El Lucero,* Oct. 1, 1855.   77. *El Hablador,* Sept. 19, 1855.

78. For a study of the elites' disaffection and worries regarding immigrants, see Solberg.

CHAPTER 5

1. Ariès, *Centuries of Childhood,* p. 411.

2. Weinberg, "Historical Perspective," p. 45.

3. *El Censor,* Apr. 24, 1817.

4. *El Lucero*, Oct. 21, 1829.

5. Grew, Harrigan, and Whitney, pp. 27–30.

6. AGN X-6-1-6, Inspección de Escuelas, 1826–36.

7. AGN X-6-1-2, Instrucción Pública, 1821–36.

8. The concept of "model" or "style" of education as an expression of the elites' dominant values is argued in Weinberg, "Historical Perspective," pp. 39–41.

9. *El Censor*, Apr. 24, 1817.

10. AGN X-6-1-1, Instrucción Pública, 1812–35.

11. *El Censor*, Apr. 24, 1817; AGN X-6-1-1, Instrucción Pública, 1812–35.

12. AGN X-6-1-1, Instrucción Pública, 1812–35.

13. AGN, Censos 1405–6, *Censo nacional de escuelas del 20 de Diciembre de 1872*, Provincia de Buenos Aires, Cuadros de Capital, B. III–B. IV.

14. República Argentina, p. 26.

15. Halperín Donghi, *Revolución y guerra*, p. 61.

16. Quoted in Solari, p. 41.

17. AGN X-6-1-1, Instrucción Pública, 1812–35.

18. Ibid.

19. Di Tella, "Raíces," p. 291.

20. AGN X-6-1-6, Inspección de Escuelas, 1826–36.

21. Maynes, pp. 80–81.

22. García, p. 96.

23. *El Censor*, May 15, 1817; emphasis in original.

24. *Crónica Política y Literaria de Buenos Aires*, June 16, 1827.

25. AGN X-6-1-1, Instrucción Pública, 1812–35.

26. Juan Probst, "La educación en la República Argentina en la época colonial," in Facultad de Filosofía y Letras, *Documentos* (vol. 18), p. 208.

27. AGN X-6-1-2, Instrucción Pública, 1821–36.

28. Ibid.

29. *Recopilación*, "Decreto restableciendo el Colegio de San Carlos," June 2, 1817, pp. 120–21; Beruti, p. 3905.

30. *La Gaceta de Buenos Ayres*, Sept. 13, 1810.

31. AGN X-6-1-2, Instrucción Pública, 1821–36.

32. *El Argos de Buenos Ayres*, June 23, 1821.

33. *Circular* of Jan. 22, 1830, in *El Lucero*, Jan. 23, 1830.

34. See the *Considerando* of the edict of Sept. 28, 1830, which closed down the Colegio de la Provincia de Buenos Aires.

35. Halperín Donghi, *Guerra y finanzas*, pp. 169–83.

36. AGN X-6-1-6, Inspección de Escuelas, 1826–36.

37. *El Lucero*, Oct. 1, 1829.

38. Ibid., Dec. 16, 1829.

39. See, for example, *El Lucero*, Dec. 18, 1829.

40. AGN X-6-1-1, Instrucción Pública, 1812–35.

41. See, for example, *Crónica Política y Literaria de Buenos Aires*, Apr. 10, May 3, July 12, and Sept. 4, 1827; *El Lucero*, Mar. 24, 1830.

42. For example, see *El Lucero*, July 23, 1830, for complaints from medical students.

43. Ibid., Nov. 30, 1830.   44. Ibid., Dec. 1, 1830.

45. Ibid., Dec. 2, 1830.   46. Ibid.

47. *La Gaceta de Buenos Aires*, Dec. 1, 1830.

48. *El Lucero*, Dec. 4, 1830.

49. Halperín Donghi, *Historia*, pp. 40–42.

50. Véliz, pp. 88–89.

51. Murilo de Carvalho.

52. Data for Spain can be found in Kagan.

53. Di Tella, "Raíces," pp. 289–92.

54. Weinberg, *Modelos*, pp. 164–65.

55. Ariès, *Centuries of Childhood*, esp. pp. 241–68, on matters of school discipline.

56. AGN X-6-1-1, Instrucción Pública, 1812–35.

57. Ibid.

58. Ibid.

59. AGN X-6-1-2, Instrucción Pública, 1821–36.

60. Ibid.

61. AGN X-17-6-3, Culto, Educación, 1845.

62. AGN X-6-1-1, Instrucción Pública, 1812–35.

63. Ibid.

64. AGN X-6-1-6, Inspección de Escuelas, 1826–36.

65. For a view of parental evasions and resistance in France, see Strumingher, pp. 34–47; for similar conflicts between parents and school authorities in New England, see Kaestle, "Social Change," esp. pp. 8–14.

66. For the mixed results of the compulsory education law, see Spalding.

67. Felipe Senillosa to Minister of War, May 22, 1816, AGN X-6-1-1, Instrucción Pública, 1812–35.

68. For a formulation of adolescence as an apposite construct, see Demos and Demos.

69. Lancaster, p. 25.   70. Lancaster, p. 26.

71. Lancaster, pp. 34–38.   72. Browning, p. 59.

73. Solari, p. 60.

74. Solari, pp. 44–45. The argument that even the unitarians in exile, sworn enemies of Rosas, came in the course of time to agree with some of the conservative values ingrained in Argentine political culture since the revolution is found in Saldías, *Vida*, pp. 244–45.

75. Vedoya, pp. 11–14.

76. In fact, Lancaster (p. 3) confidently asserted that "a class may consist of any number of scholars, without limitation to any particular number."

77. AGN X-6-1-1, Instrucción Pública, 1812–35.

78. The point of parental alienation is made by Browning, pp. 58–59, as one of the features of the Lancasterian system in general, and it appears to have caused problems elsewhere.

79. AGN X-6-1-1, Instrucción Pública, 1812–35.

80. Ibid.   81. Ibid.

82. Ibid.   83. Ibid.

84. *El Argos de Buenos Ayres*, Aug. 25, 1821.

85. Solari, p. 89.

86. Sarmiento, *Constitución*, p. 17.

87. For an overview of the tenets held by the Generation of '37, see J. Romero, *History*, pp. 126–54.

88. AGN X-6-1-1, Instrucción Pública, 1812–35.

89. Sarmiento, *Constitución*, pp. 17–18.

90. Ibid., p. 24.

91. García Márquez, pp. 23–24.

92. García, p. 97.

93. AGN X-6-1-2, Instrucción Pública, 1821–36.

94. AGN X-6-1-1, Instrucción Pública, 1812–1835.

95. *El Argos de Buenos Ayres*, June 9, 1821.

96. Ibid., Feb. 9, 1822.

97. AGN X-6-1-1, Instrucción Pública, 1812–35.

98. AGN X-6-1-6, Inspección de Escuelas, 1826–36.

99. Ibid.

100. AGN X-6-1-1, Instrucción Pública, 1812–35.

101. See the exchange of notes between the Minister of State, José Barros Pazos, and the officers of the Sociedad de Beneficencia, María de las Carreras and María Sánchez de Mendeville, between July 6 and 21, 1857. AGN X-28-11-1.

102. AGN X-6-1-6, Inspección de Escuelas, 1826–36.

103. Ibid.

104. AGN X-17-8-5, Enseñanza Pública, 1847.

105. AGN X-17-8-4, Enseñanza Pública, 1847.

106. AGN X-6-1-1, Instrucción Pública, 1812–35.

107. Ibid.

108. Ibid.

109. Ibid. The humiliation heaped on university students who dared to question the educational system was not significantly different; for attitudes toward such students at the School of Medicine of the University of Buenos

Aires, see the exchanges published in *El Lucero*, July 23, Dec. 2, and Dec. 4, 1830.

110. AGN X-6-1-1, Instrucción Pública, 1812–35.
111. Spalding.   112. Quoted in Solari, p. 93.
113. Solari, pp. 138–39.   114. Haskell, pp. 551–55.
115. Halperín Donghi, *Revolución y guerra*, p. 417.
116. Esteban Echeverría, *Manual de enseñanza moral*, quoted in Ingenieros, pp. 316–17.
117. Esteban Echeverría, *Dogma socialista*, in J. Romero, *History*, p. 145.
118. Dealy, "Prolegomena," p. 57; R. Newton.
119. Halperín Donghi, *Una nación*, p. 12.
120. See Adler.
121. See Ramos Mejía (1912), esp. pp. 75–102 and 201–18.
122. Domínguez, *Historia argentina*.
123. Ibid., p. 5.
124. Ibid.; emphasis in original.
125. Ibid., pp. 361–84.
126. Sarmiento, "Política arjentina, 1849–1851," quoted in Bosch, pp. 142–43.
127. Quoted in Solari, pp. 97–98.
128. Ibid., p. 98.
129. For the thoughts of Echeverría on the matter, see his *Mayo y la enseñanza popular en el Plata*.
130. Lazerson, pp. 37–39.
131. Elizabeth Palmer Peabody, *Lectures in the Training School for Kindergartners* (Boston, 1893), quoted in Lazerson, p. 39.
132. Kett, p. 297.
133. The data on schools come from AGN, Censos 1405–6. Censo Nacional de Escuelas del 20 de Diciembre del Año 1872, Provincia de Buenos Aires, Cuadros de Capital. B.III–IV; and Censos 1407–9, B.V–VII, Censo Nacional de Escuelas del 20 de Diciembre de 1872, Comprobantes de los cuadros.
134. Buenos Aires, *Memoria*, pp. 24–26.
135. Ibid., p. 24.
136. E. Quesada, *Reseñas y críticas*, p. 517.
137. Concejo Nacional de Educación, p. 166.
138. Spalding.

CHAPTER 6

1. Raw demographic data come from the manuscript census schedules for the city of Buenos Aires of 1810, 1827, and 1855. The schedules of 1827 have been employed minimally, and the schedules of 1855 not at all in lon-

gitudinal studies. They are located in AGN IX, 10-7-1 (1810); X, 23-5-5 and 23-5-6 (1827); X, 1.390–1.404 (1855). Among the most frequently used published works on the population of Buenos Aires are Ravignani, *Territorio*; *Registro estadístico del Estado de Buenos Aires*; Ravignani, "Crecimiento"; Besio Moreno; *Registro estadístico de la Provincia de Buenos Aires*; Maeder; García Belsunce, *Buenos Aires: su gente*; Goldberg; Lattes; L. Johnson, "Estimaciones"; Moreno.

2. Julio Irazusta, *Vida política de Juan Manuel de Rosas a través de su correspondencia*, 8 vols. (Buenos Aires, 1940), quoted in Lynch, p. 27.

3. For an overview of the impact that English liberals had on the revolutionary generation, see Belgrano, "Fuentes anglo-sajonas."

4. Ingenieros, p. 178.

5. For excellent analyses of mercantile activities in viceregal Buenos Aires, see Socolow, *Merchants*; Brown.

6. Klein.

7. For a review of military costs during the revolutionary period, see Halperín Donghi, *Guerra y finanzas*, pp. 73–144.

8. Halperín Donghi, *Revolución y guerra*, pp. 329–64.

9. On the insistent measures of law and order, see Szuchman, "Disorder."

10. Lattes, p. 854.

11. Goldberg, p. 86.

12. Socolow, "Buenos Aires," p. 23; AGN X, volumes for 1.390–1.404, *Censo de la Ciudad de Buenos Aires, 1855*. The city figures for 1810 and 1827 are based on Socolow's populations of 23,391 and 38,308.

13. Andrews, pp. 52–53.

14. Slatta, *Gauchos*, p. 130.

15. Andrews, p. 115, and pp. 113–37 passim.

16. Slatta, *Gauchos*, p. 127.   17. *El Censor*, Oct. 3, 1816.

18. Beruti, p. 3703.   19. Beruti, pp. 3703–6.

20. *El Lucero*, July 5, 1830.

21. *Teatro de la Opinión*, June 13, 1823.

22. Vilaseca, p. 9.

23. Socolow, *Merchants*, p. 38. Spaniards in contemporary Mexico also married later in life than native Mexicans. In 1811, Mexico City reported a minimum of 5 years' difference in the age at marriage between peninsulars and creoles: Arrom, "Marriage Patterns."

24. From a set of private letters furnished to me by Professor Carlos Mayo of the Universidad de la Plata.

25. For discussions of widowhood in the 18th and 19th centuries, see J. Smith; Cott.

26. Balmori and Oppenheimer, p. 240.

27. Stone, "Social Mobility," esp. pp. 40–42. Balmori and Oppenheimer

found such close similarities in their nineteenth-century data, together with such strong indications of colonial continuities from other areas of the Spanish Empire, that they were moved to suggest that "indeed, so strong and seemingly inexorable was this process in both countries that one wonders whether perhaps it was a phenomenon common to all Latin America." Balmori and Oppenheimer, p. 261.

28. For a discussion of changes in attitudinal behaviors responsible for quick and dramatic alterations of Chilean marital and fertility patterns in the twentieth century, see McCaa, *Marriage*, p. 140–44.

29. Hareven, "Modernization," pp. 191–93.

30. Landes, *Unbound Prometheus*, p. 6.

31. Isabelle, *Viaje*, p. 186; emphasis in original.

32. Mellafe, p. 16.

33. Computed from Hajnal, "Age at Marriage."

34. Mitterauer and Sieder, pp. 36–37; Hajnal, "European Marriage Patterns in Perspective," in Glass and Eversley, pp. 101–43.

35. Cases where the occupations of the heads of households were unknown were not included.

36. Shorter, *Making of the Modern Family*, pp. 26–28; Mitterauer and Sieder, pp. 41–43; Stone, "Family History," p. 60; Schofield; Braun, "Early Industrialization," pp. 291, 320.

37. Goldberg, p. 90.

38. Some of the best social science literature has demonstrated the abilities of the Latin America family to forge widespread economic and political networks. Some examples of this literature are Zeitlin and Ratcliff; Balán, Browning, and Jelin; Larissa Lomnitz, "Migration and Network in Latin America," in Portes and Browning, pp. 133–50; Balmori, Voss, and Wortman; Arnold Strickon, "Carlos Felipe: Kinsman, Patron, Friend," in Strickon and Greenfield, pp. 43–69; Lomnitz and Lisaur.

39. The cornerstone of the model rests with Le Play. Fuller discussions of industrialization and family solidarities can be found in Wrigley, "Reflections"; Goode, *World Revolution*, pp. 10–26.

40. Herlihy, *Family*, p. 5; Christiane Klapisch, "Household and Family in Tuscany in 1427," in P. Laslett and Wall, pp. 278–81.

41. The elasticity of the family structure based on functional need has been demonstrated elsewhere; see Chudacoff.

42. P. Laslett, "The Family," pp. 358–59.

43. The concern is generalized throughout the periodical literature of the time. For a discussion of the measures taken by authorities in various regions, see Halperín Donghi, *Revolución y guerra*.

44. The new regulations were to be applied to the urban militia by the royal declaration in 1767. Their specific application came by way of the *Reglamento para las milicias de infantería y caballería de la isla de Cuba*, pro-

mulgated on January 19, 1769, and extended to the rest of the American possessions by Gálvez's *Circular* of June 11, 1769. Juan M. Manferini, "La historia militar durante los siglos XVII y XVIII," in Levene, *Historia de la nación*, p. 253. For reviews of the development and consequences of the military reforms of this period, see Kuethe, "Development"; Archer; Kuethe, *Military Reform*; McAlister.

45. Halperín Donghi, "Revolutionary Militarization," p. 87.

46. See *Recopilación*, pp. 353–54, 365–66, 379–83; *Registro Nacional*, 1: 28, 42.

47. See the *considerando* of the government's decree of January 8, 1830, in *El Lucero*, Jan. 8, 1830, and the decree itself in *Recopilación*, p. 1034.

48. Szuchman, "Disorder," pp. 90–91.

49. *Crónica Política y Literaria de Buenos Aires*, Aug. 8, 1827; AGN X-43-7-5, *Policía*, 1830–1838, 1850–1859, *Serenos*. Emphasis in original.

50. See the police edict of Aug. 21, 1827, in *Crónica Política y Literaria de Buenos Aires*, Aug. 22, 1827.

51. Halperín Donghi, *Guerra y finanzas*, p. 159.

52. The text of these exchanges can be found in Museo Histórico Nacional.

53. Halperín Donghi, "Revolutionary Militarization," pp. 96–97.

54. Museo Histórico Nacional.

55. Emilio Ravignani, "El Congreso Nacional de 1824–1827. La Convención Nacional de 1828–1829," in Levene, *Historia de la nación*, pp. 113–14.

56. *Circular del 20 de Agosto de 1827 en respuesta al mensaje del Gobierno del 14 de Septiembre de 1827, precedida del mensaje mismo y de una circular a las Provincias* (Buenos Aires, 1827), pp. 1–2, in Piccirilli, 2: 470–71.

57. See, for example, *The British Packet and Argentine News*, Sept. 1, 1827.

58. Halperín Donghi, *Guerra y finanzas*, p. 155.

59. Lynch, p. 36.

60. Lynch, p. 133.

61. See Burgin, pp. 249–81, for a review of the contradictions inherent in Rosas' economic policies.

62. For a discussion of desertion, see Andrews, pp. 124–25.

63. Halperín Donghi, "Revolutionary Militarization," p. 106.

64. Halperín Donghi, *Guerra y finanzas*, pp. 222–23.

65. British Foreign Office, 6/152, Southern to Palmerston, Oct. 19, 1850, quoted in Lynch, p. 313.

66. British Foreign Office, 6/167, Gore to Palmerston, Feb. 2, 1852, quoted in Lynch, p. 324; Scobie, *La lucha*, p. 18.

67. For an excellent description of the emotions among the city dwellers

immediately following the battle of Caseros, see Scobie, *La lucha*, pp. 17–26.

68. Lynch, p. 100.

69. Levene, *El proceso histórico*, p. 146.

70. El Lucero; Sept. 19, 1829; emphasis in original.

71. Wrigley, *Population and History*, pp. 68–69.

72. The cross-sequential design comes out of the research paradigms of behavioral scientists who are concerned with investigating changes across the life span. Thus, various sequential methodologies have been devised: see Hultsch and Deutsch, pp. 40–45; Elias, Elias, and Elias, 32–35; Botwinick, pp. 388–93; Baltes, Reese, and Nesselroade, pp. 132–38; Salthouse, pp. 20–25.

73. Andrews, pp. 64–77.

74. Quoted in Chávez, *La cultura*, pp. 105–6.

75. Sarmiento, *Obras completas*, p. 123.

76. Alberdi, *La República Argentina*, quoted in Lynch, p. 306.

77. Alberdi, *Cartas quillotanas*, pp. 85–86.

78. H. Davis, p. 148. Davis was discussing Latin American political liberalism by way of the Mexican liberal José María Luis Mora.

79. For an overview of the transactional and cultural models of social processes, see R. Smith, "Introduction," in *Kinship Ideology*, pp. 5–14.

80. Stone, "Family History," p. 56.

81. For a good example of the difficulties of empiricism on the subject of changes in attitudes and mentalities over time, see the recent debates on female sexual attitudes among Shorter, Tilly, Scott, Cohen, Fairchilds, Flandrin, and others; the articulation of the debate is as fascinating as it is illustrative of the rich complexity that the historical literature can gain from such debates. Shorter, "Illegitimacy, Sexual Revolution" and "Female Emancipation"; Tilly, Scott, and Cohen; Fairchilds, "Female Sexual Attitudes"; Flandrin, "A Case of Naivete"; Fairchilds, "Reply."

82. Social historians may benefit from understanding the nature and consequences of limited evidence and symbolic meanings by comparing their problems to the limitations of other social scientific communities; see, for example, Ullman.

83. Finley, p. 139.

84. Noonan, "Intellectual and Demographic History," p. 463.

85. Stone, "Family History," pp. 72–73. The literature on changes in *mentalités* is too long to list, but the more recent works that are consciously linked to the family and household include Hill; Braun, "Early Industrialization"; Balmori; Berkner and Mendels; Bloom-Feshbach; Carlos and Sellers; Demos, "Developmental Perspectives"; Flandrin, "Contraception"; P. Laslett, "The Family"; Seed, "Parents." Excellent studies that relate

household changes to changes in production include Archetti; Gudmund-son, "Household Structures"; A. Johnson; Kuznesof, "Household Compo-sition."

86. P. Laslett, "The Family," p. 369.

87. For an overview of relations between blacks and Rosas, see An-drews, chs. 6 and 8; for Rosas' relations with *estancieros*, see Lynch, chs. 2–3.

88. Coser, p. 151.

CONCLUSIONS

1. Echeverría, *Dogma socialista*. On liberal ideology, see J. Romero, *History*, pp. 126–64; Sánchez Viamonte; Viñas.

2. On the political ideology of conservatives of the Rosas era, see Lynch, pp. 92–125.

3. The argument for the colonial tradition of allowing for local privi-leges was first codified by Phelan. More recent examples of the flexible style and the dangers incurred by deviating from it can be found in McFarlane.

4. For the twentieth-century variant of the principle of oligarchical con-trol of middle and upper levels of society by way of adjudicating educa-tional places, see Rock, pp. 21–24.

5. Kern, "Spanish Caciquismo," p. 42; Banfield, p. 83.

6. Halperín Donghi, *Revolución y guerra*, pp. 311–15; various decrees, including those of Aug. 9, 1813; Aug. 30, 1815; Nov. 27, 1821; and Feb. 28, 1823. In another Spanish American setting, Sinkin notes a similarly per-vasive concern on the part of Mexican liberals for law-and-order issues in the Constitutional Convention of 1856–57.

7. Dealy, *Public Man*, p. 27.

8. For a view of Spanish American leadership based on moral authority, see Morse, "Heritage," pp. 142–59.

9. *Gaceta de Buenos Ayres*, Dec. 13, 1811, in Binayán, p. 325.

10. Figgis, p. 72.

11. Burguiére, pp. viii–ix.

12. Morse, "Prolegomenon," p. 371; emphasis in original.

13. Furet, pp. 123–24.

14. Obligado, p. 87. The list of *cronistas* of the Generation of '80 is ex-tensive. Some of the more notable authors include: Bilbao, *Tradiciones*; R. Cárcano; Cané; López; Mansilla; Wilde.

15. República Argentina.

16. Sarmiento, "Arquitectura," p. 101.

17. The more famous and troublesome of these movements were led by Angel Vicente Peñaloza, known as "El Chacho," and Felipe Varela. Peñalo-za led his forces in the province of La Rioja in 1863, and Varela operated

in the western provinces in 1867–68. See Luna; Chávez, *Vida del Chacho*;
J. Newton.

APPENDIX

1. Estimated on the basis of average family sizes in each block and
neighborhood covered during the period under consideration in this study.

2. Scobie, *Buenos Aires*, chs. 1–2.

3. Andrews, p. 80.

4. Willigan and Lynch, pp. 199–200; Raj, p. 59; Fuente, p. 20; Arkin
and Colton, p. 145.

5. Laslett and Wall, pp. 88–89; emphasis in the original.

Bibliography

Primary Sources

Archivo General de la Nación (AGN)

SALA IX
10-7-1. Censo de Buenos Aires, 1810.

SALA X
1.390–1.404. Censo de Buenos Aires, 1855.
6-1-1. Instrucción Pública.
6-1-2. Instrucción Pública.
6-1-6. Inspección de Escuelas.
9-5-5, no. 30. Censo fiscal de españoles.
9-5-5, no. 31. Censo fiscal de extranjeros.
13-2-3. Beneficencia.
15-8-5. Pulperías. Inspección General.
16-9-2. Correspondencia Beneficencia.
16-10-7. Matrimonios.
17-2-7. Registros Parroquiales.
17-3-1. Beneficencia y Biblioteca.
17-6-3. Culto. Educación.
17-8-4. Enseñanza Pública.
17-8-5. Enseñanza Pública.
23-5-5/23-5-6. Censo de Buenos Aires, 1827.
25-2-2. Juzgado. Beneficencia.
25-6-2. Censo de Buenos Aires, 1838.
27-4-5. Tasaciones, 1810–24.
27-4-5A. Tasaciones, 1825–39.
28-1-1. Departamento de Gobierno. Sociedad de Beneficencia.

31-9-3. Basura.
31-9-4. Policía, 1825–31.
31-9-5. Policía, 1823–50.
31-11-3. Cuartel Policía, 1821–33.
31-11-3, no. 39. Censo de Buenos Aires, 1833.
31-11-4. Cárcel, 1845–52.
31-11-5. Sociedades Africanas, 1845–64.
32-1-1. Policía. Correspondencia.
32-1-7. Censo de Buenos Aires, 1854.
32-2-3. Censo de Buenos Aires, 1854.
32-3-1. Serenos, 1858–59.
32-3-7. Desertores, etc.
32-6-5. Correccional, 1867–69.
32-10-1. Policía. Ordenes superiores. Libro de Policía, 1816–22.
32-11-2. Partes de Campaña. Libro de Policía, 1827.
33-5-5. Cuartel Policía, 1847.
33-10-1. Notas de ciudad, 1854.
35-11-11. Alumbrado, 1825.
36-1-12. Cárcel, 1827.
36-2-2. Cárcel, 1828.
36-2-9. Cárcel, 1829.
36-2-13. Policía. Alquileres.
36-2-14. Cárcel, 1830.
36-4-6. Alumbrado, 1834.
42-5-7. Pulperías. Hacienda.
42-7-5. Asociaciones Filantrópicas.
42-7-11. Instrucción Pública.
42-8-2. Educación.
42-8-5. Censos, 1813–61.
42-8-5, no. 37. Análisis de población, 1829.
42-8-5, no. 38. Análisis de población, 1831.
42-10-9. Censos y Avaluación.
42-10-12. Pulperías. Alcabalas.
43-7-5. Serenos.
43-8-8. Comisarías.
43-8-9. Comisarías.
43-10-6. Censo de Catamarca y San Luis, 1812; Montevideo, 1814.
43-11-6. Pío IX. Bulas.
44-3-2. Instrucción Pública.
44-3-5. Instrucción Pública.
44-9-6. Culto e Instrucción Pública.

Archivo Histórico de la Provincia de Buenos Aires (AHPBA)
Disensos: 7.5.14, 7.5.15, 7.5.17, 7.5.18.

Newspapers
Los Amigos de la Patria y de la Juventud, 1815–16.
El Argos de Buenos Ayres, 1821–25.
The British Packet and Argentine News, 1826–32, 1835–47, 1854–57.
El Censor, 1815–19.
Crónica Política y Literaria de Buenos Aires, 1827.
Las Cuatro Cosas o el Antifanático, 1821.
El Despertador Teofilántrópico, Místico-Político, 1820–22.
Doña María Retazos, 1821–22.
El Espíritu de Buenos Ayres, 1822.
La Gaceta de Buenos Aires, 1810–11.
El Hablador, 1855.
El Lucero, 1829–30.
La Matrona Comentadora . . . , 1821–22.
La Moda, 1837–38.
Teatro de la Opinión, 1823.

Secondary Sources

Adler, Alfred. *The Neurotic Constitution.* New York, 1917.
Alberdi, Juan B. *La barbarie histórica de Sarmiento.* Buenos Aires, 1964.
———. *Cartas quillotanas.* Buenos Aires, 1916.
———. *Cartas sobre la prensa y política militante de la República Arjentina.* Buenos Aires, 1873.
———. *Fragmento preliminar al estudio del derecho.* Buenos Aires, 1837. (Repr. Instituto de Historia del Derecho; Buenos Aires, 1942.)
———. *Obras completas.* Buenos Aires, 1887.
———. *La República Argentina, treinta y siete años después de su Revolución.* Santiago, 1847.
Alvarez, Agustín. *Adónde vamos?* Buenos Aires, 1934.
Alvarez Andrews, Oscar. "El problema de la familia en Chile." *Revista Mexicana de Sociología*, 20 (May–Aug. 1958), 413–28.
Anderson, Michael. *Family Structure in Nineteenth-Century Lancashire.* Cambridge, Eng., 1971.
———. "Household Structure and the Industrial Revolution: Preston in Comparative Perspective." In *Household and Family in Past Time*, ed. Peter Laslett and Richard Wall. Cambridge, Eng., 1972.
Andrews, George Reid. *The Afro-Argentines of Buenos Aires, 1800–1900.* Madison, Wisc., 1980.

Araoz de la Madrid, Gregorio. *Memorias autógrafas*. Buenos Aires, 1968.

Archer, Christon J. *The Army in Bourbon Mexico, 1760–1810*. Albuquerque, 1977.

Archetti, Eduardo. "Rural Families and Demographic Behavior: Some Latin American Analogies." *Comparative Studies in Society and History*, 26 (Apr. 1984), 251–79.

Ariès, Philippe. *Centuries of Childhood*. London, 1962.

———. "The Family and the City." *Daedalus*, 106 (Spring 1977), 227–35.

Arkin, Herbert, and Raymond Colton. *Tables for Statisticians*. New York, 1963.

Arrom, Silvia M. "Marriage Patterns in Mexico City, 1811." *Journal of Family History*, 3 (Winter 1978), 376–91.

———. *The Women of Mexico City, 1790–1857*. Stanford, Calif., 1985.

Ashen, R., ed. *The Family: Its Function and Destiny*. New York, 1949.

Aufderheide, Patricia A. "Order and Violence: Social Deviance and Social Control in Brazil, 1780–1840." Ph.D. dissertation, University of Minnesota, 1976.

Augustine. *The City of God*. Trans. William Chase Greene. Cambridge, Mass., 1960.

Ayarragaray, Lucas. *La anarquía argentina y el caudillismo*. Buenos Aires, 1904.

Bailey, Victor, ed. *Policing and Punishment in Nineteenth-Century Britain*. New Brunswick, N. J., 1981.

Baily, Samuel L. "Marriage Patterns and Immigrant Assimilation in Buenos Aires, 1882–1923." *Hispanic American Historical Review*, 60 (Feb. 1980), 32–48.

Baker, J. H. "Criminal Courts and Procedure at Common Law, 1550–1800." In J. S. Cockburn. *Crime in England, 1550–1800*. Princeton, N.J., 1977.

Balán, Jorge, Harley Browning, and Elizabeth Jelin. *Men in a Developing Society: Geographic and Social Mobility in Monterrey*. Austin, Tex., 1973.

Balmori, Diana. "The Changing Role of Women and Family in Nineteenth-Century Argentina." Unpublished paper, 1979.

Balmori, Diana, and Robert Oppenheimer. "Family Clusters: Generational Nucleation in Nineteenth-Century Argentina and Chile." *Comparative Studies in Society and History*, 21 (Apr. 1979), 231–61.

Balmori, Diana, Stuart Voss, and Miles Wortman. *Notable Family Networks in Latin America*. Chicago, 1984.

Baltes, Paul, Hayne W. Reese, and John Nesselroade. *Life-Span Developmental Psychology: Introduction to Research Methods*. Monterey, Calif., 1977.

Banfield, Edward. *The Moral Basis of a Backward Society*. New York, 1958.

Banks, J. A. "Historical Sociology and the Study of Population." *Daedalus*, 97 (Spring 1968), 397–414.

Barclay, George W. *Techniques of Population Analysis*. New York, 1958.

Barker, Ernest, ed. *The Politics of Aristotle*. New York, 1964.

Barker-Benfield, Ben. "The Spermatic Economy: A Nineteenth-Century View of Sexuality." *Feminist Studies*, 1 (1972), 45–74.

Barrow, R. H. *Introduction to St. Augustine, The City of God*. London, 1950.

Bauer, Arnold J. "Rural Workers in Spanish America: Problems of Peonage and Oppression." *The Hispanic American Historical Review*, 59 (Feb. 1979), 34–63.

Baulant, Micheline. "The Scattered Family: Another Aspect of Seventeenth-Century Demography." In *Family and Society: Selections from the* ANNALES, ed. Robert Forster and Orest Ranum, pp. 104–16. Baltimore, Md., 1976.

Bazán Lezcano, Marcelo. "Inventario analítico de la Serie Criminales (1756–1810)."*Revista del Archivo General de la Nación*, 4 (1974), 279–402.

Beales, Ross W., Jr. "In Search of the Historical Child: Miniature Adulthood and Youth in Colonial New England." *American Quarterly*, 27 (Oct. 1975), 379–98.

Beattie, J. M. "The Pattern of Crime in England, 1600–1800." *Past & Present*, 62 (Feb. 1974), 47–95.

Beaumont, J. A. B. *Travels in Buenos Aires*. London, 1828.

Beckett, John V. "English Landownership in the Later Seventeenth and Eighteenth Centuries." *Economic History Review*, 30 (Nov. 1977), 566–81.

Bejarano, Manuel. "Inmigración y estructuras tradicionales en Buenos Aires (1854–1930). In *Los fragmentos del poder*, ed. Torcuato S. Di Tella and Tulio Halperín Donghi, pp. 75–149. Buenos Aires, 1969.

Belgrano, Mario C. "Fuentes anglo-sajonas en la formación intelectual de Manuel Belgrano." *Anales*, no. 1 (n. d.).

———. *Historia de Belgrano*. 2d ed. Buenos Aires, 1944.

Bell, Rudolph M. *Fate and Honor, Family and Village: Demographic and Cultural Change in Italy Since 1800*. Chicago, 1979.

Berkhofer, Robert F., Jr. *A Behavioral Approach to Historical Analysis*. New York, 1969.

Berkner, Lutz K. "The European Peasant Life Cycle: The Stem Family and the Joint Family." *Proceedings of the World Conference on Records*, vol. 12. Salt Lake City, 1980.

———. "Inheritance, Land Tenure, and Peasant Family Structure: A German Regional Comparison." In *Family and Inheritance*, ed. John Goody et al., pp. 71–95. Cambridge, Eng., 1976.

———. "The Use and Misuse of Census Data for the Historical Analysis of Family Structure." *Journal of Interdisciplinary History*, 5 (Spring 1975), 721–38.

Berkner, Lutz K., and Franklin F. Mendels. "Inheritance Systems, Family Structure, and Demographic Patterns in Western Europe, 1700–1900." In *Historical Studies of Changing Fertility*, ed. Charles Tilly, pp. 209–24. Princeton, N. J., 1978.

Bernárdez, F. "La crisis de 1820." In *Documentos para la historia argentina*, vol. 1, pp. 97-128. Buenos Aires, 1981.

Beruti, Juan M. "Memorias curiosas." In *Biblioteca de Mayo*, vol. 4: *Diarios y crónicas*, pp. 3647–4147. Senado de la Nación, República Argentina. Buenos Aires, 1960.

Besio Moreno, Nicolás. *Buenos Aires, puerto del Río de la Plata . . . 1536–1936*. Buenos Aires, 1939.

Bilbao, Manuel. *Buenos Aires desde su fundación hasta nuestros días*. Buenos Aires, 1902.

———. *Tradiciones y recuerdos de Buenos Aires*. Buenos Aires, 1934.

Binayán, Narciso, ed. *Ideario de Mayo*. Buenos Aires, 1960.

Blackwelder, Julia K., and Lyman L. Johnson. "Changing Criminal Patterns in Buenos Aires, 1890–1914." *Journal of Latin American Studies*, 14 (Nov. 1982), 359–80.

Blank, Stephanie. "Patrons, Clients, and Kin in Seventeenth-Century Caracas: A Methodological Essay in Colonial Spanish American Social History." *Hispanic American Historical Review*, 54 (May 1974), 260–83.

Bloom-Feshbach, Jonathan. "Historical Perspectives on the Father's Role." In *The Role of the Father in Child Development*, ed. Michael E. Lamb, pp. 71–112. New York, 1981.

Bonfield, Lloyd. "Marriage Settlements and the 'Rise of Great Estates': The Demographic Aspect." *Economic History Review*, 32 (Nov. 1979), 483–93.

Bosch, Beatriz. *Urquiza y su tiempo*. Buenos Aires, 1971.

Botwinick, Jack. *Aging and Behavior: A Comprehensive Integration of Research Findings*. New York, 1984.

Bourdieu, Pierre. "Marriage Strategies as Strategies of Social Reproduction." In *Family and Society: Selections from the* ANNALES, ed. Robert Forster and Orest Ranum, pp. 117–44. Baltimore, Md., 1976.

Branca, Patricia. *Silent Sisterhood: Middle Class Women in the Victorian Home*. Pittsburgh, Pa., 1975.

Braun, Rudolf. "Early Industrialization and Demographic Change in the Canton of Zurich." In *Historical Studies of Changing Fertility*, ed. Charles Tilly, pp. 289–334. Princeton, N. J., 1978.

———. "The Impact of Cottage Industry on an Agricultural Population." In *The Rise of Capitalism*, ed. David Landes, pp. 53–64. New York, 1966.

Brown, Jonathan C. *A Socioeconomic History of Argentina, 1776–1860.* Cambridge, Eng., 1979.

Browning, Webster E. "Joseph Lancaster, James Thomson, and the Lancasterian System of Mutual Instruction, with Special Reference to Hispanic America." *Hispanic American Historical Review*, 4 (Feb. 1921), 49–98.

Buenos Aires (Municipalidad). *Arquitectura del Estado de Buenos Aires (1853–1862).* Buenos Aires, 1965.

———. *Memoria de la Municipalidad de Buenos Aires . . . 1856–57.* Buenos Aires, 1858.

Bunge, Octavio. *Nuestra América.* Buenos Aires, 1903.

Burgin, Miron. *The Economic Aspects of Argentine Federalism, 1820–1852.* New York, 1971.

Burguière, André. "From Malthus to Weber: Belated Marriage and the Spirit of Enterprise." In *Family and Society: Selections from the* ANNALES, ed. Robert Forster and Orest Ranum, pp. 237–50. Baltimore, Md., 1976.

Burnett, John. "Autobiographies of Childhood: The Experience of Education," parts 1–2. *History Today*, 32 (Sept. 1982), 8–12; (Oct. 1982), 23–31.

Burns, E. Bradford. "Ideology in Nineteenth-Century Latin American Historiography." *Hispanic American Historical Review*, 58 (Aug. 1978), 409–31.

———. *The Poverty of Progress: Latin America in the Nineteenth Century.* Berkeley, Calif., 1980.

Bushman, Richard L. "Family Security in the Transition from Farm to City, 1750–1850." *Journal of Family History*, 6 (Fall 1981), 238–56.

Bushnell, David. *Reform and Reaction in the Platine Provinces, 1810–1852.* Gainesville, Fla., 1983.

Cain, M. "Perspectives on Family and Fertility in Developing Countries." *Population Studies*, 36 (July 1982), 159–75.

Caldcleugh, Alexander. *Travels in South America.* London, 1825.

Cancian, Francesca, et al. "Capitalism, Industrialization and Kinship in Latin America: Major Issues." *Journal of Family History*, 3 (Winter 1978), 319–36.

Cané, Miguel. *Juvenilia.* Buenos Aires, 1884.

Cárcano, Miguel Angel. *El estilo de vida argentino.* Buenos Aires, 1969.

Cárcano, Ramón J. *Mis primeros ochenta años.* Buenos Aires, 1965.

Carlos, Manuel, and Lois Sellers. "Family, Kinship Structure, and Modernization in Latin America." *Latin American Research Review*, 7 (Summer 1972), 95–124.

Carter, Anthony T. "Household Histories." In *Households: Comparative and Historical Studies of the Domestic Group*, ed. Robert McC. Netting, Richard R. Wilk, and Eric J. Arnould, pp. 44–83. Berkeley, Calif., 1984.

Caspard, Pierre. "Conceptions prénuptiales et développement du capitalisme dans la Principauté de Neufchâtel (1678–1829)." *Annales*, 29 (1974), 989–1008.

Casterline, John, and J. Trussell. "Cross-National Summaries: Age at First Birth." *Comparative Studies of the World Fertility Survey*, No. 15, May 1980. London, 1980.

Chandler, David L. "Family Bonds and the Bondsman: The Slave Family in Colonial Colombia." *Latin American Research Review*, 16, 2 (1981), 107–31.

Chávez, Fermín. *La cultura en la época de Rosas*. Buenos Aires, 1973.

——. *Vida del Chacho, Angel Vicente Peñaloza, General de la Confederación*. Buenos Aires, 1965.

Cheney, Rose A. "Seasonal Aspects of Infant and Childhood Mortality: Philadelphia, 1865–1920." *Journal of Interdisciplinary History*, 14 (Winter 1984), 561–85.

Chevalier, Louis. *Laboring Classes and Dangerous Classes in Paris During the First Half of the Nineteenth Century*. Princeton, N. J., 1981.

Chudacoff, Howard P. "Newlyweds and Family Extension: The First Stage of the Family Cycle in Providence, Rhode Island, 1864–1865 and 1879–1880." *Family and Population in Nineteenth-Century America*, ed. Tamara K. Hareven and Maris Vinovskis, pp. 179–205. Princeton, N. J., 1978.

Clavero, Bartolomé. *Mayorazgo, propiedad feudal en Castilla (1369–1836)*. Madrid, 1974.

Clay, Christopher. "Marriage, Inheritance, and the Rise of Large Estates in England, 1660–1815." *Economic History Review*, 21 (Dec. 1968), 503–18.

Cochran, Thomas C., and Ruben E. Reina. *Entrepreneurship in Argentine Culture*. Philadelphia, Pa., 1962.

Cockburn, J. S., ed. *Crime in England, 1550–1800*. Princeton, N. J., 1977.

Concejo Nacional de Educación. *Historia de la instrucción primaria en la República Argentina, 1810–1910*. Buenos Aires, 1910.

Concolorcorvo (pseud.). *El Lazarillo*. Bloomington, Ind., 1965.

Coni, Emilio R. *Movimiento de la población de la ciudad de Buenos Aires*. Buenos Aires, 1889.

Cooper, J. P. "Patterns of Inheritance and Settlement by Great Landowners From the Fifteenth to the Eighteenth Centuries." In *Family and Inheritance: Rural Society in Western Europe, 1200–1800*, ed. J. Goody, Joan Thirsk, and Edward P. Thompson, pp. 192–327. Cambridge, Eng., 1976.

Cordero, Clodomiro. *El problema nacional*. Buenos Aires, 1911.

Correa Luna, Carlos. *Historia de la Sociedad de Beneficencia*. Buenos Aires, 1923.

Cortes Conde, Roberto. *The First Stages of Modernization in Spanish America*. New York, 1974.

Coser, Lewis. *The Functions of Social Conflict*. New York, 1956.

Cott, Nancy F. "Divorce and the Changing Status of Women in Eigh-teenth-Century Massachusetts." *William and Mary Quarterly*, 33 (Oct. 1976), 586–614.

Cott Watkins, Susan. "Variations and Persistence in Nuptiality: Age Pat-terns of Marriage in Europe, 1870–1960." Unpublished paper, Social Science History Association Meeting, 1979.

Crafts, N. F. R. "Illegitimacy in England and Wales in 1911." *Population Studies*, 36 (July 1982), 327–31.

Craig, John E. "The Expansion of Education." *Review of Research in Ed-ucation*, 9 (1981), pp. 151–213.

Cushner, Nicholas. *Jesuit Ranches and the Agrarian Development of Colonial Argentina, 1650–1767*. Albany, N.Y., 1983.

Darroch, A. Gordon. "Migrants in the Nineteenth Century: Fugitives or Families in Motion?" *Journal of Family History*, 6 (Fall 1981), 257–77.

Davies, Mel. "Corsets and Competition: Fashion and Demographic Trends in the Nineteenth Century." *Comparative Studies in Society and History*, 24 (Oct. 1982), 611–41.

Davis, Harold E. *Latin American Social Thought*, 2d ed. Washington, D.C., 1966.

Davis, Natalie Z. "The Reasons of Misrule: Youth Groups and Charivaris in Sixteenth-Century France." *Past & Present*, 50 (Feb. 1971), 41–75.

Dealy, Glen Caudill. *The Public Man: An Interpretation of Latin America and Other Catholic Countries*. Amherst, Mass., 1977.

———. "Prolegomena on the Spanish American Political Tradition." *The Hispanic American Historical Review*, 48 (Feb. 1968), 37–58.

Degler, Carl. "What Ought to Be and What Was: Women's Sexuality in the Nineteenth Century." *American Historical Review*, 79 (Dec. 1974), 1468–2490.

Delasselle, Claude. "Les infants abandonnés à Paris au XVIII siècle." *An-nales*, 30 (1975), 187–218.

De Mause, Lloyd. "The Evolution of Childhood." In *History of Childhood*, ed. Lloyd De Mause, pp. 1–74. New York, 1974.

———. *The History of Childhood*. New York, 1975.

Demos, John. "Developmental Perspectives on the History of Childhood." *Journal of Interdisciplinary History*, 2 (1972), 315–27.

———. *A Little Commonwealth: Family Life in Plymouth Colony*. New York, 1970.

———. "Old Age in Early New England." In *The American Family in So-cial-Historical Perspective*, ed. Michael Gordon, pp. 209–21. New York, 1973.

Demos, John, and Virginia Demos. "Adolescence in Historical Perspec-tive." *Journal of Marriage and the Family*, 31 (Nov. 1969), 632–38.

Depauw, Jacques. "Illicit Sexual Activity and Society in Eighteenth-Century Nantes." In *Family and Society: Selections from the* ANNALES, ed. Robert Forster and Orest Ranum, pp. 145–91. Baltimore, Md., 1976.

Di Tella, Torcuato S. "Las clases peligrosas a comienzos del siglo XIX en México." *Desarrollo Económico*, no. 48 (Jan–Mar. 1972), 761–91.

————. "Raices de la controversia educacional argentina." In *Los fragmentos del poder*, ed. Torcuato S. Di Tella and Tulio Halperín Donghi, pp. 289–323. Buenos Aires, 1969.

Domínguez, Luis L. *Historia argentina*. Buenos Aires, 1861.

Domínguez, Manuel Augusto. "La vivienda colonial porteña." *Anales del Instituto de Arte Americano e Investigaciones Estéticas*, no. 1 (1948), 65–85.

Donzelot, Jacques. *The Policing of Families*. New York, 1979.

Duby, Georges. "In Northwestern France: The 'Youth' in Twelfth-Century Aristocratic Society." In *Lordship and Community in Medieval Europe*, ed. Frederick L. Cheyette, pp. 198–209. New York, 1968.

————. "Lineage, Nobility and Chivalry in the Region of Macon during the Twelfth Century." In *Family and Society: Selections from the* ANNALES, ed. Robert Forster and Orest Ranum, pp. 16–40. Baltimore, Md., 1976.

Dupaquier, Jacques. "Naming-Practices, Godparenthood, and Kinship in Vexin, 1540–1900." *Journal of Family History*, 6 (Summer 1981), 135–55.

Durch, Jane S. "Nuptiality Patterns in Developing Countries: Implications for Fertility." *Reports on the World Fertility Survey*, no. 1. Washington, D.C., 1980.

Easterlin, Richard. "Does Human Fertility Adjust to the Environment?" *American Economic Review*, 61 (May 1971), 399–407.

————. "Factors in the Decline of Farm Family Fertility in the United States: Some Preliminary Research Results." *Journal of American History*, 63 (1976), 600–614.

Echeverría, Esteban. *La cautiva. El matadero*. Buenos Aires, 1971.

————. *Dogma socialista*. La Plata, 1940.

————. *Mayo y la enseñanza popular en el Plata*. Montevideo, 1844.

Elder, Glen H., Jr. "Scarcity and Prosperity in Postwar Childbearing: Explorations from a Life Course Perspective." *Journal of Family History*, 6 (1981), 410–33.

Elias, M. F., P. K. Elias, and J. W. Elias. *Basic Approaches in Adult Development Psychology*. St. Louis, 1977.

Elton, Geoffrey Rudolph. "Introduction: Crime and the Historian." In *Crime in England, 1550–1800*, ed. J. S. Cockburn, pp. 1–14. Princeton, N.J., 1977.

Engels, Friedrich. *The Origins of the Family, Private Property and the State*. New York, 1972.

Estrada, Jose Manuel. *Lecciones sobre la historia de la República Argentina*. Buenos Aires, 1898–1927.

Evans-Pritchard, Edward E. "The Study of Kinship in Primitive Societies." *Man*, 29 (1969), 190–93.

Facultad de Filosofía y Letras. *Documentos para la historia argentina*. Vol. 8. Buenos Aires, 1919.

———. *Documentos para la historia*. Vol. 9, *Administración edilicia (1776–1805)*. Buenos Aires, 1918.

———. *Instituto de Investigaciones Historicas: Documentos para la historia argentina*. Vol. 18, *Cultura: Enseñanza durante la época colonial (1771–1810)*. Buenos Aires, 1924.

Fairchilds, Cissie. "Female Sexual Attitudes and the Rise of Illegitimacy." *Journal of Interdisciplinary History*, 8 (Spring 1978), 627–67.

———. "A Reply." *Journal of Interdisciplinary History*, 9 (Autumn 1978), 316–21.

Farber, Bernard. *Guardians of Virtue: Salem Families in 1800*. New York, 1972.

Farrell, Betty. "Family Strategies and Business Alliance in the Nineteenth-Century Boston Elite." Unpublished paper, Social Science History Association Meeting, 1979.

Fausto, Boris, "Controle social e criminalidade em São Paulo: um apanhado geral (1890–1924)." In Paulo Sergio Pinheiro, ed. *Crime, violencia e poder*, pp. 194–210. São Paulo, 1983.

———. *Crime e cotidiano: a criminalidade em Sâo Paulo (1880–1924)*. São Paulo, 1984.

Felstiner, Mary Lowenthal. "Family Metaphors: The Language of an Independence Revolution." *Comparative Studies in Society and History*, 25 (Jan. 1983), 154–80.

Ferns, H. S. *Britain and Argentina in the Nineteenth Century*. London, 1960.

Ferrer, Aldo. *The Argentine Economy*. Berkeley, Calif., 1967.

Figgis, John Neville. *Political Thought from Gerson to Grotius: 1414–1625*. 2d ed. New York, 1960.

Finley, Moses I. "'Progress' in Historiography." *Daedalus*, 106 (Summer 1977), 125–42.

Flandrin, Jean-Louis. "A Case of Naivete in the Use of Statistics." *Journal of Interdisciplinary History*, 9 (Autumn 1978), 309–15.

———. "Contraception, Marriage, and Sexual Relations in the Christian West." In *Biology of Man in History*, ed. Robert Forster and Orest Ranum, pp. 23–48. Baltimore, Md., 1975.

———. *Families in Former Times: Kinship, Household and Sexuality*. Cambridge, Eng., 1979.

Flory, Thomas. *Judge and Jury in Imperial Brazil, 1808–1871: Social Control and Political Stability in the New State*. Austin, Tex., 1981.

Folbre, Nancy R. "The Wealth of Patriarchs: Deerfield, Massachusetts,

1760–1840." Unpublished paper, Social Science History Association Meeting, 1984.

Forster, Robert, and Orest Ranum, eds. *Family and Society: Selections from the* ANNALES. Baltimore, Md., 1976.

Foucault, Michel. *Discipline and Punish: The Birth of the Prison*. New York, 1977.

Fox-Genovese, Elizabeth, and Eugene Genovese. "The Political Crisis of Social History: A Marxian Perspective." *Journal of Social History*, 10, no. 2 (1976), 205–20.

Freeman, Susan Tax. *Neighbors: The Social Contract in a Castilian Hamlet*. Chicago, 1970.

Frisch, Michael H. *Town into City: Springfield, Massachusetts, 1840–1880*. Cambridge, Mass., 1972.

Fuente, Diego G. de la. *Primer censo de la República Argentina (1869)*. Buenos Aires, 1872.

Furet, François. *Interpreting the French Revolution*. Cambridge, Eng., 1981.

Furlong, Guillermo, S. J. *Los jesuitas, su orígen, su espíritu, su obra*. Buenos Aires, 1942.

———. *Los jesuitas y la cultura ríoplatense*. Buenos Aires, 1946.

———. *Los jesuitas y la escisión del Reyno de Indias*. Buenos Aires, 1960.

Furstenburg, Frank F., Theodore Hershberg, and John Modell. "The Origins of the Female-Headed Black Family: The Impact of the Urban Experience." *Journal of Interdisciplinary History*, 6 (Autumn 1975), 211–33.

Gálvez, Manuel. *El solar de la raza*. Buenos Aires, 1913.

García, Juan Agustín. *La ciudad indiana: Buenos Aires desde 1600 hasta mediados del siglo XVIII*. Buenos Aires, 1900.

García Belsunce, César, et al. *Buenos Aires, 1810–1830: salud y delito*. Buenos Aires, 1977.

———. *Buenos Aires: su gente, 1810–1830*. Buenos Aires, 1976.

García Márquez, Gabriel. *One Hundred Years of Solitude*. New York, 1970.

Geertz, Clifford. *The Interpretation of Cultures*. New York, 1973.

Germani, Gino. *Política y sociedad en una época de transición. De la sociedad tradicional a la sociedad de masas*. Buenos Aires, 1962.

———. *The Sociology of Modernization: Studies on Its History*. New Brunswick, N.J., 1981.

Gillin, John. "Mestizo America." In *Most of the World*, ed. R. Linton, pp. 171–72. New York, 1949.

Gillis, John R. "Affective Individualism and the English Poor." *Journal of Interdisciplinary History*, 9 (Summer 1979), 121–28.

———. *Youth and History: Tradition and Change in European Age Relations*. New York, 1974.

Glass, David V., and D. E. C. Eversley. *Population and History: Essays in Historical Demography*. London, 1965.

Glenn, Norval D. "Cohort Analysis' Futile Quest: Statistical Attempts to Separate Age, Period and Cohort Effects." *American Sociological Review*, 41 (Dec. 1976), 900–904.

Glick, Thomas F. "The Naked Science: Psychoanalysis in Spain, 1914–1948." *Comparative Studies in Society and History*, 24 (Oct. 1982), 533–71.

Goldberg, Marta B. "La población negra y mulata de la ciudad de Buenos Aires, 1810–1840." *Desarrollo Económico*, no. 61 (Apr.–June 1976), 75–99.

Goldthwaite, Richard. *The Building of Renaissance Florence*. Baltimore, Md., 1980.

Gondra, Luis Roque. *Historia económica de la República Argentina*. Buenos Aires, 1960.

———. *Las ideas económicas de Manuel Belgrano*. Buenos Aires, 1923.

Goode, William J. "Marriage Among the English Nobility in the Sixteenth and Seventeenth Centuries: A Comment." *Comparative Studies in Society and History*, 3 (1960–61), 207–14.

———. *World Revolution and Family Patterns*. New York, 1963.

Goody, John R., ed. *The Character of Kinship*. London, 1973.

———. *The Developmental Cycle in Domestic Groups*. Cambridge, Eng., 1971.

Goody, John R., Joan Thirsk, and Edward P. Thompson, eds. *Family and Inheritance: Rural Society in Western Europe, 1200–1800*. Cambridge, Eng., 1976.

Gordon, Michael, ed. *The American Family in Social-Historical Perspective*. New York, 1973.

Goubert, Pierre. "Legitimate Fecundity and Infant Mortality in France During the Eighteenth Century: A Comparison." *Daedalus*, 97 (Spring 1968), 593–603.

Grau, Carlos A. *La sanidad en las ciudades y pueblos de la Provincia de Buenos Aires*. La Plata, 1954.

Greenberg, J. H., ed. *Universals of Language*. Cambridge, Mass., 1973.

Greven, Phillip J. "Family Structure in Seventeenth-Century Andover, Massachusetts." *William and Mary Quarterly*, 23 (1966), 234–56.

———. *Four Generations: Population, Land and Family in Colonial Andover, Massachusetts*. Ithaca, N.Y., 1970.

———. *The Protestant Temperament: Patterns of Child-Rearing, Religious Experience, and the Self in Early America*. New York, 1977.

Greven, Phillip J., ed. *Child-Rearing Concepts, 1628–1861: Historical Sources*. Itasca, Ill., 1973.

Grew, Raymond, Patrick J. Harrigan, and James Whitney. "The Availability of Schooling in Nineteenth-Century France." *Journal of Interdisciplinary History*, 14 (Summer 1983), 25–63.

Gudmundson, Lowell. "Costa Rica Before Coffee: Society and Economy on the Eve of Agro-Export Based Expansion." Ph.D. diss., University of Minnesota, 1983.

―――. "Household Structures and Inheritance in an Emerging Export Economy: Costa Rica Before and After Coffee." Unpublished paper, Social Science History Association Meeting, 1984.

Guest, Avery M., and S. Tolnay. "Children's Roles and Fertility: Late Nineteenth-Century United States." *Social Science History*, 7 (Fall 1983), 355–80.

Guido, Angel. *Fusión hispano-indígena en la arquitectura colonial*. Rosario, 1925.

Güiraldes, Ricardo. *Don Segundo Sombra*. Buenos Aires, 1926.

Gutman, Herbert G. "Persistent Myths about the Afro-American Family." *Journal of Interdisciplinary History*, 6 (Autumn 1975), 181–210.

Gutmann, Myron, and Renee Leboutte. "Rethinking Protoindustrialization and the Family." *Journal of Interdisciplinary History*, 14 (Winter 1984), 587–607.

Guy, Donna J. "Women, Peonage, and Industrialization: Argentina, 1810–1914." *Latin American Research Review*, 16, no. 3 (1981), 65–89.

Habakkuk, John H. "Family Structure and Economic Change in Nineteenth Century Europe." *Journal of Economic History*, 15 (1955), 1–12.

Hackenberg, Robert, Arthur D. Murphy, and Henry A. Selby. "The Urban Household in Dependent Development." In *Households: Comparative and Historical Studies of the Domestic Group*, ed. Robert McC. Netting, Richard Wilk, and Eric Arnould, pp. 187–216. Berkeley, Calif., 1984.

Hahner, June E. "Women and Work in Brazil, 1850–1920: A Preliminary Investigation." In *Essays Concerning the Socioeconomic History of Brazil and Portuguese India*, ed. Dauril Alden and Warren Dean, pp. 87–117. Gainesville, Fla., 1977.

Haigh, Samuel. *Sketches of Buenos Ayres, Chile and Peru*. London, 1831.

Hajnal, John. "Age at Marriage and Proportions Marrying." *Population Studies*, 7 (Nov. 1953), 111–36.

Halperín Donghi, Tulio. *The Aftermath of Revolution in Latin America*. New York, 1974.

―――. "La expansión ganadera en la campaña de Buenos Aires (1810–1852)." *Desarrollo Económico*, nos. 1–2 (Apr.–Sept. 1963), 57–110.

―――. "Gastos militares y economía regional: el Ejército del Norte (1810–1817)." *Desarrollo Económico*, no. 41 (Apr.–June 1971), 87–99.

―――. *Guerra y finanzas en los orígenes del Estado Argentino (1791–1850)*. Buenos Aires, 1982.

―――. *Historia de la Universidad de Buenos Aires*. Buenos Aires, 1962.

————. *Una nación para el desierto argentino*. Buenos Aires, 1982.

————. *Revolución y guerra. Formación de una élite dirigente en la Argentina criolla*. Buenos Aires, 1972.

Hamilton, Bernice. *Political Thought in Sixteenth-Century Spain*. Oxford, 1963.

Hammel, Eugene A. "On the *** of Studying Household Form and Function." In *Households: Comparative and Historical Studies of the Domestic Group*, ed. Robert McC. Netting, Richard Wilk, and Eric Arnould, pp. 29–43. Berkeley, Calif., 1984.

Hammel, Eugene A., and Peter Laslett. "Comparing Household Structure over Time and Between Cultures." *Comparative Studies in Society and History*, 16 (Jan. 1974), 73–109.

Hareven, Tamara K. "Family Time and Historical Time." *Daedalus*, 106 (Spring 1977), pp. 57–70.

————. "Modernization and Family History: Reflections on Social Change." *Signs*, 2 (Autumn 1976), 190–206.

Hareven, Tamara K., ed. *Family and Kin in Urban Communities: 1700–1930*. New York, 1977.

————. *Transitions: The Family and the Life Course in Historical Perspective*. New York, 1978.

Hareven, Tamara K., and Maris Vinovskis. "Introduction." In *Family and Population in Nineteenth-Century America*, ed. Tamara K. Hareven and Maris Vinovskis, pp. 3–21. Princeton, N.J., 1978.

————. "Patterns of Childbearing in Late Nineteenth-Century America: The Determinants of Marital Fertility in Five Massachusetts Towns in 1880." In *Family and Population in Nineteenth-Century America*, ed. Tamara K. Hareven and Maris Vinovskis, pp. 85–125. Princeton, N.J., 1978.

Hareven, Tamara K., and Maris Vinovskis, eds. *Family and Population in Nineteenth-Century America*. Princeton, N.J., 1978.

Harispuru, Adela. "Grupos familiares y tenencia de la tierra en la Provincia de Buenos Aires (1880–1930)." Unpublished paper, Buenos Aires, 1978.

Harris, Olivia. *Latin American Women*. London, 1983.

Haskell, Thomas L. "Capitalism and the Origins of the Humanitarian Sensibility," part 2. *American Historical Review*, 90 (June 1985), 547–66.

Haslip, Gabriel James. "Crime and the Administration of Justice in Colonial Mexico City, 1696–1810. Unpublished Ph.D. diss., Columbia University, 1980.

Hay, Douglas. "Property, Authority and the Criminal Law." In *Albion's Fatal Tree: Crime and Society in Eighteenth-Century England*, ed. Douglas Hay, Peter Linebaugh, and Edward P. Thompson, pp. 17–64. London, 1975.

Hay, Douglas, Peter Linebaugh, and Edward P. Thompson, eds. *Albion's*

Fatal Tree: Crime and Society in Eighteenth-Century England. London, 1975.

Heer, David. "Economic Development and the Fertility Transition." *Daedalus*, 97 (Spring 1968), 447–62.

Henry, Louis. "Historical Demography." *Daedalus*, 97 (Spring 1968), 385–96.

———. "The Population of France in the Eighteenth Century." In *Population in History: Essays in Historical Demography*, ed. David V. Glass and D. E. C. Eversley, pp. 434–56. London, 1965.

Henry, Louis, and Yves Blayo. "La Population de la France de 1740 à 1860." Demographie Historique, special issue of *Population*, 30 (1975), 71–122.

Herbert, D. T., and T. Johnston, eds. *Social Areas in Cities: Processes, Patterns and Problems*. New York, 1978.

Herlihy, David. *The Family in Renaissance Italy*. St. Charles, Mo., 1974.

———. "Households in the Early Middle Ages: Symmetry and Sainthood." In *Households: Comparative and Historical Studies of the Domestic Group*, ed. Robert McC. Netting, Richard Wilk, and Eric Arnould, pp. 383–406. Berkeley, Calif., 1984.

Hernández, José. *Martín Fierro*. Buenos Aires, 1872.

Hernando, Diana. "*Casa y familia*: Spatial Biographies in Nineteenth-Century Buenos Aires." Unpublished Ph. D. diss., University of California, Los Angeles, 1973.

Hill, Christopher. "Protestantism and the Rise of Capitalism." In *The Rise of Capitalism*, ed. David S. Landes, pp. 41–52. New York, 1966.

———. *Society and Puritanism in Pre-Revolutionary England*. London, 1964.

Holley, John C. "The Two Family Economies of Industrialism: Factory Workers in Victorian Scotland." *Journal of Family History*, 6 (Spring 1981), 57–69.

Hollingsworth, Thomas H. *Historical Demography*. Ithaca, N.Y., 1969.

———. "The Importance of the Quality of the Data in Historical Demography." *Daedalus*, 97 (Spring 1968), 415–32.

Holloway, Thomas H. "The Brazilian 'Judicial Police' System and Its Replication in Desterro, Santa Catarina, 1841–1871." Unpublished paper, American Historical Association Meeting, 1984.

Honorable Concejo Deliberante de la Ciudad de Buenos Aires. *Recopilación de los debates de leyes orgánicas municipales y sus textos definitivos*. Vol. 1 (1821–1876). Buenos Aires, 1938.

Hultsch, D. F., and F. Deutsch. *Adult Development and Aging: A Life-Span Approach*. New York, 1981.

Hunt, David. *Parents and Children in History: The Psychology of Family Life in Early Modern France*. New York, 1970.

Inciardi, James A., and Charles E. Faupel, eds. *History and Crime: Implications for Criminal Justice Policy*. Beverly Hills, Calif., 1980.

Ingenieros, José. *La evolución de las ideas argentinas*. 4 vols. Buenos Aires, 1946.

Instituto de Investigaciones Históricas de la Facultad de Filosofía y Letras. *Administración edilicia de Buenos Aires (1776–1805)*. Introducción de Luis Maria Torres. *Documentos para la Historia Argentina*, vol. 9. Buenos Aires, 1918.

Isabelle, A. *Viaje a Argentina, Uruguay y Brasil en 1830*. Buenos Aires, 1943.

——. *Voyage à Buenos Ayres et Porto-Alegre*. Le Havre, 1835.

Jiménez de Azúa, Luis. *Tratado de derecho penal*. 7 vols. 3d ed. Buenos Aires, 1964–70.

Johnson, Anne Hagerman. "The Impact of Market Agriculture on Family and Household Structure in Nineteenth-Century Chile." *Hispanic American Historical Review*, 58 (Nov. 1978), 625–48.

Johnson, H. C. Ross. *Vacaciones de un inglés en la Argentina*. Buenos Aires, 1943.

Johnson, Lyman L. "Estimaciones de la poblacion de Buenos Aires en 1774, 1778, y 1810." *Desarrollo Economico*, 73 (Apr.–June 1979), 107–19.

——. "Manumission in Colonial Buenos Aires, 1776–1810." *Hispanic American Historical Review*, 59 (May 1979), 258–79.

Judt, Tony. "A Clown in Regal Purple: Social History and the Historians." *History Workshop*, 7 (Spring 1979), 66–94.

Kaestle, Carl F. *The Evolution of an Urban School System: New York City, 1750–1850*. Cambridge, Mass., 1973.

——. "Social Change, Discipline, and the Common School in Early Nineteenth-Century America." *Journal of Interdisciplinary History*, 9 (Summer 1978), 1–17.

Kagan, Richard L. *Students and Society in Early Modern Spain*. Baltimore, Md., 1974.

Kahl, Joseph A. *The Measurement of Modernism: A Study of Values in Brazil and Mexico*. Austin, Tex., 1968.

——. *Modernization, Exploitation, and Dependency in Latin America*. New Brunswick, N.J., 1974.

Kaminsky, Howard. "Noble Liberty and Privileged Estate: The Legitimation of Property Rights in the Medieval Polity." Unpublished paper, American Historical Association Meeting, 1983.

Karst, Kenneth L. *Latin American Legal Institutions: Problems for Comparative Study*. Los Angeles, 1966.

Karst, Kenneth L., and Keith S. Rosenn. *Law and Development in Latin America: A Case Book*. Los Angeles, 1975.

Katz, Friedrich. "Labor Conditions and Haciendas in Porfirian Mexico:

Some Trends and Tendencies." *The Hispanic American Historical Review*, 54 (Feb. 1974), 1–47.

Kellum, Barbara A. "Infanticide in England in the Later Middle Ages." *History of Childhood Quarterly*, 1 (1974), 367–88.

Kent, Dale V., and Francis W. Kent. *Neighbours and Neighbourhood in Renaissance Florence: The District of the Red Lion in the Fifteenth Century.* Locust Valley, N.Y., 1982.

Kent, Francis W. *Household and Lineage in Renaissance Florence.* Princeton, N.J., 1977.

Kern, Robert. "Spanish Caciquismo: A Classic Model." In *The Caciques: Oligarchical Politics and the System of Caciquismo in the Luso-Hispanic World*, ed. Robert Kern, pp. 42–45. Albuquerque, N.M., 1973.

Kern, Robert, ed. *The Caciques: Oligarchical Politics and the System of Caciquismo.* Albuquerque, N.M., 1973.

Kern, Robert, and Ronald Dolkart. "Introduction." In *The Caciques: Oligarchical Politics and the System of Caciquismo in the Luso-Hispanic World*, ed. Robert Kern, pp. 1–4. Albuquerque, N.M., 1973.

Kett, Joseph F. "Adolescence and Youth in Nineteenth-Century America." *Journal of Interdisciplinary History*, 2 (Autumn 1971), 283–98.

Kicza, John E. "The Great Families of Mexico: Elite Maintenance and Business Practices in Late Colonial Mexico City." *Hispanic American Historical Review*, 62 (Aug. 1982), 429–57.

Klein, Herbert S. "Las finanzas del Virreinato del Río de la Plata en 1790." *Desarrollo Económico*, 50 (July–Sept. 1973), 369–400.

Knodel, John E. *The Decline of Fertility in Germany, 1871–1939.* Princeton, N.J., 1974.

Kronfuss, Juan. *Arquitectura colonial en la Argentina.* Córdoba, 1930.

Kuethe, Allan J. "The Development of the Cuban Military as a Sociopolitical Elite, 1763–1783." *The Hispanic American Historical Review*, 61 (Nov. 1981), 695–704.

———. *Military Reform and Society in New Granada, 1773–1808.* Gainesville, Fla., 1978.

Kuhn, Thomas S. *The Structure of Scientific Revolutions.* 2d ed. Chicago, 1970.

Kuznesof, Elizabeth Anne. "Household Composition and Headship as Related to Changes in Mode of Production: São Paulo, 1765 to 1836." *Comparative Studies in Society and History*, 22 (Jan. 1980), 78–108.

———. "The Role of the Merchants in the Economic Development of São Paulo, 1765–1850." *Hispanic American Historical Review*, 60 (Nov. 1980), 571–92.

Ladd, Doris. *The Mexican Nobility at Independence, 1780–1826.* Austin, Tex., 1976.

Lancaster, Joseph. *The British System of Education.* 2d ed. London, 1810.

Landes, David S. *The Unbound Prometheus: Technological Change and Industrial Development in Western Europe from 1750 to the Present.* Cambridge, Mass., 1969.

Landes, David S., ed. *The Rise of Capitalism.* New York, 1966.

Langer, William L. "Infanticide: A Historical Survey." *History of Childhood Quarterly,* 1 (1974), 353–65.

Lasch, Christopher. *Haven in a Heartless World.* New York, 1977.

Laslett, Barbara. "The Family as a Public and Private Institution: An Historical Perspective." *Journal of Marriage and the Family,* 35 (Aug. 1973), 480–92.

Laslett, Peter. "The Family as a Knot of Individual Interests." In *Households: Comparative and Historical Studies of the Domestic Group,* ed. Robert McC. Netting, Richard Wilk, and Eric Arnould, pp. 353–79. Berkeley, Calif., 1984.

———. *Family Life and Illicit Love in Earlier Generations.* Cambridge, Eng., 1977.

———. *The World We Have Lost: England Before the Industrial Revolution.* 2d ed. New York, 1971.

Laslett, Peter, and Richard Wall, eds. *Household and Family in Past Time.* Cambridge, Eng., 1972.

Laslett, Peter, Karla Oosterveen, and Richard Smith, eds. *Bastardy and Its Comparative History.* London, 1980.

Lattes, Alfredo E. "Las migraciones en la Argentina entre mediados del siglo XIX y 1960," *Desarrollo Económico,* no. 48 (Jan.–Mar. 1973), 849–65.

Lautman, Françoise. "Differences or Changes in Family Organization." In *Family and Society: Selections from the* ANNALES, ed. Robert Forster and Orest Ranum, pp. 251–61. Baltimore, Md., 1976.

Lavrín, Asunción, ed. *Latin American Women: Historical Perspectives.* Westport, Conn., 1978.

Lavrín, Asunción, and Edith Couturier. "Dowries and Wills: A View of Women's Socioeconomic Role in Colonial Guadalajara and Puebla, 1640–1790." *Hispanic American Historical Review,* 59 (May 1979), 280–304.

Lawrence, Roderick J. "Domestic Space and Society: A Cross-Cultural Study." *Comparative Studies in Society and History,* 24 (Jan. 1982), 104–30.

Lazerson, Marvin. *Origins of the Urban School: Public Education in Massachusetts, 1870–1915.* Cambridge, Mass., 1971.

Lee, W. R. "Past Legacies and Future Prospects: Recent Research on the History of the Family in Germany." *Journal of Family History,* 6 (Summer 1981), 156–76.

Lehning, James R. "Immigration and the Family." *Proceedings of the World Conference on Records*, vol. 12. Salt Lake City, Utah, 1980.

Le Play, Pierre G. F. *L'Organisation de la Famille*. Paris, 1871.

Lerner, Ralph, and Mushin Mahdi. *Medieval Political Philosophy: A Sourcebook*. New York, 1963.

Le Roy Ladurie, Emmanuel. "Family Structures and Inheritance Customs in Sixteenth-Century France." In *Family and Inheritance*, ed. John Goody, Joan Thirsk, and Edward P. Thompson. Cambridge, Eng., 1976.

————. *The Peasants of Languedoc*. Paris, 1966.

————. "A System of Customary Law: Family Structures and Inheritance Customs in Sixteenth-Century France." In *Family and Society: Selections from the* ANNALES, ed. Robert Forster and Orest Ranum, pp. 75–103. Baltimore, Md., 1976.

Levaggi, Abelardo. *Historia del derecho penal argentino*. Buenos Aires, 1978.

Levene, Ricardo. *El proceso histórico de Lavalle a Rosas*. La Plata, 1946.

Levene, Ricardo, ed. *Historia de la nación argentina*. 2d ed. Buenos Aires, 1961.

Levine, David. "The Reliability of Parochial Registration and the Representativeness of Family Reconstruction." *Population Studies*, 30 (March 1976), 107–22.

Levine, Robert M. "Society, Crime and Social Control in Nineteenth- and Early Twentieth-Century Brazil." Unpublished paper, Southeastern Council of Latin American Studies Meeting, 1982.

Lewis, Oscar. "An Anthropological Approach to Family Studies." *American Journal of Sociology*, 55, no. 5 (1950), 468–75.

————. *The Children of Sánchez*. New York, 1961.

————. *La Vida: A Puerto Rican Family in the Culture of Poverty*. New York, 1966.

Lindemann, Mary. "Love for Hire: The Regulation of the Wet Nursing-Business in Eighteenth-Century Hamburg, Germany." *Journal of Family History*, 6 (1981), 379–95.

Lipset, Seymour, Reinhard Bendix, and Gino Germani. *Movilidad social en la sociedad industrial*. Buenos Aires, 1961.

Lithell, Ulla-Britt. "Breast-Feeding Habits and Their Relations to Infant Mortality and Marital Fertility." *Journal of Family History*, 6 (Summer 1981), 182–94.

Little, Cynthia J. "The Society of Beneficence in Buenos Aires, 1823–1900." Unpublished Ph.D. diss., Temple University, 1980.

Livi-Bacci, Massimo. "Fertility and Population Growth in Spain in the Eighteenth and Nineteenth Centuries." *Daedalus*, 97 (Spring 1968), 523–35.

————. *A History of Italian Fertility During the Last Two Centuries*. Princeton, N.J., 1977.

Locke, John. *Two Treatises of Civil Government.* Cambridge, Eng., 1967.

Lockridge, Kenneth. "The Population of Dedham, Massachusetts, 1636–1736." *Economic History Review,* 19 (Aug. 1966), 318–44.

Lomnitz, Larissa, and M. Pérez-Lizaur. "Dynastic Growth and Survival Strategies: The Solidarity of Mexican Grand-Families." In *Kinship Ideology and Practice in Latin America,* ed. Raymond T. Smith, pp. 183–95. Chapel Hill, N.C., 1984.

———. "The History of a Mexican Urban Family." *Journal of Family History,* 3 (Winter 1978), 392–409.

López, Lucio V. *La gran aldea.* Buenos Aires, 1894.

Love, Edgar F. "Marriage Patterns of Persons of African Descent in a Colonial Mexico City Parish." *Hispanic American Historical Review,* 51 (Feb. 1971), 71–91.

Low, Donald A. *Thieves' Kitchen: The Regency Underworld.* London, 1981.

Luna, Félix. *Los caudillos.* Buenos Aires, 1966.

Lynch, John. *Argentine Dictator: Juan Manuel de Rosas, 1829–1852.* London, 1981.

McAlister, Lyle. *The Fuero Militar in New Spain, 1764–1800.* Gainesville, Fla., 1952.

McCaa, Robert. "Calidad, *Clase,* and Marriage in Colonial Mexico: The Case of Parral, 1788–1790." *Hispanic American Historical Review,* 64 (Aug. 1984), 477–502.

———. *Marriage and Fertility in Chile: Demographic Turning Points in the Petorca Valley, 1840–1976.* Boulder, Colo., 1983.

MacCann, William. *Two-Thousand Miles' Ride Through the Argentine Provinces.* London, 1853.

MacFarlane, Alan. *The Origins of English Individualism: The Family, Property, and Social Transition.* Cambridge, Eng., 1979.

McFarlane, Anthony. "Civil Disorder and Protests in Late Colonial New Granada." *Hispanic American Historical Review,* 64 (Feb. 1984), 17–54.

Maeder, Ernesto J. A. *Evolución demográfica argentina de 1810 à 1869.* Buenos Aires, 1968.

Maier, Joseph, and Richard Weatherhead, eds. *Politics of Change in Latin America.* New York, 1964.

Mansilla, Lucio V. *Mis memorias.* Buenos Aires, 1904.

Marcy, Peter T. "Factors Affecting the Fecundity and Fertility of Historical Populations: A Review." *Journal of Family History,* 6 (Fall 1981), 309–26.

Mármol, José. *Amalia.* 2 vols. 2d ed. Buenos Aires, 1955.

———. *Poesías completas.* 2 vols. Buenos Aires, 1946.

Martínez, Alberto, and Maurice Lewandowski. *The Argentine in the Twentieth Century.* Boston, 1911.

Martini, José Xavier. "Notas para una crítica de la arquitectura colonial argentina." *Anales del Instituto de Arte Americano e Investigaciones Estéticas*, no. 24 (1971), 9–21.

Martz, Linda. *Poverty and Welfare in Hapsburg Spain: The Example of Toledo*. Cambridge, Eng., 1982.

Matamoro, Blas. *La casa porteña*. Buenos Aires, 1971.

Maynes, Mary J. *Schooling in Western Europe: A Social History*. Albany, N.Y., 1985.

Mayo, Carlos A. "'Amistades ilícitas': las relaciones extramaritales en la campaña bonaerense, 1750–1810." *Cuadernos de Historia Regional*, 1, no. 2 (1985), 3–9.

Medick, Hans. "The Proto-Industrial Family Economy: The Structural Function of Household and Family during the Transition from Peasant Society to Industrial Capitalism." *Social History*, 3 (Oct. 1976), 291–316.

Meister, Albert. "Cambio social y participación social formal en asociaciones voluntarias." *Desarrollo Económico*, no. 3 (Oct.–Dec. 1962), 5–18.

Mellafe, Rolando. "Evolución del tamaño y estructura de la familia latinoamericana en un amplio marco comparativo." Unpublished paper, Cuernavaca, Mexico, 1977.

Milden, James W., ed. *The Family in Past Time: A Guide to the Literature*. New York, 1977.

Mitterauer, Michael, and Reinhard Sieder. *The European Family*. Chicago, 1982.

Moch, Leslie Page. "Marriage, Migration, and Urban Demographic Structure: A Case from France in the Belle Epoque." *Journal of Family History*, 6 (Spring 1981), 70–88.

Moreno, José Luis. "La estructura social y demográfica de la ciudad de Buenos Aires en al año 1778." *Anuario del Instituto de Investigaciones Históricas de la Facultad de Filosofía y Letras, Universidad del Litoral*, 8 (1965), 151–70.

Morgan, Edmund S. *The Puritan Family: Domestic Relations in Seventeenth-Century New England*. New York, 1966.

Morner, Magnus. *The Political and Economic Activities of the Jesuits in the La Plata Region*. Stockholm, 1953.

Morner, Magnus, ed. *The Expulsion of the Jesuits from Latin America*. New York, 1965.

Morse, Richard M. "Cities and Society in XIX Century Latin America: The Illustrative Case of Brazil." In *El proceso de urbanización en América*, ed. Jorge Hardoy and Richard Schaedel, pp. 303–22. Buenos Aires, 1969.

———. "The Heritage of Latin America." In *The Founding of New Societies*, ed. Louis Hartz, pp. 123–77. New York, 1964.

———. "'Peripheral' Cities as Cultural Arenas (Russia, Austria, Latin America)." *Journal of Urban History*, 10 (Aug. 1984), 423–52.

———. "Primacia, regionalización, dependencia: enfoques sobre las ciudades latinoamericanas en el desarrollo nacional." *Desarrollo Económico*, no. 41 (Apr.–June 1971), 55–85.

———. "A Prolegomenon to Latin American Urban History." *Hispanic American Historical Review*, 52 (Aug. 1972), 359–94.

———. "Trends and Patterns of Latin American Urbanization." *Comparative Studies in Society and History*, 16 (Sept. 1974), 416–47.

Murilo de Carvalho, José. "Political Elites and State Building: The Case of Nineteenth-Century Brazil." *Comparative Studies in Society and History*, 24 (July 1982), 378–99.

Museo Histórico Nacional. *Acta del Cabildo de Buenos Aires (8 de Octubre de 1812)*. Buenos Aires, 1912.

Netting, Robert McC., Richard Wilk, and Eric Arnould, eds. *Households: Comparative and Historical Studies of the Domestic Group*. Berkeley, Calif., 1984.

Newton, Jorge. *Angel Vicente Peñaloza*. Buenos Aires, 1965.

Newton, Ronald C. "On 'Functional Groups,' 'Fragmentation,' and 'Pluralsim' in Spanish American Political Society." *Hispanic American Historical Review*, 50 (Feb. 1970), 1–29.

Noel, Martín S. *Contribucíon a la historia de la arquitectura hispanoamericana*. Buenos Aires, 1921.

Noonan, John T., Jr. *Contraception: A History of its Treatment by the Catholic Theologians*. Cambridge, Mass., 1965.

———. "Intellectual and Demographic History." *Daedalus*, 97 (Spring 1968), 463–85.

Obligado, Pastor S. *Tradiciones y recuerdos*. Buenos Aires, 1908.

O'Brien, Patricia. *The Promise of Punishment: Prisons in Nineteenth-Century France*. Princeton, N.J., 1982.

Palcos, Alberto. *La visión de Rivadavia*. Buenos Aires, 1936.

Parish, Woodbine. *Buenos Aires y las provincias del Río de la Plata*. Buenos Aires, 1958.

Parsons, Talcott, and Robert F. Bales. *Family Socialization and Interaction Process*. Glencoe, Ill., 1955.

Peña, Guillermo de la. "Ideology and Practice in Southern Jalisco: Peasants, Rancheros, and Urban Entrepreneurs." In *Kinship Ideology and Practice in Latin America*, ed. Raymond T. Smith, pp. 204–34. Chapel Hill, N.C., 1984.

Pérez Amuchástegui, Antonio J. *Mentalidades argentinas, 1860–1930*. Buenos Aires, 1965.

Pescatello, Ann M. "The Female in Ibero-America." *Latin American Research Review*, 7 (Summer 1972), 125–41.

———. *Power and Pawn: The Female in Iberian Families, Societies, and Culture*. Westport, Conn., 1976.

Phelan, John L. "Authority and Flexibility in the Spanish Imperial Bureaucracy." *Administrative Science Quarterly*, 5 (June 1960), 47–65.

Piccirilli, Ricardo. *Rivadavia y su tiempo.* 2 vols. Buenos Aires, 1943.

Pinheiro, Paulo Sergio, ed. *Crime, violencia e poder.* São Paulo, 1983.

Portes, Alejandro, and Harley Browning, eds. *Current Perspectives in Latin American Urban Research.* Austin, Tex., 1976.

Power, Eileen. *Medieval Women.* Cambridge, Eng., 1975.

Pred, Allan R. *Urban Growth and the Circulation of Information, 1790–1840.* Cambridge, Mass., 1973.

Quesada, Ernesto. *La época de Rosas.* Buenos Aires, 1926.

———. *Reseñas y críticas.* Buenos Aires, 1893.

Quesada, Vicente G. *Memorias de un viejo. Escenas de costumbres de la República Argentina.* Buenos Aires, 1942.

Quiroga de la Rosa, Manuel J. *Sobre la naturaleza filosófica del derecho.* Buenos Aires, 1937.

Rahe, Paul A. "The Primacy of Politics in Classical Greece." *American Historical Review*, 89 (Apr. 1984), 265–93.

Raj, Des. *The Design of Sample Surveys.* New York, 1972.

Ramos, Donald. "City and Country: The Family in Minas Gerais, 1804–1838." *Journal of Family History*, 3 (Winter 1978), 361–75.

———. "Marriage and the Family in Colonial Vila Rica." *Hispanic American Historical Review*, 55 (May 1975), 200–225.

Ramos Mejía, José. *Las multitudes argentinas.* Buenos Aires, 1899.

———. *Las multitudes argentinas.* Madrid, 1912.

Ranum, Orest, and Patricia Ranum, eds. *Popular Attitudes Toward Birth Control in Pre-Industrial France and England.* New York, 1972.

Rapson, Richard L. "The American Child As Seen by British Travelers, 1845–1935." *American Quarterly*, 17 (1965), 520–34.

Ravignani, Emilio. "Crecimiento de la población en Buenos Aires y su campaña (1776–1810)." *Anales de la Facultad de Ciencias Económicas*, 1 (Buenos Aires, 1919).

———. *Territorio y población . . . Padrones de la ciudad de Buenos Aires.* Buenos Aires, 1919.

Recopilación de las leyes y decretos promulgados en Buenos Aires desde el 25 de Mayo de 1810 hasta fin de Diciembre de 1835. Part 1. Buenos Aires, 1836.

Registro estadístico del estado de Buenos Aires. Buenos Aires, 1889.

Registro estadístico de la Provincia de Buenos Aires. Buenos Aires, 1822–26.

Registro Nacional. Vol. 1. Buenos Aires, 1879.

Reinhardt, Steven G. "Crime and Royal Justice in Ancien Régime France: Modes of Analysis." *Journal of Interdisciplinary History*, 13 (Winter 1983), 437–60.

República Argentina. *Primer censo nacional (1869).* Buenos Aires, 1872.

Rico González, Victor, ed. *Antología del pensamiento político americano: Juan Bautista Alberdi.* Mexico, D.F., 1946.

Río, Manuel E. "Consideraciones históricas y sociológicas sobre la Provincia de Córdoba." In *Córdoba: su fisionomía, su misión,* ed. Manuel E. Río. Córdoba, 1967.

Rípodas Ardanaz, Daisy. *El matrimonio en Indias: realidad social y regulación jurídica.* Buenos Aires, 1977.

Robinson, David J., ed. *Social Fabric and Spatial Structure in Colonial Latin America.* Ann Arbor, Mich., 1979.

Rock, David. *Politics in Argentina, 1890–1930: The Rise and Fall of Radicalism.* Cambridge, Eng., 1975.

Roderick, Lawrence J. "Domestic Space and Society: A Cross-Cultural Study." *Comparative Studies in Society and History,* 24 (Jan. 1982), 104–30.

Rodríguez Molas, Ricardo. *Historia social del gaucho.* Buenos Aires, 1968.

Romano, Dennis. "S. Giacomo Dall'Orio: Parish Life in Fourteenth-Century Venice." Ph.D. diss., Michigan State University, 1981.

Romero, José Luis. "La ciudad latinoamericana y los movimientos políticos." In *La urbanización en América Latina,* ed. Jorge E. Hardoy and Carlos Tobar, pp. 297–310. Buenos Aires, 1969.

———. *A History of Argentine Political Thought.* Stanford, Calif., 1963.

Romero, Luis Alberto. *La feliz experiencia, 1820–1824.* Buenos Aires, 1976.

Rosenberg, Charles E., ed. *The Family in History.* Philadelphia, 1975.

Ross, Stanley, and Thomas McGann, eds. *Buenos Aires: 400 Years.* Austin, Tex., 1982.

Rothman, David J. "A Note on the Study of the Colonial Family." *William and Mary Quarterly,* 23 (Oct. 1966), 627–34.

Safford, Frank. "Social Aspects of Politics in Nineteenth-Century Spanish America: New Granada, 1825–1850." *Journal of Social History,* 5 (Spring 1972), 344–70.

Salas, Alberto M. *Diario de Buenos Aires, 1806–1807.* Buenos Aires, 1981.

Saldías, Adolfo. *Historia de la Confederación Argentina: Rozas y su tiempo.* Buenos Aires, 1951.

———. *Vida y escritos del Padre Castañeda.* Buenos Aires, 1907.

Salthouse, Timothy. *Adult Cognition: An Experimental Psychology of Human Aging.* New York, 1982.

Sánchez Viamonte, Carlos. *El pensamiento liberal argentino en el siglo XIX.* Buenos Aires, 1957.

Sarmiento, Domingo F. "Arquitectura doméstica." *Anales del Instituto de Arte Americano e Investigaciones Estéticas,* no. 11 (1958), 97–106.

———. *Conflicto y armonías de las razas en America.* Buenos Aires, 1915.

———. *Constitución del Colegio de Señoritas de la Advovación.* Buenos Aires, 1939.

————. *Facundo*. Mexico, D.F., 1958.

————. *Life in the Argentine Republic in the Days of the Tyrants*. New York, 1868.

————. *Obras completas de Domingo F. Sarmiento*. Vol. 6, *Política arjentina*. Paris, 1909.

————. *Recuerdos de provincia*. Buenos Aires, 1929.

Sastre, Marcos. *El tempe argentino, o el delta de los ríos Uruguay, Paraguay y Paraná*. 5th ed. Buenos Aires, 1870.

Schochet, Gordon J. *Patriarchalism in Political Thought: The Authoritarian Family and Political Speculation and Attitudes Especially in Seventeenth-Century England*. New York, 1975.

Schofield, Roger. "Age-Specific Mobility in an Eighteenth-Century Rural English Parish." *Annales de Demographie Historique*, 1970, pp. 261–74.

Scobie, James R. *Buenos Aires: From Plaza to Suburb, 1870–1910*. New York, 1974.

————. *La lucha por la consolidación de la nacionalidad argentina*. Buenos Aires, 1964.

————. *Revolution on the Pampas*. Austin, Tex., 1960.

Seed, Patricia. "Miscegenation in Mexico City: A Preliminary Historical Inquiry." Unpublished paper, American Historical Association Meeting, 1983.

————. "Parents Versus Children: Marriage Oppositions in Colonial Mexico, 1610–1779." Unpublished Ph.D. diss., University of Wisconsin–Madison, 1980.

————. "Social Dimensions of Race: Mexico City, 1753." *The Hispanic American Historical Review*, 62 (Nov. 1982), 569–606.

Segalen, Martine. "The Family Cycle and Household Structure: Five Generations in a French Village." In *Family and Sexuality in French History*, ed. Robert Wheaton and Tamara K. Hareven, pp. 253–71. Philadelphia, 1980.

Sennett, Richard. *Families Against the City: Middle-Class Homes of Industrial Chicago, 1872–1890*. Cambridge, Mass., 1970.

Shammas, Carole. "Women and Inheritance in the Age of Family Capitalism." Unpublished paper, Social Science History Association Meeting, 1979.

Sheehan, W. J. "Finding Solace in Eighteenth-Century Newgate." In *Crime in England, 1550–1800*, ed. J. S. Cockburn, pp. 229–45. Princeton, N.J., 1977.

Shields, J. V. M., and Judith A. Duncan, *The State of Crime in Scotland*. London, 1964.

Shorter, Edward. "Female Emancipation, Birth Control, and Fertility in European History." *American Historical Review*, 78 (June 1973), 605–40.

———. "Illegitimacy, Sexual Revolution, and Social Change in Modern Europe." *Journal of Interdisciplinary History*, 2 (Autumn 1971), 237–72.

———. *The Making of the Modern Family*. New York, 1975.

———. "Sexual Change and Illegitimacy: The European Experience." In *Modern European Social History*, ed. Robert Bezucha, pp. 231–69. Lexington, Mass., 1972.

———. "What Family History Is the History of." *Proceedings of the World Conference on Records*, vol. 12. Salt Lake City, 1980.

Silberstein, Carina F. "Fronteras de haciendas de Tucumán. Siglos XVI y XVII." Unpublished paper, Universidad de Buenos Aires, 1978.

Sinkin, Richard. "The Mexican Constitutional Congress, 1856–57: A Statistical Analysis." *Hispanic American Historical Review*, 53 (Feb. 1973), 1–27.

Slater, Miriam. "The Weightiest Business: Marriage in an Upper Gentry Family in Seventeenth-Century England." *Past & Present*, 72 (Aug. 1976), 25–54.

Slater, Philip E. "Parental Role Differentiation." *American Journal of Sociology*, 67 (Nov. 1961), 296–311.

Slatta, Richard W. *Gauchos and the Vanishing Frontier*. Lincoln, Nebr., 1983.

———. "Pulperías and Contraband Capitalism in Nineteenth-Century Buenos Aires Province." *The Americas*, 38 (Jan. 1982), 347–62.

———. "Rural Criminality and Social Conflict in Nineteenth-Century Buenos Aires Province." *Hispanic American Historical Review*, 60 (Aug. 1980), 450–72.

Smelser, Neil. *Social Change in the Industrial Revolution*. London, 1959.

Smith, Daniel Scott. "Parental Power and Marriage Patterns." *Journal of Marriage and the Family*, 35 (Aug. 1973), 419–28.

Smith, Daniel S., and Milton Hindus. "Premarital Pregnancy in America, 1640–1971: An Overview and Interpretation." *Journal of Interdisciplinary History*, 5 (Spring 1975), 537–70.

Smith, James E. "Widowhood in an Earlier Time." *Proceedings of the World Conference on Records*, vol 12. Salt Lake City, 1980.

Smith, Peter H. "Political Legitimacy in Spanish America." In *New Approaches to Latin American History*, ed. Richard Graham and Peter H. Smith, pp. 225–55. Austin, Tex., 1974.

Smith, Raymond T. "The Family and the Modern World System: Some Observations from the Caribbean." *Journal of Family History*, 3 (Winter 1978), 337–60.

———. "Introduction." In *Kinship Ideology and Practice in Latin America*, ed. Raymond T. Smith, pp. 3–27. Chapel Hill, N.C., 1984.

Smith, Raymond T., ed. *Kinship Ideology and Practice in Latin America*. Chapel Hill, N.C., 1984.

Smith-Rosenberg, Carol, et al. "The Female Animal: Medical and Biolog-

ical Views of Woman and Her Role in Nineteenth-Century America."
Journal of American History, 60 (Sept. 1973), 332–56.

Socolow, Susan M. "Buenos Aires at the Time of Independence." In *Buenos Aires, 400 Years*, ed. Stanley R. Ross and Thomas F. McGann, pp. 18–39. Austin, Tex., 1982.

——. "La burguesía comerciante de Buenos Aires en el siglo XVIII." *Desarrollo Económico*, no. 70 (July–Sept. 1978), 205–16.

——. "Economic Activities of the Porteño Merchants: The Viceregal Period." *Hispanic American Historical Review*, 55 (Feb. 1975), 1–24.

——. "Marriage, Birth, and Inheritance: The Merchants of Eighteenth-Century Buenos Aires." *Hispanic American Historical Review*, 60 (Aug. 1980), 387–406.

——. *The Merchants of Buenos Aires, 1778–1810*. Cambridge, Eng., 1978.

——. "Women and Crime: Buenos Aires, 1757–1797. *Journal of Latin American Studies*, 12 (May 1980), 39–54.

Socolow, Susan M., and Lyman L. Johnson. "Urbanization in Colonial Latin America." *Journal of Urban History*, 8 (Nov. 1981), 27–59.

Soeiro, Susan A. "The Social and Economic Role of the Convent: Women and Nuns in Colonial Bahia, 1677–1800." *Hispanic American Historical Review*, 54 (May 1974), 209–32.

Solari, Manuel H. *Historia de la educación argentina*. Buenos Aires, 1976.

Solberg, Carl. *Immigration and Nationalism: Argentina and Chile, 1890–1914*. Austin, Tex., 1970.

Soler, Ricaurte. *El positivismo argentino*. Buenos Aires, 1968.

Soliday, Gerald L., ed. *History of the Family and Kinship: A Selected International Bibliography*. New York, 1980.

Sommerville, C. John. "Towards a History of Childhood and Youth." *Journal of Interdisciplinary History*, 3 (Autumn 1972), 438–47.

Sopher, David. "Place and Location: Notes on the Spatial Patterning of Culture." In *The Idea of Culture in the Social Sciences*, ed. Louis Schneider and Charles Bonjean, pp. 101–17. London, 1973.

Sosa de Newton, Lily. *Las argentinas*. Buenos Aires, 1967.

Spagnoli, Paul G. "Philippe Ariès, Historian of the Family." *Journal of Family History*, 6 (Winter 1981), 434–41.

Spalding, Hobart A. "Education in Argentina, 1890–1914: The Limits of Oligarchical Reform." *Journal of Interdisciplinary History*, 3 (Summer 1972), 31–61.

Splenger, Joseph J. "Demographic Factors and Early Modern Economic Development." *Daedalus*, 97 (Spring 1968), 433–46.

Spufford, Margaret. *Contrasting Communities: English Villagers in the Sixteenth and Seventeenth Centuries*. Cambridge, Eng., 1974.

Stern, Mark J. "Differential Fertility in Rural Erie County, New York, 1855." *Journal of Social History*, 16 (Summer 1983), 49–63.

————. "The Influence of Age of Marriage, Occupation, and Ethnicity on Fertility, Erie County, New York, 1855–1915." Unpublished paper, 1979.

Stone, Lawrence. "Family History in the 1980s: Past Achievements and Future Trends." *Journal of Interdisciplinary History*, 12 (Summer 1981), 51–87.

————. *The Family, Sex and Marriage in England, 1500–1800*. London, 1977.

————. "Social Mobility in England, 1500–1700." *Past & Present*, 33 (Apr. 1966), 16–55.

Strickon, Arnold, and Sidney M. Greenfield, eds. *Structure and Process in Latin America*. Albuquerque, N.M., 1972.

Strumingher, Laura S. *What Were Little Girls and Boys Made of? Primary Education in Rural France, 1830–80*. Albany, N.Y., 1983.

Szuchman, Mark D. "Continuidades no controle social: a criminalidade na area urbana de Buenos Aires, 1810–1860." In *Crime, Violencia e Poder*, ed. Paulo Sergio Pinheiro, pp. 45–93. São Paulo, 1983.

————. "Disorder and Social Control in Buenos Aires, 1810–1860." *Journal of Interdisciplinary History*, 15 (Summer 1984), 83–110.

————. "Family and Household in the Absence of a Central State." Unpublished paper, American Historical Association Meeting, 1984.

————. "Household Structure and Political Crisis: Buenos Aires, 1810–1860." *Latin American Research Review*, 21, no. 3 (1986), 55–93.

————. "Labor and Childhood in Buenos Aires, 1810–1860." Unpublished paper, Center for the Study of Industrial Societies, University of Chicago, 1985.

Taullard, A. *Nuestro antiguo Buenos Aires*. Buenos Aires, 1927.

Taylor, William B. *Drinking, Homicide and Rebellion in Colonial Mexican Villages*. Stanford, Calif., 1979.

Thompson, Edward P. "The Crime of Anonymity." In *Albion's Fatal Tree: Crime and Society in Eighteenth-Century England*, ed. Douglas Hay, Peter Linebaugh, and Edward P. Thompson, pp. 255–344. London, 1975.

Thornton, Arland. "Marital Dissolution, Remarriage, and Childbearing." *Demography*, 15 (Aug. 1978), 361–80.

Tilly, Charles. "The Historical Study of Vital Processes." In *Historical Studies of Changing Fertilities*, ed. Charles Tilly, pp. 3–56. Princeton, N.J., 1978.

Tilly, Charles, ed. *Historical Studies of Changing Fertility*. Princeton, N.J., 1978.

Tilly, Louise, and Joan W. Scott. *Women, Work, and Family*. New York, 1978.

Tilly, Louise, Joan W. Scott, and Miriam Cohen. "Women's Work and European Fertility Patterns." *Journal of Interdisciplinary History*, 6 (Winter 1976), 447–76.

Torre Revello, José. "La vivienda en el Buenos Aires antiguo. Desde los orígenes hasta los comienzos del siglo XIX." *Anales del Instituto de Arte Americano e Investigaciones Estéticas*, no. 10 (1957), pp. 84–125.

Torres, Horacio. "Evolución de los procesos de estructuración espacial urbana. El caso de la ciudad de Buenos Aires." *Desarrollo Económico*, no. 58 (July–Sept. 1975), 281–306.

Trifilo, Samuel S. *La Argentina vista por viajeros ingleses, 1810–1860*. Buenos Aires, 1959.

Trudgill, E. "Prostitution and Paterfamilias." In *The Victorian City*, ed. Harold J. Dyos and Michael Wolff, pp. 693–705. London, 1973.

Tutino, John. "Power, Class, and Family: Men and Women in the Mexican Elite, 1750–1810." *The Americas*, 39 (Jan. 1983), 359–81.

Ullman, Stephen. "Semantic Universals." In *Universals of Language*, ed. J. H. Greenberg, 2d ed., pp. 217–61. Cambridge, Mass., 1973.

Universidad de Buenos Aires. *Estudios y documentos para la historia del arte colonial*. Buenos Aires, 1934.

Van de Walle, Etienne. "Alone in Europe: The French Fertility Decline Until 1850." In *Historical Studies of Changing Fertility*, ed. Charles Tilly, pp. 257–88. Princeton, N.J., 1978.

———. "Marriage and Marital Fertility." *Daedalus*, 97 (Spring 1968), 486–501.

———. "Motivations and Technology in the Decline of French Fertility." In *Family and Sexuality in French History*, ed. Robert Wheaton and Tamara K. Hareven, pp. 135–78. Philadelphia, Pa., 1980.

Vann, Richard T. "History and Demography." *History and Theory*, 9, no. 9 (1969), 64–78.

Vedia y Mitre, Mariano de. *La vida de Monteagudo*. Buenos Aires, 1950.

Vedoya, Juan Carlos. *Historia de la instrucción primaria en la República Argentina*. Tandil, 1984.

Véliz, Claudio. *The Centralist Tradition of Latin America*. Princeton, N.J., 1980.

Vilaseca, Clara, ed. *Cartas de Mariquita Sánchez*. Buenos Aires, 1952.

Viñas, David. *La crisis de la ciudad liberal*. Buenos Aires, 1973.

Wachter, Kenneth, et al. *Statistical Studies of Historical Social Structure*. New York, 1978.

Wainerman, Catalina H. "Family Relations in Argentina: Diachrony and Synchrony." *Journal of Family History*, 3 (Winter 1978), 410–21.

Weeks, Jeffrey. *Sex, Politics and Society: The Regulation of Sexuality Since 1800*. London, 1981.

Weinberg, Gregorio. "A Historical Perspective of Latin American Education." *CEPAL Review*, no. 21 (Dec. 1983), pp. 39–55.

———. *Modelos educativos en la historia de América Latina*. Buenos Aires, 1984.

Weinberger, Barbara. "The Police and the Public in Mid-Nineteenth-Century Warwickshire." In *Policing and Punishment in Nineteenth-Century Britain*, ed. Victor Bailey, pp. 65–93. New Brunswick, N.J., 1981.

Weissman, Ronald. *Ritual Brotherhood in Renaissance Florence*. New York, 1981.

Wells, Robert V. "Demographic Change and the Life Cycle of American Families." *Journal of Interdisciplinary History*, 2 (Autumn 1971), 273–82.

———. "Family History and Demographic Tradition." *Journal of Social History*, 9 (Fall 1975), 1–19.

———. "Family Size and Fertility Control in Eighteenth-Century America: A Study of Quaker Families." *Population Studies*, 25 (March 1971), 73–82.

———. "Household Size and Composition in the British Colonies in America, 1675–1775." *Journal of Interdisciplinary History*, 4 (Spring 1974), 543–70.

———. "Quaker Marriage Patterns in a Colonial Perspective." *William and Mary Quarterly*, 29 (July 1972), 415–42.

Wheaton, Robert, and Tamara K. Hareven, eds. *Family and Sexuality in French History*. Philadelphia, Pa., 1980.

Wilde, José A. *Buenos Aires desde setenta años atrás*. Buenos Aires, 1880.

Wilk, Richard, and Robert McC. Netting. "Studying the Household: Method and Theory." In *Households: Comparative and Historical Studies of the Domestic Group*, ed. Robert McC. Netting, Richard Wilk, and Eric Arnould, pp. 1–28. Berkeley, Calif., 1984.

Williford, Miriam. *Jeremy Bentham on Spanish America: An Account of His Letters and Proposals to the New World*. Baton Rouge, La., 1980.

Willigan, J. Dennis, and Kathe Lynch. *Sources and Methods of Historical Demography*. New York, 1982.

Wirth, Louis. "Urbanism as a Way of Life." *American Journal of Sociology*, 44, no. 1 (1938), 1–24.

Wolf, Stephanie Grauman. *Urban Village: Population, Community, and Family Structure, 1683–1800*. Princeton, N.J., 1976.

Wrigley, E. Anthony. "Family Limitation in Pre-Industrial England." *Economic History Review*, 19 (Apr. 1966), 82–109.

———. "Mortality in Pre-Industrial England: The Example of Colyton, Devon Over Three Centuries." *Daedalus*, 97 (Spring 1968), 546–80.

———. *Population and History*. New York, 1969.

———. "Reflections on the History of the Family." *Daedalus*, 106 (Spring 1977), pp. 71–85.

Wrigley, E. Anthony, ed. *Identifying People in the Past*. London, 1973.

Wrigley, E. Anthony, and Roger Schofield. *The Population History of England, 1541–1871: A Reconstruction*. Cambridge, Mass., 1981.

Yans-McLaughlin, Virginia. *Family and Community: Italian Immigrants in Buffalo, 1880–1930.* Urbana, Ill., 1982.

Yasuba, Yasukichi. *Birth Rates of the White Population in the United States, 1800.* Baltimore, Md., 1962.

Yeager, Gertrude M. "Women's Roles in Nineteenth-Century Chile: Public Education Records, 1843–1883." *Latin American Research Review*, 18, no. 3 (1983), 149–56.

Yujnovsky, Oscar. "Políticas de vivienda en la ciudad de Buenos Aires, 1880–1914." *Desarrollo Económico*, no. 54 (July–Sept. 1974), 327–72.

Zehr, Howard J. "The Modernization of Crime in Germany and France, 1830–1913." *Journal of Social History*, 8 (Summer 1975), 117–41.

———. "Patterns of Crime in Nineteenth-Century Germany and France: A Comparative Study." Ph. D. diss., Rutgers University, 1974.

Zeitlin, Maurice, and Richard E. Ratcliff. "Research Methods for the Analysis of the Internal Structure of Dominant Classes: The Case of Landlords and Capitalists in Chile." *Latin American Research Review*, 10 (Fall 1975), 5–61.

Zorraquín Becú, Ricardo. *Historia del derecho argentino.* 2 vols. Buenos Aires, 1966.

Index

In this index an "f" after a number indicates a separate reference on the next page, and an "ff" indicates separate references on the next two pages. A continuous discussion over two or more pages is indicated by a span of page numbers, e.g., "pp. 57–58." *Passim* is used for a cluster of references in close but not consecutive sequence.

Bilbao, Manuel, 107
Birth control, 67
Birth rates, 67, 76
Blacks, 37–38, 40, 219–20
Bolivia, 216
Brazil, 26, 147, 215–18
Buenos Aires, 34, 48, 59, 75, 89,
    143f, 148–52 *passim*, 163, 179,
    215, 225; growth of, 1; as
    expression of progress, 2; con-
    tradictory aspects, 4; maps, 4–5;
    described, 5–8; politics in, 10,
    14, 236; mentalities in, 12;
    patriarchy in, 14; in Western
    context, 14, 16–17; indepen-
    dence and, 16–17; social control,
    16–18, 22, 64; criminality in, 18–
    19; migration to, 19, 121; law
    and order in, 23–24; University
    of, 24, 103, 107, 146f, 166, 184;
    police in, 24, 33; criminal justice
    in, 26; sections of, 27; bureau-
    cracy of, 32; taken by British,
    37; social tensions in, 38; light-
    ing in, 39; arrests in, 39, 42; pen-
    itentiary, 40; lower classes in, 46,
    222; as seen by foreigners, 47;
    judicial system, 50; stagecoach
    line to, 52; demographic fea-
    tures of, 65; family formation in,
    66ff, 198, 206, 211–12; as a Cath-
    olic society, 67; manumission in,
    69; wage labor in, 69; Industrial
    Revolution and, 72; *conchabos*
    in, 74; port of, 74; marital fertil-
    ity in, 77, 79–81; children in, 78;
    illegitimacy in, 81, 117; military
    expenditures, 82; physicians in,
    85; birth rates, 87–88, 95, 97;
    role of parish in, 89; antinomies
    in, 90; contraception in, 97;
    cafes, 106; public spaces, 106;
    after Reconquest, 109; children

in the military of, 110; militia,
    111, 213; population, 116, 188,
    204, 218–19; infant abandon-
    ment, 116–17; State of, 121;
    education, 133, 135, 164, 180–83
    passim; conservatives in, 140;
    youth of, 162; merchants of, 186;
    Intendancy of, 187; ruled by lib-
    erals, 187; as viceregal capital,
    188; decline of males, 192; con-
    scription in, 192; marriage strat-
    egies in, 197; rights and
    obligations in, 227; greater, 243;
    consensual unions in, 243
Bureaucrats, 242

Cabildo, 21
Cafes, 107–8
Caldeclaugh, Alexander, 59
Cambridge Group for the History
    of Population, 244
Campaña, 243
Carácter, 52
Cárcano, Ramón, 113
Casa, 3
Casa de Expósitos, 85, 117–18
Caseload, 242
Caseros, 217
Castañeda, Francisco, 111–12, 155
Catamarca, 198
Catholic Church, 96
Caudillos, 13f, 19, 98, 114, 185,
    230f, 234
Census, 239, 241
Chacareros, 66
Childhood, 170; as developmental
    concept, 148; defined by social
    position, 152, 180; as a construct,
    152, 178, 228; as seen by Gener-
    ation of '37, 177
Children: political strictures and,
    15, 71, 82; as proportion of pop-
    ulation, 65; orphaned, 65, 71;

156, 178; scholarships, 157;
parental concerns for, 165; as
viewed by Rosas, 171; as viewed
by Generation of '37, 172; *gente
de pueblo* and, 173; of the
masses, 174; curriculum, 176,
181; structures of, 180; value of,
181
England, 63
Entenados, 208
Entre Ríos, 177
Estrada, José Manuel, 55

Family, as analytical tool, 2; as
political construct, 12; political
society and, 13; sociopolitical
orders and, 14; political leadership and, 15; nuclear, 78, 92;
rural, 78; average, 78; formation
of, 89ff; size, 89–91, 198; composition, 90; extended 205. *See
also Casa*; Households
Fertility, 66–67, 96, 204–5; determinants of, 77–78; comparative
rates, 77–78, 80–81; age-
standardized, 81; related to
class, 81, 88; marital indices of,
84; race and, 84; national origin
and, 85, 87; decline in, 87; in
Spain, 87; in Buenos Aires, 88,
95, 97; increases in, 98
France, 97
Froebel, Friedrich, 178f
Fueros, 28, 89

García Márquez, Gabriel, 162
Generation of '37, 39, 45ff, 56, 63,
100, 121, 170, 184, 220ff, 224;
attitudes of, 159; defines the
masses, 171; views of politics,
172; on education, 172; reforms
of, 178; intellectuals of, 188
Generation of '80, 236

Gente decente, 8ff, 56, 62, 104, 108;
police and, 36–37, 56; class
antagonism, 45–46, 98ff; schools
for, 78; children of, 105; adulthood and, 117; fears of, 121;
value system, 133; resistance to
reform, 153; marital system and,
163, 194; as owners of school
properties, 183; as social category, 225; similarity to *gente
de pueblo*, 226; as political
players, 229; authoritarianism
and, 230
Gente de pueblo, 8f, 62, 78; defined,
3; class antagonism, 45, 98;
moral standards of, 120; excesses
by, 122; illiteracy, 170ff, 173;
education, 173; conscription,
192; as war victims, 202; fertility
rates, 205; as social category,
225; political sagacity of, 226ff,
230; similarity to *gente decente*,
226; terror and, 229
Gore, Robert, 217
Gorriti, Juan Ignacio de, 59
Grandchildren, 207–8
Guido, Tomás, 103, 143

Hidalgo, Miguel, 16
Homicide, 42
Households: structures of, 76, 89ff,
202ff, 205, 243; heads of, 77, 205;
pre-industrial, 77; women as
heads of, 81–82; size of, 90, 185,
205; complex, 91, 208, 211;
school and, 140; composition of,
185, 211; coherence, 190, 212,
223; effects of *leva* on, 192;
modernization theory and, 197;
number of children and, 203–4;
kinship and, 206; war and, 212;
of selective universe, 241; as unit
of analysis, 241

Library of Congress Cataloging-in-Publication Data

Szuchman, Mark D., 1948–
    Order, family, and community in Buenos Aires, 1810–1860 / Mark D.
Szuchman.
    p.   cm.
    Bibliography: p.
    Includes index.
    ISBN 0-8047-1461-4 (alk. paper)
    1. Buenos Aires (Argentina)—Social conditions.   2. Neighborhood—
Argentina—Buenos Aires—History—19th century.   3. Family—
Argentina—Buenos Aires—History—19th century.   4. Community
organization—Argentina—Buenos Aires—History—19th century.
I. Title.   II. Title: Buenos Aires, 1810–1860.
HN270.B8S97 1988
306'.0982'12—dc19   87-34479
                                                                      CIP